PE[barcode: T0167632]

Peter Marren is a [...] on wildlife and related topics and has also worked in nature conservation in Scotland and England. His books include the bestselling *Rainbow Dust: Three Centuries of Delight in British Butterflies*, *Bugs Britannica* (with Richard Mabey), *The New Naturalists*, which won the Society for the History of Natural History's Thackray Medal, and *Britain's Rare Flowers*, which won the Botanical Society of Britain and Ireland's Presidents' Award. Peter also won a Leverhulme Research Fellowship for his work on *Bugs Britannica*.

ALSO BY PETER MARREN

The New Naturalists
Britain's Rare Flowers
Bugs Britannica
Rainbow Dust: Three Centuries of Delight in
British Butterflies

PETER MARREN

Chasing the Ghost

My Search for all the Wild Flowers of Britain

VINTAGE

1 3 5 7 9 10 8 6 4 2

Vintage
20 Vauxhall Bridge Road,
London SW1V 2SA

Vintage is part of the Penguin Random House group of companies
whose addresses can be found at global.penguinrandomhouse.com.

Penguin
Random House
UK

First published in the UK by Square Peg in 2018
First published by Vintage in 2019

penguin.co.uk/vintage

A CIP catalogue record for this book is available from the
British Library

ISBN 9781784703370

Printed and bound in Great Britain by Clays Ltd, Elcograf S.p.A.

Penguin Random House is committed to a sustainable future for our
business, our readers and our planet. This book is made from Forest
Stewardship Council® certified paper.

MIX
Paper from
responsible sources
FSC
www.fsc.org   FSC® C018179

To David and Anita Pearman

Contents

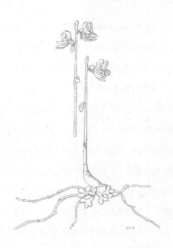

The Ghost

The ghostly flower blooms in near darkness among the rotting leaves on the forest floor. It has not so much as a speck of healthy, life-giving green. The stem is a greasy tube the colour of dead skin. The few, nodding flowers have a deathly pallor. They 'droop and dither' between pink and yellow. Some say they blacken at the touch. Sometimes a slug has been found on the half-eaten stem. Few of us have been lucky enough to find this strange plant in Britain. 'The usual experience of ghost-hunters,' noted one rueful searcher, 'is that there is nothing there.' On the rare occasion when there is, for a moment you don't quite see it – just a pale wisp, a phantom of a flower, barely visible above the blanket of decaying leaves. Then you look closer and it snaps into focus, something pale and spidery, about three inches tall, with outsize flowers on a leafless stalk. The flowers seem diseased or dying, even when they are in full freshness and vigour. They have the beauty of a lovely corpse.

Its full name is the Ghost Orchid, *Epipogium aphyllum*. It has also been called the Spurred Coralroot, the Spur-lipped Coralroot, or, with less imagination, the Leafless Epipogium. It was named the Ghost not so much for its physical appearance as for its ability to blend into its background to the point of near invisibility: a ghost in camouflage. That name was coined by the botanist David McClintock after he was taken to see the plant in 1953 and could still hardly see it until his nose was inches away from the drooping flowers.

The Ghost Orchid lacks chlorophyll, the green pigment that enables plants to manufacture their food by photosynthesis. Instead it feeds insidiously on fungi locked inside its swollen, coral-like 'root'. The science writer Richard Fortey, who lives near one of its former sites, dubbed the plant a 'parasitic piggy-back'. The orchid captures the fungus and then proceeds to digest it, as needed. Until recently the plant was assumed to be a sapro-phyte, a species that feeds on decaying matter. But when its physiology was investigated there was a surprise. It is the *fungus* that manufactures food from decaying leaves, while the orchid has turned the tables on its erstwhile fungal 'partner' in a kind of biological double-cross. Rather appropriately, its favourite food is said to be the mycelium (the mass of thread-like filaments in the soil or attached to tree roots that make up the body of the fungus) of poisonous toadstools of the genus *Inocybe*.

The Ghost sits at one corner of a *ménage à trois* between orchid, fungus and the roots of a beech tree. The imprisoned fungi, which are themselves growing with the help of trees, tap the beech roots for sugar and water and offer in exchange foodstuffs such as phosphates that are essential for the growth of a healthy tree. Trees and fungi commonly work in such a partnership, but in the Ghost Orchid's case, this partnership has morphed into slavery and then predation. Like a spider that consumes its mate, the orchid has taken full and unsentimental advantage of an evolutionary opportunity. It takes food from the fungus, and then turns the fungus into food.

So, with a belly full of macerated mushroom, the Ghost has no need of leaves. It doesn't need proper roots, either, for its 'coral root' is technically an underground stem with tuberous pseudo-roots. For most of the time it gets along without flowers, either. On the rare occasions when they are produced, the flowers are as bizarre as you might expect. The Ghost's scientific name, *Epipogium*, means 'over-beard' or 'upside-down beard' (*aphyllum* means 'no-leaves'). The 'beard' in question is the main petal, shaped like Darwin's generous face-hair, except that it sticks upwards by means of a twist in the flower's ovary (and that's another thing it doesn't have: what appears to be a flower stalk is in fact the ovary, the bit that swells after flowering into a capsule for the seeds within). It is this big petal that provides the Ghost's only definite colour, a spotty, washed-out pink. The rest of the flower, and indeed the whole plant, is cast in shades of sickly greyish-yellow.

The flowers look a little like rose-bodied spiders, perhaps dead ones, for they dangle flaccid and motionless from their hollow stem. They have a faint scent, some say of vanilla or fermenting bananas; but others have sniffed only mould and decay. Perhaps the Ghost smells of vanilla when the flowers are fresh and turns musky later on. In Britain, at least, these flowers seem to be a pointless luxury. Although they attract flies and bees in search of pollen and nectar, no ripe seed capsules have ever been found. Presumably cross-pollination seldom – if ever – takes place, simply because there are never enough flowers in bloom at any moment. Some flowers get devoured by slugs (or picked by botanists) before they get a chance to seed. So, in addition to managing without roots or leaves, and for most of the time without flowers either, it seems that the British Ghost has to manage even without fertile seed. Instead, among its swollen coral 'root', it produces little bulbils that push out more underground stems. These can be quite long; in the Ghost's best-known site they seem to have burrowed right under the road. Hence, if you are ever lucky enough to find a group of Ghost flowers, they probably all belong to the same network of underground stems, and hence to the same genetic plant.

It is possible, even likely, that there are more Ghosts out there than we know of, lurking among the leaf-mould, flowering so rarely and quietly that they defy detection. But the absence of flowers, or ripe seed, brings heavy penalties. It means that the Ghost cannot colonise new sites, but can only perpetuate itself in old ones. If a disaster afflicts its home ground, it cannot return. It seems predestined to decline. And disaster has indeed overtaken many of its former sites, through gale damage, felling and replanting, the rutting and churning of heavy vehicles, and even the trampling feet of its human admirers. The number of places where the Ghost could reappear is getting smaller all the time.

The plant shown to David McClintock was the first to be found in more than twenty years. Some thought the Ghost had departed the scene and was in fact extinct, but others imagined it had merely gone to ground – quite literally so – living on out of sight, below the carpets of leaf-mulch, with worms and fungus for company. It was finally rediscovered by Rex Graham (1915–58), an amateur botanist and dedicated Ghost-hunter, who had spent years searching for the plant in some of the shadiest woods in southern England. One July day in 1953 he was tramping the ground in a wood near Henley – a place hardly different from hundreds of other beechwoods in the Chilterns – and rested on a tree stump to light his pipe. And just then, over the bowl of the pipe, he spotted something: a pale flower poking up like a periscope from the ocean of brown leaves. 'To be honest,' he told David McClintock, 'I was ready to give up, and the feeling when I saw it was of relief more than anything. It was [only] the following day that I felt euphoria.' It was just luck, he told another friend. A subsequent, very thorough search of the wood revealed no fewer than twenty-five flowering Ghosts belonging to what were thought to be twenty-three individual plants. Never before, or since, have so many been found all at once. Moreover, at least one vigorous plant continued to produce flowers almost annually, always in late summer, for more than thirty years, right up to 1986.

In most of its other sites, the Ghost has been more fickle. It comes and goes, spookily, and no one knows where or when it will appear next, or indeed if it will appear at all. It was found for the first time in 1854 on the bank of Sapey Brook near Tedstone Delamere on the then-border between Herefordshire and Worcestershire. Its discoverer dug it up for her garden, where the plant promptly expired (and I hope the Ghost's ghost haunted her garden and mildewed her roses). It was not seen again until 1876, and then in a different place: Ringwood Chase, sometimes called Bringewood Chase, in Shropshire, where, once again, it appeared and then disappeared. A third appearance – one is tempted to call it an *apparition* – was near Ross-on-Wye in 1910, and it was the last for a long while.

Then, in the 1920s, word got around that the Ghost had begun to haunt a new area, the beechwoods near Henley. It was first found by Eileen Holly, a local schoolgirl, and had evidently flowered there for a year or two, for a botanist who managed to track her down noticed the sickly bloom among flowers in a vase on her windowsill. More years went by, until 1931 when Vera Paul found another Ghost, also in the Henley area and not far from her cottage. This one was unusually tall – a foot high, peering from the hollow of a rotting stump. It was photographed *in situ*, perhaps for the first time; and it was that hand-coloured image by Robert Atkinson that was reproduced in the orchid-hunter's Bible, *Wild Orchids of Britain* by V. S. Summerhayes. All previous Ghost portraits were drawings and paintings made from picked or pressed plants. Vera Paul's plant flowered, on and off, over the next thirty years.

A local resident, Joanna Cary, recalled years later how, as a child, she had been frightened by the sight of 'funny men in gaiters' rummaging around in the wood by her cottage. She thought they might have been flashers, or criminals intent on burying something. But it was only Victor Summerhayes and his band of Ghost-hunters, out on their annual, always unsuccessful attempt to track down another specimen.

And that was the tally of Ghosts, until the moment when Rex Graham lit his pipe. Many people visited his site between 1953 and 1986. On one remarkable occasion a plant was found growing out of a mattress abandoned in a ditch by the road. I have been to the spot several times, but always found a very Ghost-free wood. The site was easy enough to locate, by the side of a wooded lane where it was bordered by a steep bank. On my first visit, someone had banged a post into the ground to mark the spot and, to make doubly sure, had placed a brick next to it. Fortunately my trips there were never wasted, for this used to be a marvellous place for woodland flowers, including Violet, Narrow-lipped and Broad-leaved Helleborine, and the plant that most nearly resembles a Ghost, the Yellow Bird's-nest, another species that lacks any green coloration. But my Ghost-hunts were always failures. I would lie among the damp leaves, flashing a torch this way and that – for I'd been told the Ghost shines white, when struck by a beam of light. One time I found a little tepee made of twigs and suspected there had once been a Ghost inside that makeshift cage. Another time I found a dead, brown stem close to that wooden Ghost post, possibly the husk of a previous Ghost, but just as likely the remains of a Yellow Bird's-nest. I wonder now why I did not excavate the earth around the stem as far as the root, which might have confirmed its identity. That is what the prolific botanical diarist Eleanor Vachell did in 1926, after being shown the exact spot where the schoolgirl had picked her Ghost flower. She and a companion had 'crept stealthily' to the place and, 'kneeling down carefully, with [our] fingers removed a little soil, exposing the stem of the orchid, to which were attached tiny tuberous rootlets'. They replaced the earth reverently, covering the tiny hole with 'twigs and leaf-mould, and fled home triumphant'.

The last time I visited that wood I was shocked at the change. Until 1987 the Ghosts had bloomed beneath smooth, soaring beech trunks whose branches met eighty feet above your head, like the nave of a cathedral. Light filtered down in greenish shafts, dappling and pooling on the floor far below. But those majestic trees were hit hard by the great gale of October 1987. Down they crashed, pulling up great saucers of chalk and clay in their mighty roots. And, after that, the ground was further rutted and furrowed and scraped by work teams and timber lorries. Sunlight poured down through great ragged holes in the canopy. Thickets of bramble sprang up and the special, sepulchral atmosphere of the place was lost. It now looked like what it was: a wood shattered by wind, ground up by heavy vehicles and, lately, chewed up by increasing numbers of deer. Few orchids get the chance to flower now, much less set seed. Before they can, the deer bite their heads off.

The year 1987 was, in fact, the last British record of the Ghost for more than twenty years – or, at least, the last authenticated sighting. The previous year nearly a thousand botanical pilgrims had gone there to see just a single plant: a small Ghost with two flowers, one of the most-photographed flowers ever. What had been a fairly well-kept secret had been blown apart by a birders' hotline offering exact particulars. Since then, it has been a case of finders-keepers. If Ghosts still linger among the archipelago of beechwoods in the southern Chilterns, no one is saying so.

I wanted very badly to see a Ghost. But if the plant had indeed gone for ever, it meant I could at least cross it off my list of plants-to-see. For I was planning a project I'd been waiting half a lifetime to fulfil: a grand tour of Britain to see every native wild plant, including all those that had eluded me over forty years of plant-hunting. For the first time I had the leisure and enough money to spend much of the summer chasing wild flowers. We have a lot of wild flowers – around 1,500 species, if you include ferns and their allies (the exact figure depends on how you define 'native' and how you define 'wild'). There are five native flowers for every breeding bird, twenty for every species of butterfly and thirty for every kind of wild mammal. It is often said that our island flora is impoverished compared with that of our continental neighbours, but even so not many people have seen all our plants. You would need a lifetime to find them all. We have, for instance, around fifty orchids, one hundred ferns and fern-allies, fifty sedges, twenty-four rushes, twenty speedwells, twenty-two pondweeds, nineteen bedstraws, even a dozen buttercups. There is a lot of plant diversity packed into Britain.

Why did *I* want to see them all? Mainly because I love wild plants and wanted to meet them all in the flesh, in the beauty of their natural settings. The journey would, I realised, be a long one, but it would offer adventure and companionship in corners of Britain that still, miraculously, retain their wild beauty and natural diversity. It would, I reckoned, be possible to do it in a year, if I restricted myself to plants I hadn't yet seen. There was, of course, a train-spotting element to this, a nerdish desire for completion. And a very good – in fact overwhelming – chance that I would fail. If so, I knew who to blame. It was all the fault of a dead Devon vicar called William Keble Martin.

Rosa tomentosa
Cumberland Westmorland
July 2 1927

The Country Vicar who
Wrote a Bestseller

On my fifteenth birthday I was given a copy of the publishing sensation of the year: W. Keble Martin's *The Concise British Flora*. I cannot remember whether I had asked for it or whether it was my parents' idea. I wasn't especially interested in wild flowers just then. My thing was butterflies and moths. But there it was, already in its fourth impression, and it changed my life.

I was roughly the 100,000th person to own a 'Keble Martin'. By 1980 another million-and-a-half people had joined me. The reason so many of us bought it was that this was a different kind of field guide to any that had gone before. It was the first book printed for a mass market that illustrated nearly every species of wild flower accurately, in colour, and at more or less life-size (trees were represented by leaves and twigs). The flowers were carefully arranged on each plate, often overlapping, in a way that was uncannily lifelike. Pale flowers were shown against green foliage, as in a hedgerow. 'The draughtsman's aim,' explained the author in his old-fashioned way, 'has been to show an average fragment [of a plant], with its essential features, and to give each a place in the sun without crowding.' In their exquisite detail Martin's drawings resembled the past masters of flower illustration, but, unlike theirs, his pictures were available to all at thirty-five bob, or £1.75. *The Concise British Flora* was a labour of love that had taken this dutiful and preoccupied vicar the best part of his lifetime to complete.

I used Keble Martin to tick off wild flowers as I found them – to me, it was a good way of learning them. Fifty years on, my tattered copy is annotated with dates and places in much the same way as Martin himself had labelled his sketches. Beginning with Plate 1, Meadow Rues and Anemones, I see that I ticked my first Alpine Meadow Rue on Ben Lawers in the Scottish Highlands during a family holiday in July 1969. The most luscious flower on the plate, Pasqueflower, had to wait until a spring walk on Aston Upthorpe Down, Oxfordshire, in 1985. And I didn't see the now nearly-extinct Pheasant's Eye, whose intense red flowers lent it its old name of 'red Morocco', until July 2012, in a 'cornfield near Dunsden, Oxon'. Ticking became a habit. Many of Keble's 100 plates now have a near-complete set of ticks. But, especially towards the back of the book, among the grasses, sedges and rushes, there were many gaps. I used to brood over those gaps. Not all the missing plants were rare. Some were species I might have walked straight past, unrecognised – there were plenty of those among such lookalike groups as chickweeds, eyebrights and forget-me-nots.

When I found a new flower I would check its likeness on the page and then double-check it against Keble Martin's terse text notes opposite. When I first opened Keble I hardly knew a daisy from a dandelion. With his help, I was soon able to sort out buttercups, umbellifers (they look tricky, but are in fact quite easy) and eventually even those problematic lookalikes, the 'yellow composites'. I graduated to plants without colourful flowers, to sedges, pondweeds and even grasses – which, since they are all shades of green, Keble had left as uncoloured drawings. As I delved deeper into the world of plants. I learned that nearly every species has its own 'look', a kind of botanical personality – its 'jizz', as they used to say. In the process I learned the names of parts, like 'umbel', 'sepal' and 'cyme'; understood that an 'arcuate' stem is one bent like a bow, and that a 'lanceolate' leaf is one shaped like a spear-point. Botanical jargon might seem arcane and unnecessary, but it enables a plant to be described precisely, stripped down to its component parts for the purposes of identification. With the help of such words, I learned to tell the difference between very similar-looking plants, not just from the details of the flowers, but also their leaves (are they 'lanceolate' or 'cordate'?), their seed-heads or their sepals (are they hairy or are they reflexed?). Botanical terms aren't difficult to learn, and they enable you to use the keys in a field guide or flora. Without them, a buttercup will probably always remain a buttercup, and not a Creeping one, or a Bulbous one, or a Small-flowered one. Your delight in buttercups will remain generalised, and not specific.

Why, in general, aren't more of us interested in wild flowers? After all, they are all around us, even in a city, and their colours make a powerful, if easily underrated, contribution to the beauty of the landscape. They have wonderful names and intriguing back-stories and, unlike garden flowers, they don't cost anything (seeing beauty in a weed can change your life – and the way you garden). We should love and cherish them more, and in Keble Martin's boyhood, a century ago, people did. Wild flowers have retreated in the public consciousness since then. At least a million of us are sufficiently interested in birds to take out a subscription to the RSPB. But the equivalent charity, Plantlife, has to struggle along with just 1 per cent of that number.

This made the rapid ascent to best-seller status of *The Concise British Flora* all the more surprising. Who was he, this man who, accidentally, almost unintentionally, created a surge in wild-flower awareness? By the time his book appeared, he was nearing the end of a long and busy life. William Keble Martin was born halfway through the reign of Queen Victoria, in 1877, the son of the rector of Staverton in Devon. He was a comfortable member of the educated upper-middle-class, a scion of a large West Country family with connections to Winchester College and the patriarchal home at Overbury Park in Gloucestershire. Among his siblings and cousins were vicars and deans, naval captains and engineers, schoolmasters and architects. A boyhood spent in rural surroundings in Devon and Wiltshire nurtured his love of the outdoors. The young Keble spent his holidays walking and camping on the moors, bird-nesting in the hedgerows and pressing plants in a book. He learned to shoot, and to ice-skate, not on a rink but on a frozen pond near the house. More unusually, he was interested in mosses. He collected and reared butterflies and moths and, indeed, it was 'the desire to know their foodplants', he explained, 'that first promoted the effort to identify the plants required'. At Oxford University he read an unconventional mixture of Greek philosophy and botany. But there was never any doubt about his vocation, and it wasn't botany. Naturally religious, with an evangelical bent, Keble Martin was ordained, like his father, and spent the rest of his life in the service of the Church of England.

He was that now near-vanished species, a naturalist who was interested in everything, or (as he put it) in 'all branches of natural history'. While at Oxford he learned to draw flowers mainly because 'fellow students complained of the difficulty of identifying them from the long, wordy descriptions in works then available'. In 1899, aged twenty-one, he made the very first drawing for what would become *The Concise British Flora*: a snowdrop highlighted against a leaf of ivy – the only drawing in the book to bring in a fragment of a different plant.

In those days, when photography was still cumbersome and monochrome, painting wild flowers was a popular hobby. One way of learning them was to 'paint in your Bentham' – the standard handbook of the day, by George Bentham and Joseph Dalton Hooker, which included a set of drawings printed on strong paper suitable for watercolours. These drawings, by William Hood Fitch, set a lasting example to Keble Martin by always including the date and locality where the plant had been gathered.

In the 1920s a Wildflower Society was formed, of which Keble Martin was a keen member. It encouraged its members not only to draw and paint flowers, but to keep a diary of all the species they found. After reaching a certain level of proficiency, members could be promoted to the Society's higher echelon, which was called, with romantic whimsy, 'Valhalla', and then, beyond that, to 'Parnassus', the Garden of the Gods. The select few who grazed the verdant lawns of Parnassus would be expected to have coloured in most of their Benthams. They now dwelled in the airy spaces reserved for those of uncommon attainment.

Keble Martin, funnily enough, would not have qualified for Parnassus, and perhaps not even for Valhalla. Forever busy with parochial matters, he never learned to drive and had a large family to support. He went botanising only where he could and when he could find the time. Many of the scarcer plants he painted were brought to him by friends, or even resuscitated from dried, pressed specimens. Perhaps the first *rare* flower he ever painted was the Heath Lobelia, *Lobelia urens* on his Plate 54, which he discovered at a 'strong new locality' at Yarner Wood in Devon, and first drew for the *Journal of Botany* in 1901. Earlier that year he had also painted Mossy Saxifrage, 'a mass of flower like a white tablecloth', which he had come across during a walking holiday in the Brecon Beacons. While serving as curate at Ashbourne in the Peak District a few years later, he spotted the rare Jacob's Ladder on the steep bank of Bentley Brook, and took a sprig for painting later, 'my fiancée holding me by an ankle to prevent my falling'.

By 1906 he had conceived his ambition to paint the entire British flora, including that of Ireland and the Channel Islands. At that time it consisted of around 1,400 native or well-established species. His principal guide was the *London Catalogue of British Plants*, which was marked off into 100 sections, each with about fifteen plants. 'This method,' he noted, 'led almost unawares to the plotting of the 100 plates of the *Concise British Flora*.' Perhaps for reasons of space, he decided against including ferns and their allies in the project. His flora would consist entirely of *flowering* plants, except for a single plate showing the three native conifers: Scots pine, yew and juniper. His *modus operandi* was to place a drawing in the corner of each plate and fill the rest of the space with related species as he found them. This required many rethinks, as he worked over and over to fit drawings on the same plate without overcrowding. For some species, fruits, as well as flowers, had to be drawn; and, for difficult groups, magnifications of other diagnostic features: florets, capsules, stamens. Each drawing had to include everything necessary to identify the plant. And they would all have to be done at approximately life-size – which meant, of course, that in many cases the whole plant could not be shown, only a representative sprig of blossom or catkins. A pair of acorns and a leaf were sufficient for the Pedunculate Oak.

By 1932, by which time he was fifty-four, married and with four grown-up children, Keble Martin had completed about half of 'the 1,480 figures proposed'. Some he needed to replace because the original paper had discoloured. Always a perfectionist, he repainted many more after discovering a superior grade of green paint. Some of the more elusive flowers were painted on 'little holidays', such as his family's excursion to The Lizard in 1923, to Berry Head in 1924, to Upper Teesdale in 1927 and to Ben Lawers in 1933. It was at the last named that Martin famously 'walked miles in mountain mist and rain to restore a small rare plant to its own niche'; the plant was Drooping Saxifrage, *Saxifraga cernua*, which at that time was known only from Ben Lawers. For his plate of lookalike fumitories (Plate 6, one of his best), he was able to enlist the services of the acknowledged authority, H. W. Pugsley – himself no mean botanical artist – and tour Cornwall in Pugsley's car. More usually Martin travelled by rail or on his 'lightless auto-bike'. For those plants that still remained out of reach, he relied on friends. Over five decades, eighty-two botanists sent him 360 specimens, a tribute to the generosity and fellowship that still lives on in botanical circles.

Keble Martin retired in 1949, aged seventy-two, moving to a bungalow near Chagford on the edge of Dartmoor – always his favourite corner of Britain. With increased leisure, but now in intermittent ill-health, he repainted or rearranged many of the older pictures whilst slotting in the last remaining plants as he found them, including Common Spike-rush, *Eleocharis palustris*, which he picked on a walk in Dovedale in 1952. The very last plate to be completed was the one chosen for the book's jacket: an arrangement of wild roses 'redrawn after kind criticism of N. Y. Sandwith'. The full set of plates was exhibited at the Royal Horticultural Society in 1958. Everyone who saw them agreed on their consistently outstanding quality. The Society's President, Sir David Bowes-Lyon, headed an appeal for funds to get them published.

The publication of botanical art was then an expensive business. Gorgeous pictures printed by lithography in limited editions were affordable only by wealthy collectors or institution libraries. The mass-production of all-colour field guides was still in its infancy and, as far as wild flowers were concerned, the results had been decidedly unimpressive. The standard-setter was the *Collins Field Guide to Wild Flowers* by David McClintock and R. S. Fitter, first published in 1956. The text, with its Michelin star-system (great rarities such as Ghost Orchid merited three stars), was excellent, but the drawings were not much of an advance on Bentham and Hooker, and they were separated from the text, in a bank of plates. The only really good published pictures then available were the *Drawings of British Plants* by Stella Ross-Craig, but they were not coloured and were of more use to specialists working in a herbarium than to amateur botanists in the field. The only other recourse of enthusiastic amateurs was to wrestle with the scientific descriptions in the standard flora by A. R. Clapham, T. G. Tutin and E. F. Warburg; but, good as it was, it was not intended for beginners.

Martin's work was offered to seven publishers, one after the other, and they all turned it down. The pictures would be impossible to reproduce, they said, at an affordable price to anything like the required standard; it was a pity, but it just couldn't be done – sorry. Then the Duke of Edinburgh got to hear of it and asked to see them. He, too, was impressed, but another year went by until his equerry, David Checketts, decided to show them to George Rainbird, who was a pioneer of a new kind of publishing – book packaging. He specialised in illustrated books, often printed outside Britain, at presses where the quality of colour printing was high and the prices more reasonable. He also reduced costs by putting together large print-runs – getting publishers and book clubs all around the world to club together to achieve economies of scale. He is said to have taken one look at Keble Martin's plates and exclaimed, 'Every schoolboy will want one!' With Rainbird's know-how, allied to his absolute faith in the broad appeal of this book, the unit costs of production began to come down. This kind of illustrated book – a 'coffee-table book' in more recent parlance – was his forte; Rainbird had already made cheaply printed successes out of *Beautiful Butterflies* and *Birds of Heath and Marshland*, which had cost just twelve shillings each. Keble Martin's more delicate work was more demanding. Rainbird had to put together a print-run of 25,000 copies to achieve a retail price of thirty-five shillings (the equivalent price today would be £27). Prince Philip helped things along by penning a foreword praising the 'dedicated and painstaking skill which has gone into each plate'.

The Concise British Flora in Colour was published in May 1965 by Ebury Press, a subsidiary of the National Magazine Company owned by Michael Joseph (and now part of Random House). It sold out in four months. By the following Christmas the book had been reprinted four times. By 1980 one-and-a-half million copies had been sold all over the world. Despite the ponderous title (but, even so, a better one than Martin's first thought, 'Comparative Figures of British Flora'), it was the greatest success of George Rainbird's long career.

By now a widower, Martin remarried in 1965 and presented his bride with all the original coloured drawings, the work of a lifetime. 'What greater proof of my devotion could I give?' he said.

The retiring and now retired vicar, aged eighty-eight, was suddenly famous. He was honoured with a science doctorate at Exeter University. Hatchards bookshop flung a party for their 'author of the year'. He was invited to design a set of stamps for the Post Office. And he wrote an autobiography, *Over the Hills*, described by Wilfred Blunt as a work 'of quiet charm – the sort of book to be read at ease in a deck-chair in a garden full of Madonna lilies and delphiniums'. He died at home in Woodbury, Devon, on 26th November 1969, aged ninety-two and lies in the local churchyard.

The Concise British Flora isn't perfect. Although the colour printing was remarkably good for its time, there was some loss of definition and a slight colour distortion, which grew worse as the book was reprinted. And, as the historian and naturalist David Allen has remarked, Martin's taxonomy was 'rather noticeably out of date', and the short descriptions of the text 'too meagre for comfort'. There were mistakes (the Lizard Orchid doesn't flower in May), corrected in later editions, which added more naturalised species and widespread hybrids. But the drawings still stand up well to modern field guides. Keble Martin did not have room – and perhaps not the material, either – to reproduce every species. I totted up nearly 200 species described in the text that he was unable to illustrate, including eleven sedges, twenty-eight grasses, seven lady's-mantles and, more surprisingly, seven orchids (including the Ghost Orchid). There are even a few species that he forgot to include, such as Norwegian Mugwort, Alpine Coltsfoot, Mat-grass Fescue, Hairy Lady's-mantle, *Alchemilla monticola*, and Vigur's Eyebright, *Euphrasia vigursii*.

Some of the drawings – and this is not really a criticism – are not an exact match for the living plant. Martin had made subtle changes to make identification easier. Take the orchids, where the spikes of flowers are looser than you usually find in the wild, so that the structure of each individual flower can be better appreciated. Many lanky plants were cut short to fit the space. And, of course, his trees and shrubs are minimal: his stand-in for sycamore is a simple double-winged seed; his alder, a mere catkin.

Modest to the last, Keble Martin would have been the first to acknowledge the book's shortcomings. As he noted in the last line of his short, rather formal preface, 'we hope that the plates may have a chance of speaking for themselves. The author is very conscious of their limitations.'

The Grand Design

My original plan had been simple: I wanted to find and tick every plant in Keble Martin. But I soon realised that the task was impossible. As early as Plate 5, I found a plant that no longer exists wild in Britain, the Violet Horned-poppy, last seen in a Suffolk chicken-run sixty years ago. Martin included this and other vanished species because they were illustrated in the Victorian floras he grew up with: in Bentham and Hooker, and in the *London Catalogue of British Plants*. Contrariwise, there are other plants that Martin did not include because he did not know of their existence, including recent discoveries such as Radnor Lily and Suffolk Lungwort.

My new plan was to see all the *native* wild plants found in Britain, including ferns, but to ignore the 'introductions'. I would also ignore 'critical' plants such as the brambles and hawkweeds, on the grounds that they are far too difficult and not proper species anyway (they are usually described as 'micro-species'). I also decided to omit species found only in Ireland or the Channel Islands, on the grounds that they are not really British, but Irish or French respectively. Even so, this still left around 1,500 species, including those, like the common Field Poppy, that might not be strictly native but which had certainly been in the landscape for hundreds of years. Had anyone, I wondered, managed to see them all? A few luminaries of the past seem to have done so. George Claridge Druce (1850–1932) was probably one of them, for I had examined his herbarium, in Oxford, and found a sheet of an entrancingly dim little plant called Guernsey Centaury, *Exaculum pusillum*, on which Druce had written: 'my last plant'. What satisfaction those words must have given him! David McClintock is also said to have seen every native plant. Richard Fitter, doyen of field guides written in the 1950s and 1960s, told me he had too, so long as you discount the hawkweeds and the more ephemeral garden escapes known as 'casuals'. Perhaps there are today a few quiet, modest souls who have twitched the whole lot. If there are, I feel appropriately humble.

I got out my battered old copy of *The Concise British Flora* and counted the native plants without a tick. To my surprise, it came to a round number: exactly fifty. Fifty un-ticked species. How hard could it be to find all those in a year? Quite hard, on closer inspection. There were good reasons why I had never found those fifty. A few are plants that flower erratically, while others are found only in remote corners of Britain, and some bloom underwater. Finding them all would require a lot of travel. It might in some cases demand a degree of personal fitness. Well, I thought, I can swim and climb a bit, and still walk up a hill without collapsing in a wheezing heap. I hoped that would be sufficient. More problematic was that some of them flowered at the same time at opposite ends of Britain. Just how badly did I want to do this? Was it any more than a passing whim? Was it going to be worth the trouble, for that small inner satisfaction?

I made a table of flowering times and places, and began to work out a rough itinerary. I called it The Quest. But over the whole enterprise hung the spectre of *Epipogium*, the Ghost Orchid – a plant almost as unobtainable as the Holy Grail. Unless someone found it during the year, which, on recent form, seemed unlikely, it was a built-in guarantee of almost certain failure. Its non-availability haunted the whole project. It was impossible. But all the same, having thought about it, and imagining where The Quest would take me, I wanted to try.

Setting Out

Until now, I had never set out, systematically, to try and find every plant in the flora. Mostly, flowers, trees and ferns turned up in the course of walks, camping trips, ecological surveys and the like. The one family where I did once make an effort to locate and photograph every British species was the Orchidaceae, the wild orchids, in my gap year between school and university. I failed miserably, finding only two-thirds of them by the season's end. Even now, there were two missing British orchids on my list, the Irish Lady's-tresses and, of course, the Ghost.

The first county whose plants I got to know fairly well was Devon: a big county with a big flora and a fine range of plant habitats, ranging from the bogs and tors on Dartmoor to the limestone headlands of Tor Bay and the wilderness of sand at

Braunton Burrows – not to mention the island of Lundy and its unique wild 'cabbage' – the subject of my first published paper. During my three years at Exeter University I was able to find most of Devon's special plants, including the magnificent display of white rockroses at Berry Head, the intense blue stars of Blue Gromwell where the cliff had slumped into the sea near Axmouth, and the little, spring-flowering Sand-crocus on the golf links at Dawlish Warren – where, after having taken its picture, I was kicked out by a grumpy official.

Keble Martin assured his readers that botanists 'take no risks'. We do, though. Sometimes we have to. When you have driven a hundred miles, and trudged another ten over moor and hill to find a cliff with your flower halfway up it, you are definitely going to climb that cliff. I've fallen off a few times. I'm probably lucky to be alive, after attempting to get within touching distance of Tufted Saxifrage. What seemed like a reasonable toehold gave way, and down I went, with flailing limbs in a spray of gravel, turf and rock. I was alone, and miles away from any help. Perhaps it was the malice of the flower's guardian spirit, which had mistaken my purpose and thought I was about to pick her precious bloom. I fell off Ben Lawers, too, but that is a more comfortable mountain, with soft turf to ease the return of the plummeting botanist. Welsh Mudwort played a nasty trick on me once, when, eagerly peering into pools for its spiky rosette and dim little submerged flowers, I failed to notice that the rising tide was flooding the river, and that the mudwort and I were about to be stranded on a fast-diminishing patch of *terra firma*. Remarkably few botanists seem to have died for their hobby; at least not since 1861, when the plant collector William Williams was found at the bottom of a cliff with a tuft of Alpine Woodsia in the clutch of his stiffened fingers. For most of us, natural caution usually wins.

'We commend botanising as a means of healthy recreation for young and old,' continued Keble in his best, sermonising style; one that should 'last to the end of our pilgrimage'. His own pilgrimage lasted nine decades, active to the end. Field botanists, I've noticed, often reach a great age; in fact the *average* age of members of botanical societies tends to be in the fifties or sixties. We hear a lot about the distance that has grown up between people and nature, and how this severance has had malign effects on our well-being, leading to obesity, listlessness and morbid self-absorption. Without nature, we lose our sense of rootedness. Wild flowers offer an antidote to computer-age neurosis. You don't need to be a botanist to feel uplifted by the mist of bluebells tracing the woodland floor; or a meadow full of buttercups, bright as sunshine; or even the stellar sprinkle of daisies on the lawn. Birdwatching can be exciting, but plants offer something else, a feeling that is hard to describe: a kind of inner calm, a feeling of oneness with nature. It is a good feeling and it makes us happy.

Yet, sadly, field botany is not as popular as it was a century ago. Television has sidelined flowers in favour of animals and birds that move about and do things (flowers do things too, but less obviously, and often too slowly for the camera to catch). To newspaper editors, the most thoroughly urban of human stereo-types, wild flowers are usually relegated to the gardening section. Those who write nature notes are warned to stick to the birds and bees. Even the academic world has spurned us, for not a single British university now offers an undergraduate course in botany (they still do in Ireland). By contrast, in the age Keble Martin was born into, 'plants were just about the most interesting things on the planet', as Richard Mabey puts it in his revivalist book, *The Cabaret of Plants*. Readers then were entranced by the wonderful new plants brought to Kew and Edinburgh from all over the world – huge, carnivorous plants that could swallow a mouse, flowers you could smell a mile off, water lilies whose enormous leaves have inspired architects. Darwin spent a lot of time with plants, studying how they reverse the tables by catching and devouring animals and insects, or fooling them into doing their bidding as pollinators. Plants made people think. They tweaked our imaginations and inspired wonder and respect. Whatever happened to all that? We still love trees – witness the growth of charities such as the Woodland Trust – but we tend to think of them not as wild plants but, in the memorable words of the woodland scholar and author Oliver Rackham, as 'gateposts with leaves'. We stick them into the ground and harvest them later on, like slow-growing corn. When did we lose our respect for wild plants?

Twitching birds has grown up in my lifetime into a popular hobby with its own established hotlines and culture. It even has its own language – 'crippler', 'megatick', 'dip-out'. Plant twitching, is, by contrast, socially invisible. I have met people, even quite young people, who tick plants. However, it is not Keble Martin that they tick, but Clive Stace, the author of the present standard British flora. Stace-tickers (a tricky phrase to say out loud) make less distinction than I do between which flowers are native and which aren't. Thanks to plants that 'escape' into the wild, Stace has nearly three times as many species to tick as Keble Martin, and no one will ever complete that particular quest, for garden escapes are endless, a continually unfurling list of exotica.

Plant-tickers are often people who tick everything – 'pan-listers' as they are known – naturalists who try to identify every animal, vegetable or bug. The champion pan-lister is Jonty Denton, who has seen and identified an incredible 12,000+ species of wildlife in Britain, including 2,000 wild flowers. They post their tallies and new species on websites, along with their favourite 'grippers' and 'cripplers', or Best Find Ever, or bogey-species, which are the ones that ought to be findable but just cannot be located. They also have 'grails', the species that, above all others, they long to see. The Ghost Orchid tends to make its way onto such lists. It is both a grail and a bogey-species, and also the ultimate crippler.

I had already enjoyed a couple of years in which I had whittled down my own missing plants from more than a hundred to the Last Fifty. These trips were entirely pleasurable. I cleared up the remaining plants of Dorset and Cornwall with the help of my old botany-buddy, David Pearman. We tracked down Greek Spurrey in a National Trust car park close to a parked lorry, and Lesser Tree-mallow along a suburban street by a Tesco superstore (but it has been known there long before the superstore, or even the street). I raced through Sussex, pinning down Red Star-thistle in a farmyard behind a historic tiled barn, Wall Germander close to a signpost at the Seven Sisters, and Stinking Hawksbeard inside a charged fence on which I casually electrocuted myself. I caught up with the two missing plants from my home county, Wiltshire: Tuberous Thistle on the army ranges on Salisbury Plain, and Loddon Pondweed in the middle of the river near Bradford-on-Avon. Another natural-history friend, Brett Westwood, showed me Grey Hair-grass at a place with the wonderful name of Burlish Top. Phil Pullen took me to see Field Eryngo in a convincingly native site on a hillside overlooking the grey sprawl of a Plymouth housing estate.

And so, by degrees, I reached the Last Fifty: to me, the most elusive plants in Britain. I assumed I would find the missing plants in their approximate order of flowering, but in practice it didn't work out like that. In fact, I sought them in the following order:

50 Radnor Lily or Early Star-of-Bethlehem, *Gagea bohemica*
49 Early Sand-grass, *Mibora minima*
48 Unspotted or Suffolk Lungwort, *Pulmonaria obscura*
47 Slender Cotton-grass, *Eriophorum gracile*
46 Interrupted Brome, *Bromus interruptus*
45 Fen Woodrush, *Luzula pallescens* (or *L. pallidula*)
44 Crested Cow-wheat, *Melampyrum cristatum*
43 Few-flowered Fumitory, *Fumaria vaillantii*
42 Spiked Rampion, *Phyteuma spicatum*
41 Childing Pink, *Petrorhagia nantuelii*
40 Least Whitebeam, *Sorbus minima*
39 Ley's Whitebeam, *Sorbus leyana*
38 Fen Ragwort, *Senecio paludosus*
37 Early Marsh-orchid, cream-coloured form, *Dactylorhiza incarnata* subspecies *ochroleuca*
36 Proliferous Pink, *Petrorhagia prolifera*
35 Purple-stem Cat's-tail, *Phleum phleoides*
34 Yarrow or Purple Broomrape, *Orobanche purpurea*
33 Wild Gladiolus, *Gladiolus illyricus*
32 Holy-grass *Anthoxanthum nitens* (or *Hierochloe odorata*)
31 Crested Buckler-fern, *Dryopteris cristata*
30 Holly-leaved Naiad, *Najas marina*
29 Elongated Sedge, *Carex elongata*
28 Leafless Hawk's-beard, *Crepis praemorsa*
27 Thread Rush, *Juncus filiformis*

26 Alpine Enchanter's Nightshade, *Circaea alpina*

25 Creeping Spearwort, *Ranunculus reptans*

24 Alpine Catchfly, *Silene suecica* (or *Lychnis alpina*)

23 Whorled Solomon's-seal, *Polygonatum verticillatum*

22 Diapensia, *Diapensia lapponica*

21 Iceland Purslane, *Koenigia islandica*

20 Alpine Rock-cress, *Arabis alpina*

19 Norwegian Mugwort, *Artemisia norvegica*

18 Purple Oxytropis, *Oxytropis halleri*

17 Estuarine Sedge, *Carex recta*

16 Upright or Tintern Spurge, *Euphorbia serrulata* (or *E. stricta*)

15 Tasteless Water-pepper, *Persicaria mitis* (or *Polygonum mite*)

14 Copse Bindweed, *Fallopia dumetorum*

13 Strapwort, *Corrigiola litoralis*

12 Triangular Club-rush, *Schoenoplectus triqueter* (or *Scirpus triqueter*)

11 Irish Lady's-tresses, *Spiranthes romanzoffiana*

10 Slender Naiad, *Najas flexilis*

9 Pipewort, *Eriocaulon aquaticum*

8 Slender-leaved Pondweed, *Potamogeton filiformis*

7 Hartwort, *Tordylium maximum*

6 Sickle-leaved Hare's-ear, *Bupleurum falcatum*

5 Pedunculate Sea-purslane, *Atriplex (Halimione) pedunculata*

4 Thistle or Yorkshire Broomrape, *Orobanche reticulata*

3 Blue Heath, *Phyllodoce caerulea*

2 Ribbon-leaved Water-plantain, *Alisma gramineum*

1 Ghost Orchid, *Epipogium aphyllum*

What a set of names they are. Even though some botanists prefer the scientific names, as they have to do in journals, nearly all native plants have been given common names. Some of them – like buttercup, dandelion and pimpernel – date back to the Middle Ages. Shakespeare knew the cowslip, primrose, pansy and columbine. In more recent times, common names have become standardised, but some people still use folk names, such as my Wiltshire speciality, the fritillary, which is also known by many people as crowcups or snake's-heads (or, according to the poet and plant-lover Geoffrey Grigson, as the Mourning Bells of Sodom). But rare and little-known flowers do not attract folk names and so tend to have just one name, the one allocated to them by botanical authors – which, in many cases, is a straight translation of the scientific name. All the same, there is a kind of unintentional poetry in the names of my Last Fifty. Some names seem to hint at a secret nook where a rarity survives, such as Tintern Spurge or Radnor Lily. Others suggest that our plant might be more at home elsewhere, such as the Iceland Purslane or the Norwegian Mugwort. Yet others indicate a resemblance to some unlikely object: a pipe, or the ear of a hare, or the tail of a cat. Some are just odd: what, for instance, is a naiad? What kind of plant looks like a hawk's-beard, assuming a hawk even has a beard? A few seem to grasp at negatives: a plant that is 'tasteless', or distinguished by its *lack* of spots. One is simply 'Diapensia' – like rhododendron, a scientific name that has wandered into the common language and so has become English.

The obscurity of these plants is, to me, part of their allure. Some are little-known beauties. The first on my list, the Radnor Lily, has a glorious golden flower that blooms in the depths of winter. Holy-grass is a plant you can sniff out of the landscape by its powerful scent. Our one and only wild gladiolus is a luscious gem that has somehow managed to remain all but unknown.

There was a time when the whereabouts of such plants was known only to intimates. It was no accident that an earlier incarnation of the Botanical Society of the British Isles (the BSBI, lately renamed the Botanical Society of Britain and Ireland) was the Botanical Exchange Club: members exchanged the localities of rare plants just as they exchanged plant material. Tracking down a rare and elusive flower was part of the fun. I own a folder of 'Botanical Directions', sealed with a leather strap, made by an eager flower-finder half a century ago: a collection of letters, postcards and little maps with crosses to mark the spot. You could find a plant by clues in the landscape: a stand of trees, or a bend in the stream, or a curiously shaped rock. That agreeable form of botanical treasure-hunting has, alas, been consigned to history by the GPS. Hand-drawn maps have given way to twelve-figure grid references. But I have kept my own notebooks with their coloured maps of where to find Monkey Orchid or Wild Tulip: green for the woods, blue for water, and red for the bull's-eye – the magic circle, the secret place.

The reasons for missing these particular fifty plants were various. Plant lists tend to reflect where we live, or have lived, or where we have been on a course or on holiday. I live in the south of England, and so many of my missing plants occur at the other, far end of Britain. Some of them, as I say, may be plants I have simply failed to recognise. Others are among our rarest wild flowers. I knew from the outset that I was unlikely to be able to find them all on my own, and, besides, I didn't want to. Part of the pleasure of any quest is the chance to go botanising with old friends and also to meet new enthusiasts. The world of flower-finding is fairly small, but it is warm and welcoming. I was lucky to meet local plant recorders who were willing, even eager, to help. Companionship in the field is not only safer, but more stimulating. We talk plants and lunch in a nice pub and get to know one another, or renew an old acquaintance. The twin summits of field botany are finding a flower and making a friend.

Perhaps finding just fifty wild plants does not sound much of a challenge. After all, unlike birds, flowers can't fly away. They stay put, rooted to the soil, right under your nose. But you do need to be able to spot your plant in the tangle of vegetation, in the glare of the sun or in deep shadow. You also need knowledge of what you are looking for and how to recognise it; and some idea of the places where such plants grow. You need to be something of an ecological detective, one who, *pace* Keble Martin, is prepared to take mild risks. For some places that are good for flowers are difficult of access, uncomfortable or even dangerous – quaking bogs, cliffs, cold northern lakes, tidal marshes, or simply places owned by someone who plainly hates botanists. Flower-finding is also a battle against the perennially changeable British weather. In dull light, a flower may remain tight shut. In rain, droplets condense on a chap's specs until he can hardly see his boots, let alone some tiny sandwort. Your feet tire; so do your eyes. The trail can grow weary; you may long to give up and go home. Yes, it is possible – just – to see all the native plants. But you need to really, *really* want to.

The Quest for the Last Fifty

The Winter Lily

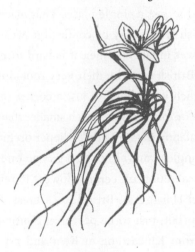

50

Radnor Lily or Early Star-of-Bethlehem
Gagea bohemica

A winter-flowering bulb plant with golden flowers
and linear, grass-like leaves
Stanner Rocks, Radnor
10th February
Helper: Andy Shaw

Some wild flowers are found all over Britain, from Land's End to John o' Groats, and even offshore islands beyond. Wherever we are, we are never far from Common Dog-violet or Spear Thistle, and plantains, stinging nettles and brambles seem to follow human beings around wherever we live or work. Within a mile of any home in Britain there could be at least a couple of hundred kinds of wild flowers. Within a county, it may be closer to a thousand.

On the other hand, there are flowers so rare that you need to travel to a distant corner of Britain to have any hope of finding them. By my count, there are around sixty native wild flowers that are confined to just a single place. That place may be quite large: the Cornish Heath may be confined to western Cornwall, but when in flower in late summer, it is hard to miss. But other species cling to British earth by their very root-tips. The Downy Woundwort, which is confined to just a corner of Oxfordshire, consists of three or four colonies, each smaller than your kitchen. The native population of the Lady's Slipper orchid was believed to consist of a single plant (although a second one is rumoured). The extreme localisation of certain flowers is reflected in their names: Somerset Hair-grass, Bristol Rock-cress, Cheddar Pink, Lundy Cabbage (but, just to be perverse, Nottingham Catchfly is widespread from Kincardine to Kent and no longer occurs naturally in Nottingham).

My first, earliest flower – the number 50 of my missing fifty – is one of these. Radnor Lily, also known as Early Star-of-Bethlehem, is not only confined to the old Welsh county of Radnor (botanists still use the historical counties when recording wild flowers), but to a single rocky hill within it. To make it still harder to find, the lily's golden flowers appear only in late winter, sometimes as early as January, and they are nearly always over by Easter. To make it more difficult still, less than one plant in a thousand ever produces a flower. But for this exceptional flower, all you normally see are the leaves: narrow, spidery tendrils that reflect the sunlight and so, on a sunny day, seem to shine. Nor do you have any certain means of knowing exactly when or where that flower is going to appear. The only way to tell is to go there and look. All this is why, despite its golden beauty, Radnor Lily was not known wild in Britain until 1974, even though its locality at Stanner Rocks is well known and has been visited by hundreds of botanists.

How does a plant get by without flowers? In this case, by producing tiny balls of tissue known as bulbils, which germinate as though they are seeds. Each one contains a full kit of genetic material but, since no sexual reproduction is involved, the offspring of bulbils is identical to the parent plant. As a mode of increase, it seems to work well enough. But it may have prevented the plant from colonising other rocky hills, and may be the reason why Radnor Lily is now marooned on a solitary crag. When it does flower, it seems to be a waste of energy. Our plant has never been known to produce ripe seed, not even in cultivation. Perhaps it is genetically inbred and incapable of doing so.

Wintertime botanising belongs to the bryologists, the moss-hunters. This is the season when mosses are at their healthiest and best, before heat dries them out and vegetation grows over them. Appropriately enough, the first, faded plant of Radnor Lily was found by a moss-hunter, in 1965, but was misidentified as the related Snowdon Lily, *Gagea serotina*, in a new and unexpected location. It took another nine years for the botanist Ray Woods to peer more closely at another sun-bleached flower that he found and notice it had a hairy stem – and that ruled out Snowdon Lily. Next year he visited Stanner several weeks earlier and this time he was rewarded not with a white flower, but with a bright golden one. He had found a new British plant. It was subsequently identified by Martin Rix, an expert on bulb plants, as *Gagea bohemica*, a wholly unexpected species whose nearest sites are in continental Europe hundreds of miles away. In March 1978, Woods and Rix managed to find twenty-five flowers, an exceptional number for this species. It was Ray Woods who christened it the Radnor Lily, to match the Snowdon Lily – surely a better name than the more botanically correct Early Star-of-Bethlehem.

Unless you know someone who can scout the place for you, you must trust to luck to find Radnor Lily in flower. I was in luck. Andy Shaw, a consultant ecologist based in Builth Wells, was willing, indeed keen and eager, to show it to me. The question was whether it would decide to flower this year – for, by my makeshift rules, a mere tuft of leaves or a thimble full of bulbils would not count. It had to be a flower. Just four days into the New Year, while the rocks were still rimed in frost, Andy explored the hill and eventually spotted a single plant in bud on the floor of a disused quarry. With a bit of help from the sun, he thought the flower might open in a couple of weeks. But there was very little sunshine that January. One rainy, blowy week followed another, as western Britain found itself at the tail end of a succession of Atlantic gales. Hurricanes Desmond, Eva, Frank, Henry and Imogen each passed over, lashing the hill with their respective burdens of wet. The little bud sat tight. Visiting again on 27th January, the eagle-eyed Andy spotted a second bud, this time at the top of a beetling cliff. It, too, was sitting out the storms, waiting patiently for a sunny day. The buds were slowly colouring up and one short spell of blessed warmth was all he thought they needed. I arranged a date with the flower, but both buds remained stubbornly shut. 'I've never known a season like it,' said Andy. 'It's been painfully slow. Normally it would have been out weeks ago. It used to be easier than this. Back in the early Nineties, you could expect to find a dozen flowers at peak time. The record was thirty-seven in 1991. You even saw the odd plant making a stupendous effort and producing *two* flowers.' But these days you are lucky if you find one or two.[1]

It was now 7th February, five weeks since Andy had located a bud, and at last the flowers showed signs of opening. We made a new date. 'Hopefully the gale-force winds and driving rain won't damage them,' he said. Should the petals be closed, as they normally are except in sunshine, he would bring his most powerful torch. The flowers, Andy told me, can be encouraged to open with the help of a sun-lamp.

Our new date, 10th February, arrived bright and sunny, though with the probability of rain later. For once there was no wind. My old friend Bob Gibbons, the wildlife photographer, wanted to see the Radnor Lily too, so there were now three of us standing below the cliff at Stanner Rocks where Victorian quarrymen had

---

1   Why Radnor Lily is flowering less and less frequently is uncertain, but Andy thinks climate change is a possibility. The perfect winter would be cold but relatively dry and sunny. But the recent trend is for milder but cloudier, wetter winters. All the same, in February 2017 no fewer than ten flowers appeared, the most for many a year.

blasted half the hill away for road stone. The Rocks are the remains of an ancient volcano, a mass of hard, dark-grey diorite whose chemical composition supports a number of rare plants, including Sticky Catchfly and Western Spiked Speedwell, as well as a suite of specialised mosses and liverworts. Stanner also has its own microclimate, warmer than the surrounding land. There were puddles in every dip of the road that day, but the south-facing cliff at Stanner was already dry. It was, as we panted up the steep track, surprisingly warm; the sheltered quarry is said to be one of the balmiest places in Wales.

The locations of rare flowers were traditionally kept secret, so I was rather nonplussed to see a large image of the lily on the entrance sign. We were not its first visitors. At the foot of the cliff, five elderly men were on their knees. We joined them. In the middle of the scrum was a single lily flower the size of a penny. It was only partly open, with malformed petals. One of the worshippers was accidentally poking it with his camera lens. He had come all the way from Mansfield, he told us, and seeing the lily in flower was worth every mile. They were like excited children at a party.

To find what we hoped would be a superior specimen, we made our way up the crag through woodland and scrub, past a succession of crumbling headlands, each with a fine view of mid-Wales above a dizzying drop. The shiny leaves of Radnor Lily sprouted by the hundred from chinks in the rock, growing from bulbs the size of peppercorns or even tinier bulbils no larger than a grain of sand. To produce a flower, said Andy, the conditions must be just right. Perhaps a dollop of dung from a passing rabbit might make the difference between flowering and not flowering. It seems to be that random.

I nibbled a leaf. It was succulent, with a neutral taste. I could see why a hungry rabbit would enjoy a winter salad of Radnor Lily. I could also understand why the plant chooses to flower in the low winter light. Come spring, these thin soils soon dry out, and once the sun starts to bake the rocks, further growth is impossible. By summer the leaves of Radnor Lily have shrivelled, but the swollen bulb, tucked inside its crevice, can sit out the heat until the autumn rains arrive.

And there it was at last: a single golden-yellow bloom imprisoned inside Andy's precautionary cube of netting. Was it worth every mile? Yes, I think it was. Radnor Lily resembles a celandine in size and shape, but is far more elegant with its circle of seven lens-shaped petals, one of which held a raindrop. An inner circle of six upright stamens surrounded the dart-like stigma in the middle, a ring around the bull's-eye. The short stem was covered with drought-resistant woolly hair, and from the base sprouted a whorl of slender leaves. Beyond its lonely vigil, high on the cliff, stretched bracken-brown, pudding-basin hills with streams and small meadows in between.

Bob took some pictures with his usual quiet proficiency. Then we reverently replaced the netting and retraced our steps. The five men had gone, but Andy had other clients waiting to pay their respects: a trio of enthusiasts from Bournemouth, a gardening group from Hereford, a pair of university lecturers from Oxford.

So, that was the first tick. For that, Andy had climbed the hill half a dozen times to locate two pinhead-sized buds. I had to travel about 200 miles (and had a parking ticket waiting for me at the motorway service station). We had managed to see the plant in flower on the one day in a month when the sun was shining. There were forty-nine more plants to go.

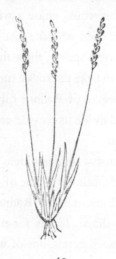

49
Early Sand-grass
Mibora minima

A stiff, purplish grass, just an inch tall, said to be the world's
smallest
On bare sand at Aberffraw Dunes (*Tywyn Aberffraw*),
Anglesey
27th March
Helpers: Ian Bonner, James Robertson,
Ivor and Jane Rees

The second plant of my quest was a grass. A very small grass,
some say the smallest in the world, a grass for the lawn of a
doll's house. Its name is Early Sand-grass, though more usually
botanists refer to it by its scientific name, *Mibora minima* – a
minimal presence on certain dunes facing the Irish Sea in late

winter. It meant a long journey to Anglesey – all that way to see an inch-high grass – but it doubled as a reunion with some old friends, Jamie and Joanna Robertson, who have a small farm on the island. They had warned me not to leave it too late to tick *Mibora minima*. As an annual growing in loose sand, it has to flower and set seed before the ground dries out. So it pokes forth its stiff little head in the first warm pools of winter sunshine, flowers and seeds quickly, and then dies back, long before the first bathers are spreading their beach towels.

Being an annual also means that this is a plant that comes and goes. A decade ago I might have tootled down to Dorset to see it. Or I could have headed to the Gower Peninsula, where patches of *Mibora* used to face the sea at Whiteford Burrows. But the best place to see it today is Anglesey. That morning, another sunny day towards the end of March, we met at the dunes of Aberffraw, a great half-moon bay of sand facing the Irish Sea. We were joined there by another old acquaintance, Ian Bonner, who is the BSBI's county recorder for Anglesey, and by two naturalist friends, Ivor and Jane Rees. Between us, we reckoned we could find it. Bearded, enthusiastic and with an encyclopaedic knowledge of the island and its wild flora, Ian told me that, although he had shown a great many botanists the beauties of the island, I was the very first person to come here to see *Mibora*. 'Come back later,' he urged, 'and I can show you some very nice hybrid horsetails.'

Crests of sand traverse Aberffraw's bay like frozen waves. The locals call it *Traeth Mawr* – the Big Beach – but it is also known with pawky humour as 'Anglesey's Sahara'. Nearest the sea the sand is fine and yellow, but inland it turns grey as its minerals are leached by the rain. Frogs and toads breed in the dips between the cliffs of sand where the water reaches the surface. These west-coast dunes are wonderfully rich in plants because they are made up partly of broken seashells, made of the same substance as chalk and limestone. On this warm morning, when the dunes were still winter-brown, the scent of wild thyme hung in the air, to be displaced further inland by the tang of drying seaweed and the whiff of decay from the estuary.

It was almost warm out on the sand. When the wind dropped I could hear the swoosh of the sea, the skylarks singing overhead and the occasional cronk of a raven: the songs of Aberffraw. That winter had been drier than usual. The frogs and toads had spawned in whatever shallow puddles and ruts they could find. Their dried and frazzled eggs littered the path: black strings of bootlace, teaspoons of caviar from a millionaire's picnic. 'You never can tell any more,' sighed Ivor. 'Last year this slack was a lake. This year it's a desert.'

Mibora wasn't hard to find. The trick, instructed Ian, is to look wherever the turf has been scratched by rabbits. 'Over the next headland, at Cymyran,' he added, 'it even flourishes in the ruts left by motorbike scramblers.'

All the same, Early Sand-grass is difficult to spot from head height. So down we went on our knees, crawling about the rabbit scrapes with our noses to the ground, and there it was: inch-high green and purple spikes, with the odd violet stamen sticking out between the florets. *Mibora* obtains its dole of nourishment from decaying weed, rabbit dung and dew. It survives against the drying winds with the help of a layer of wax so thick that both leaves and flowers are as stiff as fairy bayonets. The stamens seem too big for the grass-head and stick out like ears. You wouldn't call it pretty; you probably wouldn't want to grow it in a garden; but *Mibora* is rather charming in its coquettish minimalism – with the necessary magnification of a lens, it looks somewhat like a cactus. It is a much finer thing than the nondescript, wispy little plant in Keble Martin. He had evidently never seen a living *Mibora*.

'*Mi*-borough,' insisted Ian. He made it sound like a small manufacturing town in the Midlands. 'I've always called it "My-*bore*-er",' I said. 'Hmm. What about "*Me*-boh-ra"? I've heard it called that.' How botanical names are pronounced is a question that has never been fully settled, for Cicero is no longer around to tell us how Latin was spoken. Some insist the stress should be on the second syllable; others that you should use an equal stress throughout, as far as possible. The truth is that no one way of saying '*Mibora*' is better than any other. Mi-borough? My-borer? We take whatever path seems best through the maze of a dead language, and no one seems to mind so long as they know, more or less, which species we are talking about.

We left the mini-grass in its scented desert and headed for the nearby village – the seat of the kings of old Gwynedd – for a cup of tea and an ice-cream. Two down, forty-eight to go. A fine morning at the seaside with old friends, and a long journey home.

48
Unspotted or Suffolk Lungwort
Pulmonaria obscura

A woodland flower with blue flowers and heart-shaped leaves
and without the telltale spots of garden lungwort
Ancient woods near Diss, Norfolk–Suffolk border
24th April
Helper: Alex Prendergast

I *won't* call it Unspotted Lungwort: probably the least-inspired
name in the whole flora. We are forced to assume that a plant
named from a negative must be an exceptionally dull one. This
lungwort's scientific name *obscura* says as much. It could mean
'darkened', or 'hidden' in the sense of a plant that is hard to
identify because it so closely resembles another species. So it
came as a pleasant surprise that *Pulmonaria obscura* is not only

attractive and grows in a lovely, wild location, but is also reasonably distinctive and not 'obscure' at all. Its alternative name, Suffolk Lungwort, is much better, for this plant is indeed confined to that county.

Common lungwort is a familiar spring-flowering flower of cottage gardens, so named from its oval, blotched leaves, which vaguely resemble the human lung. But there are also two fully wild lungworts in Britain, both rare: the Unspotted one and the (also often unspotted) Narrow-leaved Lungwort, *Pulmonaria longifolia*. I had tracked down the latter at Exbury Gardens the previous year, growing among primroses in a pleasant glade overlooking the Beaulieu River. It had flowers of a piercing dark blue – pretty enough for it to be gathered in the past in bunches as 'Virgin Marys' – and long, oval, bluish-green leaves. I was curious to see how the recently discovered Suffolk Lungwort compared, for, to judge from the books, the differences seemed to be slight. That may be why it wasn't until 1995 that the Suffolk Lungwort was correctly identified as a new and apparently native British species.

My guide for the morning was Alex Prendergast. In his twenties, he had spiky, green-dyed hair, perhaps in sympathy with the plants he clearly loves. Alex is a botanist at Natural England, based in Norwich. His enviable job is to keep an eye on rare flowers, mosses and lichens, and to come up with plans to conserve them in our ever-changing world. He monitors their populations and the state of their habitat, and advises accordingly. Alex's knowledge and expertise were impressive. He instantly understood the purpose of my quest, for he himself is a self-confessed 'Stace-ticker', eager to see as much of our wild flora as possible. His knowledge of the plant world extends beyond flowers and ferns to include mosses and liverworts, and even stoneworts – those neglected aquatic plants that look like tiny fir trees, but are in fact algae. Alex carried a well-used vasculum, a botanical box on a strap, made of metal to maintain a cool, humid environment for the plants inside. Every Victorian botanist used to own a vasculum, but most of them are now in museums. Alex's was made in 1820.

The predicted showers never came and the sky remained a reassuring, ethereal blue. We had permission to visit the lungwort woods, all of which are private and are used to rear pheasants. You could see the woods from the road as smudges of trees not yet in full leaf, each crowning a low rise. I wasn't sure what to expect. Woods reserved for pheasants are typically full of tracks and feeders and overrun with brambles and tall grass. In other words, I was ready to be disappointed.

In fact this one was one of the prettiest small woods I have ever seen. One reads of the 'tapestries' of flowers, of primroses, anemones and violets, that used to carpet our woods before the explosion in deer numbers and the onslaught of modern machinery on stable woodland soil. Bluebells excepted, it is now unusual to see real carpets of flowers. But this one would have caused gasps of admiration at the Chelsea Flower Show – a glorious display of celandines, violets, primroses and anemones, plus the odd dash of the exotic: the purple towers of Early Purple Orchid and the sinister, oddly insect-like flower of that devil's lily, the Herb Paris. The wood itself was a coppice of ash, maple and hazel with ancient, moss-grown stumps. You wouldn't be surprised to see a fairy sitting on a primrose.

There were plenty of lungwort too, not confined to the sides of tracks as I had been led to believe, but mingling with the anemones and bluebells. It even had its own bee, *Anthophora plumipes*, a big black buzzing one that was doing a grand job of pollination, to judge from the many seedling lungworts about. Alex told me that 95 per cent of seed collected from here for the seed-bank at Kew has proved viable – a sign that the Suffolk Lungwort really is an overlooked native species and not a garden escape that had somehow found its way into an isolated ancient copse. Lungwort flowers lack scent and the bees find them by sight. Maybe that is why the flowers are blue (they change colour as they grow, from pink buds to blue or purple flowers). With its sensitivity for the violet end of the spectrum, the bee sees them better than we do. Indeed, for an insect whose vision extends to the ultraviolet, the flowers may appear to them as incandescent beacons, shining like lamps in the semi-shade.

'How many people ever see this?' I wondered, wide-eyed at the beauty. 'We get the occasional group,' answered Alex. 'The local branch of the Wild Flower Society comes here as part of a yearly open day organised by a local nursery. They sit on hay bales in a trailer and get towed in by tractor.' But in general, visitors are not encouraged. Apart from the keepers, who know about the lungwort and do not harm it, the only person to see it regularly is Alex himself. He's talking to another landowner who is keen to establish the plant in a place where visitors are more welcome. Maybe the main reason why the Suffolk Lungwort was overlooked for so long is that so few people ever saw it. It is confined to three small woods, none of them with public access. Moreover, its flowering season is short and early, and the plant would be hard to spot at any other time.

The other lungwort wood we visited was larger and more overgrown, on stiff clay rather than sand, and less rich in flowers.

Yet the lungwort seems to be thriving here too, in open glades within the wood and centred on one broad grassy ride. The keeper refrains from mowing them until later in the year, not so much for the lungwort's sake as for the displays of 'milkmaids', the local name for Lady's Smock. Alex decided to do a quick lungwort count. Using his hands and arms for scale, he calculated the rough area occupied by 100 lungworts and then 'proportionated it up'. By his calculation, the biggest patch held roughly 900 mature plants. All told, he thought there must be in the 'low thousands' of them. 'It has definitely increased,' concluded Alex. I came away feeling that I had seen something special: a pretty and seldom-seen wild flower that, for whatever reason, happens to be the only plant confined to Suffolk.

So far my quest had presented few problems in terms of timing. The three early plants were comfortably separated, leaving plenty of time to plan the journeys – and for doing other things. But the time was fast approaching when everything would be coming into flower at once, the peak time of late May through June to early July, the season the French once called *Floréal*. To make things worse, I was taking a week off to go on a wildlife holiday in Hungary with some friends. To fit the bulk of my missing flowers in a few crowded weeks would need military timing, some help from the weather and, it was dawning on me, a certain amount of luck. Quite a lot of luck, in fact.

47

Slender Cotton-grass
Eriophorum gracile

A small cotton-grass with creamy, powder-puff heads rooted
in open water and moss
A wet valley bog near Sway in the New Forest
28th May
Helper: Andrew Branson

Cotton-grass is the humble plant that dapples the wetter moors
of northern Britain in late spring with fluffy spots of pure white.
The puffs of cotton are what pass for the flowers: long white
bristles with an ovary at their base. At a slightly earlier stage
the male parts appear as a mass of yellow stamens. Individually
the plants look nothing special but, en masse, they cheer up
some of our most barren moorlands. There is even a Cotton

Grass Appreciation Society, dedicated to the art and music of the hills. The wonder is that no one has tried spinning these cotton balls into fabric. The mill-owners of Lancashire seem to have ignored an abundant source of pseudo-cotton growing on their very doorsteps.

There are four kinds of cotton-grass in Britain. The commonest, *Eriophorum angustifolium* – the Greek and Latin mean 'narrow-leaved wool-bearer' – has multiple, drooping heads, though in wet weather they tend to stick together, while the Hare's-tail Cotton-grass, *Eriophorum vaginatum*, has solitary puffs, as the common name implies. More localised, and so less likely to be noticed, is Broad-leaved Cotton-grass, *E. latifolium*, which prefers moving water, such as spring-heads with a touch of dissolved lime. And finally, and by far the rarest, is Slender Cotton-grass, *E. gracile* – small, delicate and ecologically exacting. It was this cotton-grass that I had come to the New Forest to see, with the help of Andrew Branson who, for reasons he will explain, has a particularly soft spot for it.

We were in one of the valley bogs of the New Forest, called 'bottoms'. A boggy channel with a stream in the middle, it formed a narrow, gently curving strip of wetland of the kind botanists call 'poor fen': that is, not quite acid enough to be a bog, but not sufficiently lime-rich to be a proper fen, either. It was a fine spring morning, the air sweet with the coconut fragrance of gorse. From some recess within the thorns, a Dartford Warbler was singing. Andrew, in his early sixties, with red hair and a well-trimmed, greying beard, was enjoying his freedom. For the past quarter-century he had been pinned to his keyboard as a publisher and editor, most notably of *British*

Wildlife, a journal he founded in 1989, at the dawn of the environmental movement.

He was surveying our soggy bottom with a practised eye. 'That's *Scorpidium cossonii*,' he pointed out happily: a brownish little moss with curly leaves. 'It's more or less confined to springs with limewater in them: a signature species. Drain the spring and it's gone.' That meant we were standing in an unusually well-preserved bottom, full of flowers with bog in their name: Bogbean, Bog Pondweed, Bog St John's-wort, Bog Pimpernel. And with them was another signature species of New Forest valley bottoms: Southern Damselfly, *Coenagrion mercuriale*, a needle of piercing blue on glistening wings.

'I spy cotton-grass.' I said.

'Ah, well done. Oh, *Common* Cotton-grass. Pure white, more or less. Now look over *there* where it's really wet, down by the stream. Do you see how *those* cotton puffs aren't white? More of a dingy creamy-yellow, looking like well-used paint brushes? *That*'s our plant.'

The Slender Cotton-grass wasn't going to make it easy for us. To reach it we had first to wobble over an obstacle course of quaking tussocks. The surface peat was only a crust over what was probably a lost lake – a devil's domain of sooty water bubbling up under our wellies. If you want to touch Slender Cotton-grass, you are going to get muddy and wet. I found a vantage point from which to look over its finer points. Not for the first time, I found the real thing more plausible, better than the pictures. As expected, it was a slenderer, slighter version of its relatives, but with more distinctive features. Its cotton puffs are more dainty, less drooping and, as Andrew pointed out, tinged with pale grey and yellow, enabling the experienced cotton-grass hunter to pick them out at a distance. The heads are also blunt-ended, exactly as though someone has trimmed them with a pair of nail scissors. The leaves are short and as narrow as needles and, since they tend to die back early, the flowering stems are often all there is to see. In fact a blind person could distinguish Slender Cotton-grass, said Andrew, by licking. The flower stalks (pedicels) feel rough, due to tiny bumps or 'papillosities' that are just visible with a lens. Lick the other cotton-grasses and they feel smooth.

No artist has got the Slender Cotton-grass right. Keble Martin didn't even try; all he has is a text description: 'In acid bogs, rare and local', and he was wrong about the acid bogs. The best published drawing is Claire Dalby's, in Frances Rose's *Colour Identification Guide*, but even she failed to notice the distinctive shade of its cotton brushes and so has made them as white as snow.

Andrew was pleased at how well it was doing. Hundreds of the little off-white heads bobbed in the morass by the stream. Back in 1994 he had counted less than half a dozen plants in flower. At its other, better-known site in the New Forest the cotton-grass is doing less well, probably because of competition and increased shading from reeds and alder bushes. Our plant, like so many rare and declining species, is a poor competitor. To survive it has become a specialist, able to grow in places where other plants cannot. Both in Britain and across most of Europe, Slender Cotton-grass is in steep decline; its strongest showing is now in Ireland, followed by Finland. As a plant of very wet, nutrient-poor places, it is vulnerable to drainage and also to agricultural fertilisers. It used to be found in at least thirty different places in England and Wales, but now survives in only seven, of which just three are in England. The New Forest once had ten sites; now there are just two, and one of those is in trouble.

'I love it to bits,' confided Andrew, slightly apologetically. 'It's my favourite plant.' I asked him why. 'I used to be the voluntary warden at a Hampshire nature reserve, where this was once the star plant. By the time I became involved, it had already been "lost". I spent hours trying to re-find it, without success. So for me it became an icon of the lost fens of Britain.' Few plants have suffered quite so catastrophic a loss – and most of it within our lifetimes. In some counties it was discovered in one decade, only to be lost to drainage in the next. Britty Common, in Somerset, used to have all four species of cotton-grass, until the Forestry Commission stepped in and drained it. Andrew sees Slender Cotton-grass as a kind of vegetable bittern: 'There it is, standing erect at the heart of the bog, in the wettest place, blending in, hard to see and never appearing for long. We've driven it to the edge. It's a sweet little plant,' concluded Andrew. 'And a very sad story.'

Probably the main reason it survives in the New Forest is because of the ponies. 'Look at your trousers. No, not there – below the knee. See those bits of cotton-grass-heads all over them?' I hadn't noticed before, but my bog-hoppers looked as though I had just brushed through a bed of wet thistledown. Being wet and slightly sticky, the cotton is almost impossible to remove until it has dried out. Andrew believes that the cotton, along with the seeds attached to it, was once carried from one watering hole to the next on the coats of wild animals, such as the extinct wild ox or aurochs. Now free-range ponies do the same job. Possibly they also take away bits of cotton-grass rhizome (creeping stems) on their muddy hooves – necessary mud that they maintain by treading, wallowing and grazing down the invading grass. Some believe that another of the plant's former unwitting partners was the beaver, whose endless chewing and dam-building created exactly the sort of open, wet quagmires that Slender Cotton-grass likes. The loss of most of our big mammals may have been its tragedy, for in the majority of places it has now lost the ability to spread into new sites, despite flowering freely and setting fertile seed. And who will miss it once it has gone? Andrew will. And so, now, will I.

Lost and Found:
Why Extinction Isn't Necessarily the Last Word

46
Interrupted Brome
Bromus interruptus

A brome grass with a characteristic 'interrupted' look, as
though there are bits missing
At the edge of an arable field near Whittlesford, Cambridgeshire
2nd June
Helpers: Fred Rumsey and Ashley Arbon

The rarest wild plants of Britain are those classed officially as
'critically endangered', meaning 'probably doomed, without
immediate help'. But there is a category beyond that: 'extinct
in the wild', which means that the wild plants have all gone,
but that the species lives on in captivity, generally in one or

more botanic gardens.[2] Such is the case of a grass called Interrupted Brome. It is not, frankly, much to look at, and not likely to be chosen for its aesthetic qualities, but Interrupted Brome is unusual in at least one respect: it is, or was, found nowhere else in the world outside Britain. It is one of our few endemic plants. Unfortunately, as it turned out, its habitat was not a natural one, but a field of crops, sainfoin above all. That was problematical for at least two reasons. First, no one grows sainfoin any more. It was formerly cultivated as fodder for horses, although it was also attractive for bee-keepers. And second, crop fields are apt to get sprayed because no one wants a field of weeds. The result was that Interrupted Brome died out almost everywhere in the immediate post-war years, apart from a single field headland in Cambridgeshire. And by 1972 it had died out there, too.

That Interrupted Brome hasn't, after all, gone the way of the dodo and the dinosaur, and so is still available to be twitched by plant-hunters, is because someone happened to collect a few of its seeds before the grass disappeared. Philip Morgans Smith didn't know he was rescuing a doomed species. All he wanted was a few strands of the grass to keep in a pot. He was a lecturer in biology and he was interested in brome grasses. Not only was it a nice addition to his collection, but it would also make a good novelty to introduce to his class on grass identification.

As I say, Britain doesn't have many species found nowhere else in the world. So why didn't we take better care of this rare

---

2 That of course means that living material is available for a reintroduction. But first you need a suitable place to introduce it to; for it was probably the lack of such places that caused the extinction in the first place.

example? Probably because it was a grass. Despite our fondness for lawns and sports fields, most of us have a blind spot for grasses. I have talked to otherwise knowledgeable naturalists who seemed surprised to learn that not all grasses are the same. One of the tricks we tour leaders like to play is to sit people down in the middle of a field and ask them how many kinds of grasses they can see. If it is a good field – for example, what ecologists call an 'unimproved meadow' – you could easily lay your picnic cloth on a dozen different kinds. And most grasses are as different from one another as a swan is from a goose. Their uniform greenness disguises their exuberance of form. Keble Martin understood this when he drew his 150-odd species of British grasses, distributed over five plates, in pencil, and had them printed in monochrome. They look more individual that way.

Keble's portrait of Interrupted Brome is exact. Evidently he never saw it in the field, but he still managed to capture its strangeness: a grass from which bits seem to have been plucked – hence the 'interrupted' look of the heads. These are deltoid (three-sided) in shape, are covered with soft hair and bear long, stiff awns, slender spines that catch the fur of a passing mammal and so help the plant to disperse. Keble's pencil catches its top-heavy look, with a big three-way cluster of deltoids crowding the apex. The clinching botanical character is a split palea (a palea is one half of the grass flower – the petal, as it were, the other half being the lemma). Unfortunately this is not easy to see in the field, but even without it, this is a fairly distinctive-looking grass. People have known its existence since 1849, but for a long time it was thought to be a variety of the common and versatile Soft Brome, *Bromus hordeaceus*. Interrupted Brome wasn't described scientifically until 1888, forty years after its discovery, and it was seven years after that before it was elevated to a species, *Bromus interruptus* Druce.

'Clover fields,' noted Keble Martin, 'becoming rare.' In fact, the grass was already rare by then, and getting rarer fast. As a species it enjoyed less than a century of recognition. The grass probably evolved by mutation and, since it has never been found outside arable crops and grass leys, and so was always associated with farmland, it had no wild habitat. Quite likely it spread from place to place not by natural seed dispersal, but in sacks of impure grain. An attempt was made to save it at its last site, but it was too little, too late. By 1972 the Interrupted Brome was written off as extinct.

And that might have been that, if Philip Morgans Smith had not had the foresight to pick a bit and maintain the grass in cultivation. No one knew he had done so, nor did he know that he owned the last tuft of Interrupted Brome in the whole world. Some years later he was at a conference in Manchester and happened to overhear botanists bewailing the loss of the grass, and wishing something more had been done to save it. 'Ahem,' said the modest Smith. 'Would you like some seed?'

From the pot on Smith's windowsill came all the sizeable quantities of Interrupted Brome now cultivated in botanic gardens or frozen in seed-banks. The challenge now was to use some of this stock to reintroduce the plant into the wild – wild in this case being a suitable field corner or headland. One such place, owned by a farmer who was also a keen ecologist, was found in 2003 at Whittlesford, Cambridgeshire, not far from the last-known native site. Another was created by the plough on the chalky slopes of Aston Rowant nature reserve in the

Chilterns. The media picked up the story and ran it with gusto, comparing the sowing of this very modest annual grass with revivifying the corpse of a dodo. Well, it made good copy.

The experiment did well for a year or two, then less well, and finally it failed. What went wrong? The usual things, it seems. A report by Fred Rumsey of the Natural History Museum, who took over the project later, concluded that it had been 'neither documented, reported, or adequately dealt with in the absence of staff delegated to take the work forward'. A modest amount of money had been dedicated to its establishment, but not for any follow-up work or monitoring. Some 200 plants were counted on the strip at Aston Rowant in 2005, but then, 'due to difficult weather, ploughing was delayed', and after that the sheep got at it through a hole in the fence and grazed the plot flat. At Whittlesford the introduced plants did better, until herbicide spray drifted over from the nearby bean crop and killed the lot. And so, a mere six years after the much-trumpeted reintroduction, there were once again no Interrupted Bromes except those growing in pots.

More money was scraped together for a second bash in 2013, centred on the same site at Whittlesford, plus two more headlands nearby. It was to this field that I headed, one unseasonably cold, overcast day in early June. I was met there by Ashley Arbon, who farms thirty-five acres here but works mainly as a professional ecologist, and by Fred Rumsey from the Natural History Museum, who is in charge of the project. A short walk through the farmyard and out into a hedgerow facing a big square field of beans and we were there. The precious brome was in fresh flower, a whole mini-meadow of it, the top-heavy heads swirling and swaying in the bitter wind. 'It gradually keels over under its own weight,' said Fred. 'Come late summer, it will have dried and turned yellow in the sun. If we get any sun this year.' To avoid a repeat of death-by-herbicide, Ashley had left a broad, unsprayed 'buffer zone' between the grass and the crop and, interestingly, this had been colonised by other rare 'weeds': Rough Poppy, Sharp-leaved Fluellen, Venus's Looking-glass. 'Mind if I take a bit for my windowsill?' I asked, eyeing those interrupted stalks. 'I'll turn my back,' said Ashley.

How wild is 'wild'? For all practical purposes, this strip of cultivated brome is less a wild grass than a crop, a source of seed for further conservation attempts. Its survival will depend on regular cultivation, like any other crop. It might even require weeding, for mixed with the desired brome is another, far less desirable one: the aggressively colonising Sterile Brome. Ashley had sown Interrupted Brome seed at two other sites, but less successfully. At one, the tender seedlings had been crushed by a heavy vehicle operating in wet weather. The other site had been underwater for days and was now smothered in horsetail, although a few plants had nevertheless struggled through. Fred hopes to get other introductions up-and-running. His aim is to get the plant to the stage where nursing is no longer required, when the grass will, he hopes, spread naturally from field to field as it did in the past. Its best chance may lie in seed packets of 'wild flowers' attuned to unsprayed arable fields on the chalk.

Before I set off on the long road home, Ashley had something else to show me. We walked into a cul-de-sac of modern houses with cars, street lights and brick walls, the sort of street that could be anywhere. 'There it is,' he told me. 'Where?' '*There!*' We were standing on the pavement and over a low wall lay someone's front garden. What marked out this particular garden from a row of more-or-less-identical front gardens was a large patch of one of the oddest plants in the British flora: Birthwort, *Aristolochia clematitis*. It was clearly at home in these very un-wild surroundings, 'growing up straight and tall, like a field of crops', as one admirer observed, its thick, heart-shaped leaves masking the tubular, bright-yellow flowers beneath. Without any knowledge of its circumstances, anyone would suppose that the gardener liked aristolochias and had bought this one from a plant nursery along with its neighbouring columbines and Japanese roses. But, in fact, records show that Birthwort has grown wild close to this spot for more than 300 years, despite periodic attempts to get rid of it. Its whereabouts was noted in one of the first local floras, the second edition of John Ray's *Catalogue of plants growing around Cambridge*, published in 1685. The Birthwort has managed to cling to the same patch of land ever since, despite the passage of time, which has changed its patch from a rural hedge bank to an orchard to a farmyard, and now to a housing estate. The patch of Birthwort happens to be the one still point in a landscape that is no longer recognisable. It is the oldest thing visible, older than the trees or the walls or the houses.

Its original source may well have been a medieval herb garden, for Birthwort was grown for its medicinal 'virtues', as a means of speeding up labour and easing the birth, or, some say, to induce abortions. The flowers hint at their function, for they are shaped to resemble the womb and the birth passage. They could be pretty useful in cases of snake-bite too, or so noted the Tudor herbalist John Gerard, and, in powdered form, could 'beautifie, clense, and fasten the teeth'. In his day, Birthwort was wonderful. Today it is just a plant.

It's a nice question which is the wilder: an ancient plant persisting under its own means in a small garden or a wild grass deliberately sown into a field corner? Evidently the probably non-native Birthwort is better at surviving modern conditions than the probably native Interrupted Brome. Yet both may survive in this small corner of an intensively farmed and populous county simply because someone loves them. It is easy to get despondent about the fate of our wild flowers. Conservation bodies speak of the 'fragility' of a species, as a thing so easily broken or smashed. But we can just as truly see wild plants as remarkably tough and adaptable. Every one of them has its own way of surviving change, for otherwise they would not have survived at all. It might be copious seed production, or networks of creeping stems, or teaming up with fungi or bacteria, or producing toxins that suppress insects and competing plants (the toxic chemicals at work in Birthwort did not evolve for human benefit, even if we did find them incidentally useful) – or some other trick in its armoury that we have not yet discovered. Wild flowers are resilient beyond our imaginings. Interrupted Brome might be among the least successful forms of vegetation on the planet and yet, with a little imaginative help from mankind, it too may have a future.[3]

---

3   Certain plants now 'Extinct in the wild' can do very well in cultivation. The ginkgo, for instance, that survivor from the age of the dinosaurs, is grown the world over, though it may be extinct as a wild plant. A striking example from Europe is Parrot's Beak, *Lotus berthelotii*, which has lovely flame-like flowers on trailing silvery foliage. Although long gone from its only wild site, in the Canary Islands, it is sold for hanging baskets in plant nurseries, so much so that it is often known as the *Common* Parrot's Beak. There is only one snag. None of these plants have produced any seed, and the plant now seems to be completely sterile. Hence it can never again be a fully functioning wild flower.

What Makes a Species?
The Mystery of the Fen Woodrush

45
Fen Woodrush
Luzula pallescens (or *L. pallidula*)

A small, tufted rush-like plant of damp, peaty woodland; it
differs from its closest relative in various botanical characters
On disturbed damp ground at Holme Fen, Cambridgeshire
16th June, morning
Helpers: Alan Bowley and Peter Stroh

First a little-known grass, now an even less-known grass-like
plant: Fen Woodrush. Relatively few people have ever set eyes
on it in Britain and, indeed, like the Interrupted Brome, the
woodrush has been written off as extinct before now. But it still
occurs in one place, Holme Fen, although, according to the most

recent survey, it seemed to be on its last legs, with fewer than fifty plants. Finding it might be a challenge, or so I thought. A population that small could crash out of existence at any moment.

Fen Woodrush is a misleading name. It grows not in marshy places, but in open woods on winter-damp, peaty soil. In effect it is named not from a habitat but a place, or rather two places: Woodwalton Fen, in Cambridgeshire, where it was first discovered in 1907, and nearby Holme Fen. Such is the plant's waywardness that Keble Martin found no specimen to draw. Nor, until recently, did anyone else. Even Claire Dalby, the best-ever illustrator of rushes, woodrushes and their like, ducked this one. So that may be another reason why the Fen Woodrush has sometimes been lost: nobody had a very clear idea what it looked like.

Holme Fen is a place of dramatic transitions, a birch wood on what was once a bog and, before that, the largest lowland lake in England: the lost Whittlesey Mere. Today the ground level is many feet lower than the waters of that lake, for the drying peat has shrunk to below sea level. Yet the woodrush seems to have survived all the convulsions, and, indeed, the drying of the fen might have favoured it. One of the problems of finding Fen Woodrush is that it grows with another plant it much resembles, the much commoner Heath Woodrush, *Luzula multiflora*. The stated differences between them sound subtle: the leaves of the Fen Woodrush are of a 'lighter green' (but how much lighter?), the heads a 'paler brown' (but how pale is that?). Only one person seems to have taken much interest in it: Maurice Massey, a former warden of the Nature Conservancy Council, an insightful and meticulous botanist.

I had asked Massey's wiry successor, Alan Bowley, to help me track down a bona fide Fen Woodrush. We met on the main ride at Holme Fen, along with Peter Stroh of the BSBI, a fellow spirit who had been busy drawing up a new *Red Data Book* of threatened wild flowers in England and thus welcomed the chance for a day out. Luckily, Pete had brought with him a few genuine specimens of Fen Woodrush from his garden, where he cultivates them in an old stone horse-trough. 'It is easy enough,' he said. In fact it can be hard to prevent the plant from taking over the horse-trough and crowding out other, equally desirable species, such as his precious Fen Violets. To my surprise, Pete's plants looked rather distinctive, and in fact elegant. Yellow-brown clusters of seed-heads were borne on straight, stiff pedicels, sealed with an upright bract (the usually narrow leaf below the flower), held in a spray of slender, fresh-green leaves. So *that* was Fen Woodrush.

Alan had good news. He had located a patch of it deep in the wood and had marked the position with a bamboo cane, on which he had tied a strip of red ribbon. The morning was still and warm, and the wood was filled with the smoky scent of drying peat. We crossed the footbridge into the reserve and set off through beautiful, spring-fresh birch trees along a grass track bordered by half-grown fronds of bracken.

Suddenly, Pete stopped and stooped. 'Surely that's it there.' Right by the path was a tufted woodrush that certainly looked very similar to those in Pete's horse-trough. Quite a lot of it, in fact. Alan said that yes, he'd seen them before, but believed them to be hybrids, crosses with the Heath Woodrush. Not the pure thing.

The experts got their lenses out.

'How about the leaf base? Poland says it has short hairs on the leaf base' (John Poland is the author, with Eric Clement, of a vegetative key to British plants – a book that tells you how to identify plants without flowers.)

'The hair character is a bit dodgy. I think Poland was working from garden plants.'

'Are the capsules *obovoid*?'

'Seem to be. And the pedicel is definitely *papillose*.'

'This *must* be it.'

'But see how hairy it is.'

'But look at those upright, compact *panicles*. It has the right jizz of the thing. It *must* be.'

'I'm gonna take this away.'

By now we were finding similar plants all the way along the track and by the thousand. Had past surveys got it wrong? Far from being nearly extinct, our woodrush seemed to be thriving. 'How many people come here to see it?' I wondered.

'Hardly anybody. You're one of the few. Only one other person has asked me to show it to them this year.'

At length we reached Alan's marker and the bona-fide woodrush, a neat clump with classically pale heads on short, stiff stalks. By now even Alan was ready to concede that the Fen Woodrush, as we understood it, might be under-recorded. Since it did not seem to be a very demanding plant, it raised the question of why it hasn't been found anywhere else. Maybe, suggested Pete, it is because *dry* fen is a rare habitat. In East Anglia, drained fen was nearly always converted to farmland in short order. Perhaps, then, all the other surviving fens are too *wet* for the woodrush.

Alan thinks that another key is competition. Many (maybe most) uncommon plants are that way because they are poor competitors. Back in the 1970s, a large area of birch was cleared at Holme Fen and the ride was churned up in the process of dragging the logs to the trailer. Thousands of Fen Woodrushes appeared from nowhere on the broken ground, only to disappear again as the grass moved back in. Perhaps, we conjectured, this latest apparent splurge of woodrushes might owe something to the maturing woodland, with more light reaching the floor through the boughs of now-tall trees, and perhaps also to the invasion of muntjac deer, which are busy chewing up the brambles and keeping them at bay.

So that seemed straightforward enough. Fen Woodrush duly ticked! But we were in for a shock. Our plants were later examined closely by Fred Rumsey at the Natural History Museum and by Jan Kirschner in Prague, who is the world authority on woodrushes. Their conclusion was that the plant we had seen in such quantity was not, in fact, Fen Woodrush but a form of its near lookalike, the common and variable Heath Woodrush, *Luzula multiflora*. It is possible, thought Fred, that the latter had absorbed some of the genes of Fen Woodrush by hybridisation in the past. But it wasn't Fen Woodrush, and so we hadn't found it. Armed with a better understanding of the differences between the two species, Fred and Pete did eventually locate a small colony of what they called 'pukka *pallescens*' in a damp place where the ground had been disturbed after the removal of some invading scrub. Ironically the work had been done to safeguard a completely different plant, the Royal Fern. Pete sent me a photo of the find, the real deal, the pukka plant. And, yes, it was slightly paler brown, slightly lighter green, slightly more delicate. Once you see the real thing you can understand the very subtle difference, the hair's breadth that distinguishes one critical species from another. So our hunt for the Fen Woodrush turned out to be the first failure of the quest. What we had found was what nearly everybody had thought was Fen Woodrush, but wasn't. Perhaps if they mess up the soil by pulling up some more willow trees there will be a better opportunity in future to see the infinitely elusive, real thing: one of the least-known, least understood wild plants in the British flora.

44
Crested Cow-wheat
Melampyrum cristatum

A ragged plant of woodland edges and hedge banks with
tubular, bright-yellow flowers enclosed in pink, frilly bracts
On a grassy bank close to Monks Wood, a large ancient wood
near Woodwalton, Cambridgeshire
16th June, afternoon
Helpers: Alan Bowley and Peter Stroh

My plan now was to go on to Thetford to look for two more
plants on my list, but Pete had bad news. He had been there the
previous day and, this being a late year, my target flowers were
not yet out. Instead he offered to show me Crested Cow-wheat.
I was happy about that, since I had never seen this attractive plant
at its colourful best, and so felt I could squeeze it into The Quest.

Cow-wheats are plant cuckoos. Although they manufacture some of their needs in the usual way, by photosynthesis, they also sneak their roots among those of other plants and tap them for sugar, salts and water. Perhaps cow-wheats concentrate nutrients in their tissues, for they say that cows that graze on it produce particularly rich milk and golden-yellow butter. The 'wheat' bit is named after the plant's seeds, which are large and resemble unripe grains. The scientific name, *Melampyrum*, has the same idea. Originally coined by Theophrastus 2,300 years ago, it means 'black wheat' – for, although it is good for cows, too much cow-wheat seed can darken the flour and give it a bitter taste.

The real purpose of these big, fleshy wheat-grain seeds is to get the ants onside. Without their help, the plant's life-strategy wouldn't work; in no time at all the seeds would be gobbled up by foraging mice and voles. But ants love the seeds because they come with a droplet of sweet oil that they can slurp and then puke up to feed to their grubs. The seeds are also of a size and shape that are agreeable for ants to carry off to their nests, since they resemble the cocoons in their nurseries. Nor are the pink, frilly bracts enclosing the flowers present for mere decoration. They form chutes for the seeds, which roll down the channel like a child down a playground slide, gathering speed and then shooting out from the tip. Because of the plant's peculiar architecture, with shoots and flowers facing all ways, the seeds are broadcast to all points of the compass. Ants seem to remember where cow-wheat grows and so forage about the plants, picking up seeds or crawling up the stems to poke about in the ripe capsules. But what turns a good evolutionary idea into absolute genius is what happens next, after the nutritious seed-oil has been consumed. Ever anxious to keep their nests neat and tidy, the ants carry out the now-useless seeds one by one and dump them in the waste, the ant midden, which is rich in nutrients from a whole summer of shitting ants and therefore as good as fertiliser for the germinating cow-wheat seedlings.

And so cow-wheats in general, and the Crested Cow-wheat in particular, are ant plants, evolved to take advantage of an insect which, though small, is the most numerous on the planet – and, moreover, one anchored to a territory by its nest and regular foraging habits. I love it when plants outwit animals. Of course the ant gets something out of it, too – a reward for being such a helpful dumb insect – but you sense that it's the cow-wheat's game; the cow-wheat is in charge.

If only Crested Cow-wheat could cope as well with mankind. Humans have all but driven it out. There is not a single cow-wheat field left in England. Even in the odd corners which are all that is left to it, theirs is, in every sense, an edgy existence. Scrubby banks get mown or flailed before the seeds can ripen. Verges become overgrown by hogweed and nettles. Sprays wipe out the flowers. Fifty years ago, Keble Martin could describe Crested Cow-wheat as 'local'; today it is officially 'endangered'. This implies that, unless things improve, this plant of marvels could wind up extinct in Britain.

Given all that, it was heartening to find so much of it on *this* bank in Cambridgeshire, on the sheltered south-facing side of a large wood. And in good flower, too. Locally they call it the 'Melampyrum Bank' in the cow-wheat's honour. The Crested Cow-wheat is a lovely sight. Drawings and pressed flowers do not adequately show the plant's strange beauty: how it branches at exact right-angles, north, south, east and west, with the surprisingly small stem-leaves matching this symmetry. It is peculiarly angular. And each branch terminates in those pretty, pink-and-yellow frilly heads, like decorations for a fairy feast.

'It's having a good year,' said Alan. The population had 'leapt across' (Alan's phrase) a ditch, or 'popped over' (Pete's), and was now spreading into an adjacent field, which had been plough-land only a few years ago. Perhaps it is following the ants. Perhaps one day soon this field will be coloured in June by a mass of cow-wheat flowers, a lost East Anglian landscape in glorious resurrection.

I said goodbye to Alan and Pete and, with time on my hands, went for a walk in the wood, hoping to glimpse a rare butterfly for which it is famous: the Black Hairstreak. This, so a waymark informed me, was a Butterfly Trail. But the experienced butterfly-watcher doesn't need signs. To find the elusive hair-streak all you need do is look for a group of usually elderly people gazing intently at a sloe bush. Ah, there they are!

One of the gazers was an old acquaintance of mine, Brian Davis, who used to work at the former ecology research station at Monks Wood. We got talking and Brian told me his own cow-wheat story. There used to be a road verge not far away from here where the Crested Cow-wheat had been 'protected' by the local council. Just to be on the safe side, Brian had collected seed from the colony and scattered it on the opposite verge. Sure enough, it has done well there, but had failed to flourish at the original site. For the council's idea of protection was to leave the verge alone, un-mown, and in consequence it had become overgrown with nettles, thistles and docks. 'Good intentions are never enough to preserve wild plants,' he concluded. 'What you really need is knowledge.'

At least that is the story I took down. Later, Brian told me I'd got it wrong and that the cow-wheat is still present on the original verge, and in good numbers. That at least makes a happier ending, even though it ruins my story and its sturdy moral.

Earth-smokers: The Fumitories

43
Few-flowered Fumitory
Fumaria vaillantii

A small, pale-flowered annual fumitory, differing from its
relatives in various minor botanical characters
At the edge of a chalky arable field near Pegsdon,
Bedfordshire
17th June
Helper: Chris Boon

I remember the day in 2011 when Amy, our postwoman, delivered
my review copy of *Flora of Bedfordshire*. It weighed as much as
a couple of bricks. She nursed the parcel in her arms like an
obese baby. Hastening to relieve her of the burden, I nearly
dropped it on my slippered toe. 'It should come with a health
warning,' laughed Amy.

There is a tendency for county floras to get bigger and bigger, not because wild flowers are getting more numerous – far from it – but because of their authors' sense of completeness. Floras make a statement. They reflect the diversity of the county and the wonder of wild flowers, but most of all they are a record of the prodigious amount of fieldwork made by local botanists over many years. Usually they are written by men or women near the end of their recording career, as a kind of culmination. Moreover, today's floras tend to be printed on heavy coated paper so that text, maps and pictures can be colour-integrated over, in the case of *Flora of Bedfordshire*, 718 large pages.

Its author is Chris Boon (his friend Alan Outen added a shorter section on mosses and liverworts). It took him twenty-five years. Chris learned about the county and its flowers from his hero, the author of the two previous *Floras of Bedfordshire*: John Dony, a Luton schoolteacher. It is typical of the modesty of local botanists that you can read all about Dony in this latest flora, but almost nothing about its present author, Chris (if you look very hard, you will find just a tiny bit on page nine). But there is a photograph of him on the back: a fit-looking man, who appears younger than his then seventy-two years, holding a hand lens. He has the thoughtful, slightly quizzical expression of a dedicated naturalist. If a Bedfordshire flower had eyes, it is that look of intense curiosity that it would see, as the hand lens descends. Chris is a former research physicist who has been recording wild plants in the county since 1973. Early retirement has been a real boon (oh, dear!) to British botany. It has released people who still have enough energy to throw themselves whole-heartedly into ambitious mapping projects. Retirement, and the advent of desktop publishing, has created a new generation of flora-writers at a time when many believed that published floras were heading for oblivion. That is, of course, another reason why modern floras are so thick and heavy.

I had met Chris by chance on a plant tour of eastern Crete. I mentioned my forthcoming quest to see all the British wild flowers, and Chris kindly offered to show me some of the gems of his home county. So, when I got home, I dragged the great *Flora* from its bottom shelf, dumped it on the desk and turned the pages, hunting for a flower I had not yet seen, for that big, wild-Bedfordshire tick.

Bedfordshire is a bit like England in miniature. It has a tight knot of chalk downs in the south, a few heaths, meadows and marshes surviving in its agricultural heartland, and scattered small copses and woods. It has nearly every English lowland habitat apart from a coast. But there are signs that the county's wild flora is in retreat, not so much from development – though there is plenty of that – but from more insidious causes. Back in the early 1950s John Dony had established more than a hundred 'permanent plots' in interesting bits of the county, and recorded their flora in detail. After Dony died, in 1991, his plots were relocated and surveyed again by Kevin Walker of the BSBI, and only then did it become clear just how much things had changed. The wet places had been drained or polluted; many a former botanical wonderland had become over-shaded or crowded out by nettles and brambles; some of the woods had been felled; and most of the old grasslands had been ploughed up and reseeded. Native plant biodiversity had crashed. The reason why Chris Boon's flora is bigger than John Dony's is largely the hundreds of non-native 'introductions'. The new plants have escaped into the 'wild' from gardens and nurseries, from bird-seed and rubbish dumps, and possibly even from bike treads and rucksacks. They have spread along main roads and railways and now maintain themselves on walls, waste ground, even the cracks in an urban pavement. Botanists love these new species because they never know what they will find next – new species are always exciting. But the county's native wild flowers were in a much better state half a century ago in John Dony's time, and his work proves it.

Eventually I found in the *Flora* a wild flower I hadn't seen. It was a little cornfield weed called Few-flowered Fumitory, *Fumaria vaillantii*. I gave it a number: Plant 43. As chance had it, Chris had shown me this very species at the edge of a field of maize close to the shore in eastern Crete, a long way from the cornfields of Bedford. It must be a versatile plant, but it has never been an easy one to find. No one, it seemed, had seen it in Bedfordshire lately. Cornfields make an unstable habitat for flowers because one good blast of herbicide, one sharp twist of the plough, can put paid to the wild flora for another year. But, given the chance, arable flowers can still reappear from buried seed, whenever conditions permit.

According to the BSBI's handbook on fumitories, there are more than fifty ten-kilometre-square records for *Fumaria vaillantii*, mainly from the chalk in south-east England, but only eighteen since 2000. Formerly listed as 'nationally scarce', Few-flowered Fumitory is now considered 'vulnerable', which is worse than 'scarce'. The next step on the slippery slope is 'endangered'. And the one after that is 'extinct'. 'You've chosen a hard one,' said Chris.

Fumitories are a tight group with only a dozen species, technically related to poppies, though looking nothing like them.

I am fond of fumitories despite their difficulty, which is why I wanted to find this last one. They have curious long, thin flowers that reminded people of boats, so that fumitory experts talk about the flower's 'keel'. Where you might expect to find the sail is a feather-like petal they call the 'wing'. All British fumitories are annuals and their not-so-natural habitat is disturbed ground, especially arable fields and gardens. I have even seen wild fumitories in hanging baskets. Keble Martin managed to squeeze all the British species on the same plate – a mass of similar-looking flowers, which, in the words of the writer and humourist Miles Kington, 'slide imperceptibly from one to another'. All share certain general characteristics: clusters of pink-and-cream flowers and funny little fruits the shape of lollipops. Some species scramble, or 'ramp', as the botanists say, while other, generally smaller ones creep along the ground among pebbles of chalk. Fumitories are named after their finely divided leaves, which trail in a way that reminded some imaginative observer of smoke, and hence *Fumaria*, meaning 'smoke-of-the-earth', or 'the fuming plant'. They say the plants even smell faintly of bonfires.

A means of telling one fumitory from another is to look at the sepals, a pair of frilly appendages near the back of the flower where, on a ship, you might expect to find the rudder. In some species they are proportionately huge, like a pair of elephant's ears. On others they are tiny; and those of the Few-flowered Fumitory are the tiniest of all – in fact barely visible without a hand lens. The trick of identifying fumitories is therefore to forget about the leaves or the flowers and look at the sepals.

One of the rules of fumitory-finding is that in ninety-nine cases out of a hundred it will be the well-named Common Fumitory, *Fumaria officinalis*. Looking for the exceptions, therefore, is a bit like looking for a slightly differently shaped piece of hay in a haystack. All the same, Chris and I thought it worth a try in some carefully selected chalky fields in the south of the county.

The first was a sloping field bordering a gravel pit at Barton. It was a flop. The crop had been sprayed. In a good year, said Chris, this place can absolutely fume with fumitories. 'A weed-free field for the lucky farmer then?' I mused. 'Oh, please. Don't call them weeds. They are arable *flowers*. A weed is just a flower in the wrong place.'

After lunch we tried another field near Pegsdon, a square of plough-land bitten into the base of the down. The field's ripening wheat must live on fertiliser, for there was almost no topsoil. No wonder supermarket bread has no taste. But along the edge the arable flowers were wonderful. There was a long line of wild Candytuft, whose flowers are themselves chalky-white, matching the pebbles. There was a sprinkling of other choice arable *flowers*: Small Toadflax, Venus's Looking-glass, Dwarf Spurge… Where are the fumitories? Aha!

Some flowers you can admire standing. For others you need to kneel as if in worship. To admire the smaller fumitories you have to lie at full length in the dust and pull out your hand lens. 'Hello,' I said. 'You're not going to believe this.' Chris eased himself alongside and studied the little plant for what seemed quite a long while. 'Congratulations,' he said at last. 'That's the one. It's *vaillantii*. Look at these tiny sepals. Look at these rounded fruits.' I felt a moment of glowing pride. Few-flowered Fumitory, despite its mournful name, is not a bad-looking flower: a kind of mini-fumitory with pale-pink florets on twisting stalks, and strangely animated leaves like green monkey-fingers poking this way and that. There was quite a bit of it, too, growing with the common one, for ease of comparison. Well, that had been easier than expected.

'This seems to be a new site for it,' said Chris, getting up and dusting himself down. 'Don't worry,' I said, 'I'll say *you* found it. Do you mind if I pick a bit?' It seems only polite to ask, when you are in the company of the county recorder. 'There's plenty of it. Be my guest.' My Few-flowered Fumitory lasted for weeks in its tooth-glass on the kitchen windowsill. But the little flowers never ripened into those 'subglobose' (meaning inflated but not quite spherical) fruits whose seeds I hoped to sow in the garden. For that they presumably need something more nutritious than tap water.

With plenty of afternoon left, we walked over a nearby chalk hill to see the orchids. The full plant list of this particular hill makes your mouth water: Pasqueflower, Moon Carrot, Spotted Cat's-ear... It also boasts the world's most closely studied wild orchid. Back in 1962, the ecologist Terry Wells began a long-term demographic study at this place of Autumn Lady's-tresses, a small white orchid that, contrary to convention, produces its leaves first, and flowers only when they have died back. Each and every year Wells came here to count the number of little white spiky flowers, as well as the exact number of seed-capsules on each plant, and the number of leaf rosettes. Anything that could be counted in the field, he counted. By this simple but time-consuming means, he discovered that the flowers vary wildly in number, and that most are eaten by rabbits or sheep before they get the chance to ripen seed. But, counter-intuitively, this probably doesn't matter very much, for the little plants are long-lived, and seed-set is more of a long-term insurance policy than an immediate necessity. More importantly, the rabbits and sheep do a useful job in keeping the turf short and open enough for little orchids to bloom.

Terry's project had another useful result. This is now the only colony of Autumn Lady's-tresses in the Chilterns. The reason it survived, when all the others didn't, was that Terry Wells used all his charm and persuasion to save his outdoor laboratory from becoming just another patch of barley. The farmer gave his assent, and the place is now a nature reserve.

We were too early to see the lady's-tresses, but we found another of the glories of the hill, Burnt-tip Orchid, and in good flower. Another miniature orchid of short chalky turf, its white, spotted flowers dangle from dark-red sepals that, when in tight bud, produce the 'burnt-tip' effect. Orchids are the rare birds of botany. People come from far and wide to photograph them, occasionally in numbers greater than the habitat can reasonably withstand. This was such a place. To safeguard the Burnt-tips, the best colony had been protected by a circle of chicken-wire. Admirers had worn a path around it. 'Like Stonehenge,' I murmured. Other orchids had been individually caged. One Burnt-tip was poking through the wire, as if reaching out to the wind and sun from a prison window. 'People get very protective about orchids,' said Chris. 'They say it's to ensure they manage to ripen seed.' Yes, you wonder, but how do their pollinating bees feel about buzzing through holes in chicken-wire?

A mesh of metal takes away a little of the joy of discovery. I think wire cages around wild plants are about more than would-be protection. They imply, surely, a sense of possession: that this orchid has been gardened by *me*, its licensed protector, and you are forbidden to touch it. But, I wondered, if somebody thinks they own a plant, what does that say about its wildness?

42
Spiked Rampion
Phyteuma spicatum

A cream flower with a head of massed tubular flowers that
reminded someone of Rapunzel's long hair
The banks of a country lane near Heathfield, Sussex
20th June
Helpers: Steve Berry and Pat Millard

Rampions, wrote Geoffrey Grigson, are a bit like animals. Think
of a kind of sea anemone – an 'air anemone' – on a stalk. The
flowers, small bundles of violet-blue that float over banks and
downs in late summer, are formed into curly tubes that resemble
tentacles, and from each one a triple-pronged stigma projects
like an adder's tongue (the long stigma acts like a sink plunger,
pushing out pollen grains as it grows). A rampion in full bloom

looks as though it might enjoy catching and ripping apart a visiting bee. But it is only a flower. Like other flowers, it offers not a vicious claw, but a touch of nectar in exchange for the bee's unconscious duty, carrying away the tiny grains of pollen that cling to the tip of that snake-tongue stigma.

In Britain this air-anemone is the Round-headed Rampion, a late flower of the downs. It is also known as Pride of Sussex, at least in Sussex. Our only other, and much rarer, rampion is also a Sussex plant. In fact Spiked Rampion is confined to that county, especially in the well-wooded district between Heathfield and Eastbourne. Unlike the Pride of Sussex, its flowers are yellowy-cream in colour and look more like bottlebrushes or, with a bit of poetic licence, like braided hair. It might have been the plant behind the story of Rapunzel, the girl with the long, fair plaited hair. As fairy-tale fans will recall, she was the girl who was banged up inside a tall tower after her mother unwisely stole rampion from a witch's garden. Rampion has edible roots, which were highly prized in parts of Europe. Rapunzel was named after the Latin name of the rampion flower, *rapunculus* – that is, Little Rampion. Appropriately or not, Spiked Rampion's leaves are heart-shaped.

In times past, Spiked Rampion could be found in many of the copses and lightly shaded lanes of Sussex, but today it has disappeared from all but seven sites. It survives best along the sunny side of narrow lanes, often concealed under bracken. Conservationists are doing their best to maintain optimum conditions for the flower by cautious hedge-trimming or bracken-nipping. It is the kind of plant that gets fussed over: attractive(-ish), unusual and growing in the kind of pleasant, cottagey countryside that gets onto National Trust calendars.

Since this is the only plant to be absolutely confined to Sussex, local patriotism is also invoked. As the commoner rampion is the Pride of Sussex, perhaps the fair Rapunzel could become the *Hope* of Sussex?

Armed with grid references kindly donated by the Species Recovery Trust, I set off one jolly, sunny afternoon to look for Rapunzel's flower with my friends Steve Berry and Pat Millard, and their bouncing dogs, Bella and Patch. The narrow lane that is now considered to be the best site is hidden among a maze of similar lanes, and we went round in a circle twice before finding it more or less by accident. It is one of many quiet lanes in this part of Sussex, designed for horse and cart rather than the Range Rover. One side opened into fields; the other was a steep bank topped by a hedge. While Pat wrestled with the dogs, I did the botany-walk: slow step forward, look up and down, a few steps further and repeat. The first trio of rampions I spotted were nearly over. With a sinking feeling I walked on, and there, under a fretted canopy of bracken, I stumbled on the main colony. I counted fifty in flower, but there were doubtless more; and with such a rare plant, you don't want to be too intrusive. In a good year a hundred or more flowering spikes have been counted. The national total is fewer than 500 plants.

A curiosity of the Spiked Rampion is that it changes shape as the flowers mature. To begin with, the cluster of tubular florets is conical, with the flowers opening from the bottom, bristling with spiky stamens. As more open, the spike elongates until it becomes a ragged cylinder, with the fresh flowers now at the top and those at the bottom already swelling into seed. Once all have gone over, the spikes look more like plump plantain heads, greenish pompoms, still bristling with those tough little stigmas. For his picture, Keble Martin chose a plant that was a little past its best: an upwardly spiked bottlebrush, highlighted by a downturned leaf. He got the timing wrong, too. Spiked Rampion flowers in May and June, not July. It is, in fact, another tricky one to get exactly right in our changing weather.

Bracken can be an evil neighbour, crushing other vegetation under the sheer weight and toxicity of its dead fronds. On this bank, it was a friend. There was no mattress of decaying vegetation, only a loose dry litter through which grass and flowers could flourish in the dappled shade, as in open woodland. In fact the flora of this bracken-bank resembled that of old woodland. There were bluebells in flower, and spotted orchids, and a sprinkling of twayblades, primroses and woundworts. Country lanes don't come much sweeter.

Keen to see the rampion in its aboriginal setting of ancient woodland, we made our way to Abbot's Wood, one of the larger natural woods of East Sussex and once the rampion's best-known site. We had no great hope of finding it, but suddenly there it was, right in front of us – about forty flowering heads, huddled together by the side of a muddy track. The only trouble was that they were inside a cage, a wire rampart that seemed as likely to prevent their escape as to protect them. There was no sign or explanation, but it was possible to guess the reason. This is a public wood and the main rides are close-mown, presumably in obedience to health-and-safety rules. Hence most of the verges are distinctly flower-unfriendly. Only inside its cage could the rampion find refuge, along with its retinue of sedge, bluebell and pimpernel.

One of the rampion flowers had curled over the top of a slightly smaller one, as if to comfort it. Perhaps it was the cage, but I couldn't help thinking of one of those memorials for concentration-camp victims, the mother embracing her child as if to shield it from the horror all around.

Dominic Price of the Species Recovery Trust told me I'd been lucky: it had been a vintage year for rampions. The annual count of the flowers had been the best for ten years (but far fewer than thirty, or even twenty, years ago). One reason it sometimes fails to perform well is that the verges get cut before the plant has the chance to flower, as a result of a failure in communication between the county council, which is responsible for road-verge maintenance, and the contractors who actually do the work. Protected or not, road verges tend to get mown flat by bored men in cabs with the radio on. In one case a new ditch had been dug straight through the rampion patch. Yet the flower appears in everyone's plans – the council highways authority, the Forestry Commission, Natural England. No one wants to harm the flower. But it gets harmed nonetheless, because the plan is on a computer file, not in the cab of a mowing machine.

Fortunately, perhaps, the Spiked Rampion is easy to cultivate. *Ridiculously* easy, according to Belinda Wheeler, who sowed it into her Devon garden, only for the plant to make a dive for freedom, self-seeding into her borders and paving cracks and even invading plant tubs. She spent years studying the plant for a doctorate and still enjoys its ragged, urchin heads poking through the flowerbeds every spring. That Spiked Rampion can so easily turn into a plant outlaw in shaded gardens suggests that its apparent delicacy on Sussex verges is an illusion.

In fact it might be wrong to see it as an endangered native and not as a successful invader that is now encountering hard times. The rampion was grown in gardens as long ago as the sixteenth century, as a vegetable as well as a pretty flower. The lateness of its discovery in the wild (1829), in a well-botanised corner of England, does suggest an arriviste rather than an aboriginal. But I was happy to give Spiked Rampion – relative newcomer or not – the benefit of the doubt and a big, bold tick as Plant 42. We had exercised the dogs, enjoyed two short walks at the prettiest time of the year, and now it was time for pre-dinner drinks in the garden: rather a lot of them, as I recall. This is gentle English botanising at its best, I thought, as Steve splashed more gin into my tonic. The quest, I considered, is going really rather well at the moment.

41
Childing Pink
Petrorhagia nanteulii

A small annual pink with crisp flowers enclosed by a papery
bract
On bare sand at Shoreham, Sussex
21st June

There were two more flowers I wanted to tick off on the way
home. I didn't expect them to be much trouble. Both, I knew,
grew at Shoreham Beach, where it ends at the nineteenth-century
concrete fort and coastguard station. Starry Clover, *Trifolium
stellatum*, was said to grow right by the fort itself, although it was
there before the fort and survived its construction. Why it doesn't
grow anywhere else is a mystery. It is a very common flower of
waste places in southern Europe and, since it is not much grown

in cultivation, is unlikely to be a garden escape. It might, just possibly, be an overlooked native flower, clinging to one of the warmest, sunniest corners of England, but since most people think otherwise, I decided not to give it a quest number. The shingle beach here certainly has the feel of a much warmer shore, with its colourful mixture of 'escaped' silver ragworts and pink beach asters and native Viper's Bugloss and Yellow Horned-poppy.

I was expecting to have to search the beach for the tiny clover, but I spotted its little red stars and contrasting bright-green trefoil leaves almost as soon as I opened the car door. It was doing well on the banks of the parking bays in front of the fort, and nearby where walkers had worn a track to the beach. The stars of starry clover are not the pinky-orange flowers, but the enlarged sepals left behind after the petals have withered. Under a lens they are fringed with bristles. The whole plant is hairy – a useful adaptation to dry, summer-hot places, for the hair maintains a halo of relatively cool, moist air around the plant and so prolongs its life. Although it can ripen seed in warm years, the clover seems to rely mainly on its creeping stems to form patches up to six feet across.

The other famous Shoreham rarity grows just around the corner on the inland-facing bank. The place, known locally as Silver Sands, is a private beach at the back of the Harbour Club. When I pulled up at the forecourt they were rolling beer kegs from the back of a lorry, with metallic rattles and clangs. Behind the clubhouse is a narrow backwater with a few moored boats. Across the narrow inlet lies a desolation of dredgers and warehouses: VW Heritage, Travis Perkins, Screwfix ('Open 7 days!'). The only beauty lay at my feet, in the patch of a tiny flower growing in bare sand. This was the Childing Pink: little fingernails of shocking-pink, as pink as angels' cheeks. The flowers are borne on stiff little stems with just two spiky leaves near the base. They look like fairy arrows with a pink blob at one end – Cupid's heart, perhaps. Most of the colony lay within a low wooden fence, put up by the local council to prevent people from wandering outside with their beers and accidentally crushing them.

The flowers are produced one at a time inside cup-shaped, papery bracts. That is presumably what the 'childing' is about: the clusters produce just one little pink cherub, followed by another. Only a few robust plants bore twins. Unfortunately, despite the plant's name, reproduction and efficient dispersal are not its strong points. It produces plenty of seed but, since the seeds are relatively large and dense, they rattle from their dry cases like coal from a scuttle. Growing by the shore brings its own pressures, too. Most historical colonies of Childing Pink have been built over or otherwise destroyed. The best remaining one, at Pagham Harbour, is inaccessible at flowering time because it blooms inside the fence protecting a tern colony. There is not much to be said for Silver Sands as a natural habitat – though the pink itself seems wild enough. But it would have to do.

40
Least Whitebeam
Sorbus minima

A pretty, small flowering tree with tiny notched, oval leaves
and round red berries
Craig y Cilau, Brecon Beacons, Powys
24th June, morning
Helper: Tim Rich

At the start of my quest to see all the wild flowers I decided
to make certain exceptions. I would ignore the ones botanists
call 'critical', those you cannot identify without a hand lens and
a specialist manual. The first plants to be set aside were all the
many forms of brambles, hawkweeds and dandelions, which
would, in any case, require several lifetimes to see. I was less
certain whether or not to include several more groups consisting

of plants that readily hybridise with one another and which can therefore be difficult to identify, among them oraches, eyebrights and dog-roses. I decided to include them whenever I found them, or when they were shown to me by a proper expert, but that they wouldn't appear among the Last Fifty. Even I wasn't prepared to travel to the ends of Britain to see a dog-rose.

That left the whitebeams. I was reluctant to ignore them because, for one thing, whitebeams are beautiful small trees with their white-clothed leaves, their abundant blossom and the flaming spectacle later on, when a well-lit tree turns into a conflagration of orange and scarlet berries. And for another, I happened to have seen most of them at one time or another, at least those that could be described as 'classic' whitebeams – the ones known to Keble Martin when he was finishing off *The Concise British Flora*. Whitebeams take you to some of the love-liest places in Britain: wooded limestone gorges, cliffs where wind-pruned trees sweep down to the sea, landscapes of rock and stone where weather-beaten trees cling to remote ledges. The trouble is that there is now a large and growing number of new whitebeam species that cannot be easily identified, and which is leading to a hawkweed level of complexity. Many of the new ones have been discovered and described by my friend Tim Rich and his co-workers (Tim has been honoured by one of the new species, *Sorbus richii*, Tim's Whitebeam). I decided to restrict my whitebeam-hunting to just two species that I have long wanted to see, and if we saw some others on the way, that was fine, too. I asked Tim if he would act as a guide and, being an obliging soul and always fond of a windy day out, halfway up a cliff, he agreed.

Tim has been at the cutting edge of British field botany for half a lifetime. He was still studying for his doctorate when he wrote the BSBI's Handbook on the Crucifers – the cresses and cabbages – one of the trickier families in the flora. He has worked on the conservation of rare flowers for Plantlife, written a full-scale flora of his home turf, Ashdown Forest, and of course has spent a lot of time with whitebeams. He's probably the most prolific field botanist of his generation. His unquenchable enthusiasm for plants makes even the most arcane research sound fascinating. You sharpen the pencil and start a new page, for a day out with Tim.

Whitebeams are weird. The standard, common one, *Sorbus aria*, is a sexually normal species with diploid (that is, twin) chromosomes, which reproduces in the usual out-crossing way, perpetuating the species with sufficient natural variation to ensure its survival in an unstable world. But long ago things started to get more complicated when an ancestral *Sorbus*, either Rowan or Common Whitebeam, hybridised with another *Sorbus* and the resulting hybrid produced fertile seed. There must have been a large number of times over the past 10,000 years when such hybrids have stabilised and evolved into a new species – but this time one with three, four or even five pairs of chromosomes instead of the usual two. Tim and his colleagues have reconstructed an evolutionary tree of whitebeams, in which most of the present-day species form branches off the mainstream 'trunk'. For these, evolution has probably come to a juddering halt. Unlike their ancestral parents, these whitebeams produce seed asexually, so that each seedling is an exact copy of its mother. Normal sexual reproduction rarely, if ever, takes place. This means that populations consist of genetically similar mother–daughter lines, effectively clones. In theory these forms are all species, and have therefore been given names, both Latin and English. Botanists call them 'micro-species', and many of them consist of very small populations in circumscribed places, sometimes even a single cliff – quite possibly the selfsame cliff where they first evolved. Certain places, mostly on hard limestone, form hotspots for rare whitebeams. They include the Cheddar and Avon Gorges, the lower Wye Valley and the place Tim was taking me now: Craig y Cilau in the Brecon Beacons.

Craig y Cilau (pronounced 'Kill-aye'; it means 'refuge crag') is a magnificent amphitheatre of limestone capped by Millstone Grit and with a bog at its base. The cave system within is one of the longest in Europe, although only a small part of it is accessible. The setting looks natural, but of course this is Britain, and not all of it is. Part of the original cliff was quarried away for stone, for use in the nearby ironworks at Brynmawr. A horse-drawn tramway delivered stone from the seams of limestone to the wagons beneath. The place is now a nature reserve, but the most significant act of preservation took place long before. During the Second World War the army had used the place as a mortar range, casually hurling shells against the cliff face. Fortunately a campaign led by the local MP had the desired effect. The soldiers were ordered off and told to take their explosives with them. It was the presence of rare whitebeams that clinched the case for the defence. But did local patriotism also come to the aid of the botany? Did someone point out that here were English soldiers blowing up good Welsh trees?

The cliff face looked pretty formidable to me, the more so as we approached it. In the words of one visitor, Theophilus Jones, hard, steep stone 'bursts out along the whole range of [these] mountains'. Tim knows it as well as his own back yard:

with the help of a good sense of balance, he has counted every whitebeam bush and tree. He took me to a fissure in the rock shaped like a chimney. 'It's the way up,' he said. 'Just shuffle and twist, use your legs and grab whatever hand-holds look firm enough.' It was my first proper scramble of The Quest, short but exhilarating. Tim went first, I followed, and within minutes we were standing on a natural shelf of stone on which you can walk as easily as on a stair, though without a banister to separate you from the giddying drop.

From below, the bushes and trees that cling to the cliff seem ordinary enough. But this is a wonderful place. Almost every native tree found in England and Wales grows here, in a kind of vertical wood. Among them are both limes, Large-leaved and Small-leaved, native beech at its westernmost natural limit, and patches of native yew, dark green against pale rock. And there are no fewer than five kinds of whitebeam, three of them – *Sorbus minima*, *Sorbus leptophylla* and *Sorbus cambrensis* – confined to South Wales. On these unstable cliffs the trees 'self-coppice', so that they often develop multiple branches, after a tumbling rock has crushed a trunk or a landslip has dragged down the roots. Slow growth and this natural coppicing have prolonged their lives. Tim showed me a huge Large-leaved Lime with multiple trunks, protruding from a hidden woody mass ten feet across. The great, green umbrella of its canopy is visible from half a mile away. Tim thinks it could be one of the oldest limes in Britain, perhaps a thousand years old, maybe more, not gnarled and hollow like an ancient oak, but still vigorous and continually sending up new shoots from roots twisted into rock crannies. This tree may be effectively immortal, or at least until the cliff itself erodes away.

Sorbus minima, or Least Whitebeam, is Tim's favourite tree and now I could see why. There was plenty of it up here and it is a beauty, a bonsai among whitebeams, with its twisted limbs bearing bunches of small, neat leaves. We were too late to see its white blossom at its best, and too early for its cherry-red berries and red-brown autumn colours, but it was still adorable. Unlike some whitebeams, this one sets seed regularly, though it has been slow to recolonise rocks in the adjacent quarry area. Tim has counted around 700 plants here, with a few more on an adjoining cliff, and that is the entire world population of the species. He believes it evolved on this very spot within the past few thousand years. A chance union of rowan and an existing whitebeam – it is uncertain which one – has produced this little tree that not only functions well biologically, but is also, to the human eye, a near-perfect combination of form, leaf-shape, flower and berry. And with a wonderful view at its back.

Tim pointed out other notable whitebeams. The most widespread is *Sorbus rupicola*, Rock Whitebeam, whose leaves are typically stiff, upright and cupped, exposing their white-winking undersides and so making this tree seem paler than the others. It is the probable ancestor of several of the rarer whitebeams. The evolutionary patriarch and its genetic offspring occur side by side; they could almost link branches. Next door to it was a fine example of *Sorbus anglica*, English Whitebeam or – since we were in Wales – *Cerddin Saesneg*. Tim demonstrated the distinctive feathering effect on the underside of its broad, oval leaves formed by the intricate veins, and also its leathery, slightly crinkly appearance. Once you know what to look for, you can spot a likely *Sorbus anglica* from a distance as a bush with multiple stems, often leaning well over its narrow ledge as if straining for the light. Soon, on a bare rock face we found yet another one, *Sorbus leptophylla*, Thin-leaved Whitebeam, a very odd-looking small tree whose trunk – or was it a branch? – was pressed to the rock like ivy, and whose branches pointed downwards like wooden stalactites. 'Hold up a leaf,' commanded Tim. They were relatively large and kite-shaped and much thinner than those of *Sorbus anglica*, indeed almost translucent. When I held up a leaf by its stalk, it flopped over. 'That's what it does,' said Tim. 'That's *Sorbus leptophylla*. It means "thin-leaf".'

There were plenty of hawkweeds on this cliff too, and since Tim is also a leading expert on the group – a hieraciologist – I asked him about them. It was easy enough to recognise a hawkweed as such, he said, from its general appearance: from its jagged or oval leaves, spirally arranged, its overall hairiness and its clusters of yellow, composite flowers. But naming the species requires some hard peering, for there are now more than 400 of them (it was 'only' 260 in Keble Martin's time). I was keen to see one of the latest, one that had appeared in the daily papers because Tim had named it after his hero, Sir David Attenborough: *Hieracium attenboroughianum*, Attenborough's Hawkweed. It's not that hard to recognise, insisted Tim, with its 'sparse, simple eglandular hairs with many hairs in the invo-lucral bracts' (which translates as 'simple hairs, without glands, and a lot of them on the cup-shaped bit holding up the flowers'). Unfortunately it didn't grow on our cliff, and the best he could do was to point out a hawkweed very like it, Limestone Hawkweed, *Hieracium subbritannicum*, which is distinguished, said Tim, 'by a different arrangement of hairs on the bracts, and more toothed leaves'. It was quite nice. 'You can age each plant by counting the leaf scars,' said Tim. 'This one is twenty years old.' Just out of its teens and flowering nicely.

Specialists get very fond of their chosen plants. Hawkweed-finders in particular insist that theirs are the most beautiful flowers in the world – above all, the mountain ones, which tend to produce a single large lemon flower above a pretty circlet of oval leaves covered in hair. You can tell how the experts admire the plants from the names they give them. There is the Neat Hawkweed, for example, *Hieracium perscitum*, followed by the Elegant Hawkweed, *H. mundum* and the Noble Hawkweed, *H. insigne*. Then, upgrading a bit, there is the Excellent Hawkweed, *H. probum*, the Splendid Hawkweed, *H. optimum*, the Memorable Hawkweed, *H. memorabile* and the Remarkable Hawkweed, *H. notabile* (the species name means 'note it well'). It would be rude to suggest that, whether Neat, Noble, Excellent or even Splendid, they all look very similar. There is a long-running tradition in British botany to name a new species after a friend or colleague, partly in the hope that they will do the same for you one day. So there is something rather touching in the way hawkweed experts have chosen instead to express their admiration for the flowers, rather than their own cleverness.

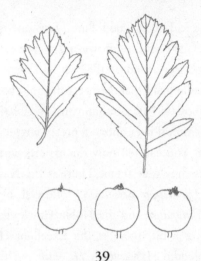

39
Ley's Whitebeam
Sorbus leyana

Another small flowering tree with distinctive lobed leaves and
small red berries
A wooded limestone cliff at Penmoelallt, near Merthyr Tydfil,
Glamorgan
24th June, afternoon
Helper: Tim Rich

Our next cliff was above a dry valley near the old mining town
of Merthyr Tydfil. *Sorbus leyana*, Ley's Whitebeam, was at one
time considered to be the rarest tree in the world, as well as one
of the rarest plants in Britain. Its world range consisted of two
cliffs of limestone on opposite sides of the valley. On one side
there were, in 2004, just eight small bushes, and on the other
three small trees, plus a few more that had been planted as a

conservation measure. Evidently the species has declined considerably since the botanist Ted Lousley noted a 'considerable number' back in 1948.

Ley's Whitebeam is deliciously obscure. Richard Mabey offered it as a conundrum of conservation in his seminal book *The Common Ground*. In the natural order of things, he suggests, these minutely different whitebeams must come and go. They arose from the random union of two parental *Sorbi*, will exist in small numbers as a short-lived 'micro-species' and then, inevitably, they will die out and be replaced by new, upcoming whitebeams. Without sharp-eyed and critical botanists like Augustus Ley, who discovered his eponymous whitebeam in 1896, no one would even notice them. 'Knowledge,' writes Mabey, 'makes extinction a moral problem as well as a material one... The ecosystem might scarcely stir if we sit back and allowed Ley's Whitebeam to vanish.' But – and it is a big 'but' – 'if we admit that any one species is not important enough to try and save, how do we argue for the next? How do we draw a convincing ethical line between an obscure whitebeam and an elm, say, or between a sperm whale and a salmon?' It is our knowledge of it that makes *Sorbus leyana* important.

But, perhaps surprisingly, it does have cultural, as well as scientific, value. Ley's Whitebeam, or *Cerddin Ley*, has become a symbol of Welshness, like the leek and the daffodil. Its notched leaf, rather like hawthorn's but larger, is now the logo of the Botanic Garden of Wales. A specimen at Garwnant Forest Centre was chosen as one of fifty 'great British trees' by the Tree Council (though, according to Tim, they planted the wrong species – it seems to be *Sorbus intermedia*, not *Sorbus leyana*).

There is even a picture of Ley's Whitebeam on a sign by the nearest car park — though the badly overgrown path suggests that few people come this way to see it.

We fought our way up the bramble-infested track past a succession of sculptures — a trenchant badger, a totemic hare, a crescent moon. It was starting to rain; the leaves were still wet from the last shower, but the midges didn't seem to mind. At last we reached the top of the cliff, a strange sort of cliff that lay concealed beneath another vertical wood with roots embedded in the rock.

'Careful where you tread,' warned Tim. He wasn't concerned for my own safety so much as for the seedlings and saplings of his precious whitebeams — and quite rightly, for they are much rarer than I am. He plunged like a jungle monkey into the leaves and disappeared. 'Don't come with me,' he cautioned, not that there was any danger of that. After a minute or two there was a commotion in the bushes and Tim's hand shot up through the leaves. '*Leyana!*' He shook the bush and I took it in with my misted binoculars: an obviously old plant, all root and branch, half-hidden in the rock with a moss-covered hollow stump in the middle. Three generations of shoots sprouted from its ancient roots. Tim had also found six saplings.

There was something else there, too. Tim disappeared again; his hand reappeared further down the cliff and another bough shook. 'Look!' It was (said Tim) *Sorbus* x *motleyi*, a natural hybrid between *Sorbus leyana* and rowan, and even rarer than Ley's Whitebeam. Just four plants, all saplings, represent the known world population. They had grown up in a gap created by the great storm of 1987, which gave a seed sleeping in the thin soil the light and space it needed to germinate and grow. Tim wanted to call it *motleyana*, after its discoverer, Graham Motley, and also happily incorporating the name of its parent plant, *leyana*. But it seems that name is ungrammatical by the rules of Latin. It had to be *motleyi* instead. 'And so,' regretted Tim, 'my fun was spoiled.' Perhaps *motleyi* will last only a few generations, lost in a blink of evolutionary time. Or perhaps the saplings will grow up, produce fertile seed and multiply, and in due course the hybrid will stabilise into yet another new species. Such is the lottery of evolution – a game of chance taking place on a single cliff, a slow pageant of whitebeams, evolving and transmuting for as long as climate and habitat allow. It felt good to be in such a place, a testing ground for new forms, where evolution has slipped into the outside lane and is currently running at top speed.

38
Fen Ragwort
Senecio paludosus

A noble ragwort up to seven feet tall with narrow, saw-
toothed leaves and two-inch daisy-flowers
A ditch by a busy road near Ely; and a glade at Woodwalton
Fen near Huntingdon
26th and 27th June

Fen Ragwort was extinct. On that everyone agreed. A towering
giant up to seven feet tall, with bright-yellow flowers the size
of moon-daisies, is hard to miss. It would have been a familiar
sight, once, in the fen ditches of East Anglia and Lincolnshire.
Each winter the plant would die back, only to shoot up rapidly
in late spring to overtop the reeds. However, all but fragments
of the wild, wet fens were drained in the mid-nineteenth

century using newfangled steam-pumps. In that mass drying many species died out, and among them was the Fen Ragwort. The last super-ragwort was recorded in 1857 by Professor Babington of Cambridge. And that was that – or at least it was for 115 years.

Then someone pausing at a lay-by on the busy road from Ely to Newmarket, perhaps to buy a coffee and a bacon roll from the ever-busy van stationed there, spotted an unusual tall yellow flower in a ditch on the opposite side of the road. It was Fen Ragwort. The ditch had been dug or re-dug, as investigation showed, only three years before. Presumably the excavator had brought up seeds that had been sleeping in the fen peat for more than a century. Seeds shed in the age of steam trains and penny-farthings had emerged into a brave new world of Concorde and computers; there were actually men on the moon on the day the Fen Ragwort was re-found. But in place of the reedbeds and grazing marsh where the ragwort's parents had flowered, the ditch now opened onto a thoroughly dry plain of wheat, past which lorries thundered, oblivious, on their way to Harwich.

Plants have senses of a kind that it is hard for a mammal like us to imagine. They pick up changes in their immediate environment: the fall of a tree, say, and the consequent explosion of light; they know a dull day from a bright one, respond when a pest attacks their leaves or bark, and can smell and hear, after a fashion. Experiments have shown that plants even respond to music, and are at least sufficiently critical to tell the difference between heavy metal and a string quartet (though what they seem to detect is volume rather than musicality). And so I wondered what the great ragwort thought of its new environment. Did it retain some distant genetic echo of horses and carts, of the swish of scythes in the meadow, the softer sounds of a quiet world? Sensing the crash and roar of traffic, did it perhaps wonder whether it had been wise to wake up? The ragwort's ditch regularly fills with rubbish; in 2001 four sackfuls were removed one day, along with 'a road sign, three drums of lubricant and a traffic cone'. The plant has also been a mute witness to several accidents. In 1998 a lorry collapsed into the ditch, just missing a budding ragwort. Another crashing vehicle shed its whole cargo of tinned cat food. You can still find the rusting tins down there, in the jungle of bindweed and coarse grass.

This unlovely ditch is still the only wild locality of Fen Ragwort in Britain. I stopped there one cool, cloudy day near the end of June. It took a while to find a few rather stunted plants just coming into flower. With only a narrow verge to separate them and me from the screaming traffic, I wasn't disposed to linger. Coils of blue piping close by suggested a rather desperate attempt to keep the ditch sufficiently wet. I'd heard that the colony was weakening. Traffic eddies batter the flowers. Herbicide sprays drifting from nearby crop fields may have taken their toll. There may even have been deliberate vandalism. When the *Daily Mail* ran a piece on the Rip van Winkle-like return of the Fen Ragwort, a lively correspondence ensued about the threat that ragwort is supposed to present to livestock and horses. 'I feel like digging it up and burning it,' roared an angry reader. Fed and misled by media stories, people have come to fear 'the yellow peril'. Some claim that ragwort is dangerous even to touch; and that sniffing the flowers, and so breathing in their pollen, risks liver damage (none of it is true, but that doesn't prevent people from believing it). To those readers, a giant ragwort represented the ultimate vegetable nightmare, a veritable invading triffid. Needless to say, the Fen Ragwort is far too rare to represent any kind of threat to anyone. In fact it is protected by law, and any zealous exterminator could be liable, on conviction, to a fine 'not exceeding £2,000'.

The future of the Fen Ragwort in Britain is not especially promising. Unlike its congeners on the opposite side of the Channel, the plant in its lonely ditch is infertile. Its puffs of seed are empty, and no seedling has ever been found among the cat-food tins. The colony could be wiped out at any moment by crashing vans, toppling lorries, burning buses. Hence its conservation plan is based on introducing the plant to other, supposedly safer places, especially nature reserves that preserve scraps of more or less natural fen. Fortunately Fen Ragwort is easy to propagate from cuttings or even from sections of its creeping stem. Grown on in pots and planted out on wet ground specially prepared for it, the plant has maintained a low-key presence in a few places for the past twenty years, though it has not spread far from them, as was hoped.

The next day I was able to visit one of those places. Woodwalton Fen, in the heart of the Fens, is one of our oldest nature reserves, originally set up to preserve – unsuccessfully, alas – the Large Copper butterfly. The Fen Ragwort grows in a glade among the reeds, not far from the entrance, but unless you know exactly where, you might walk straight past, as I did at first, for the flowers are tucked away behind a wet ditch and a belt of tall reeds. I peered through the parted stems and spotted it in a little glade among the reeds, in good flower, shaking in the breeze, tall and stately and buzzing with grateful insects. There were about a dozen of them, each about seven feet tall and looking unbelievably exotic, almost like sunflowers. They are counted ('monitored') every year and their progress noted; and it seems the Fen Ragwort has neither increased nor decreased much since they were planted there a quarter of a century ago. Two hundred more years further back and there would have been not only wild Fen Ragwort but scarlet-bronze Large Copper butterflies too, sipping nectar from those glorious floral sunbursts. Perhaps, one day, we will see such sights again, in the time-machine we call species reintroduction.

I enjoyed this encounter more than the roadside ditch, needless to say. But it is the catastrophic ditch that is home to the natural plants, while the nature reserve is really a kind of wild garden. The flowers in the ditch were the 'tick', and not Woodwalton Fen's stately plants. It's an interesting ethical question: which is the best – nature's own ragworts in a rotten location or introduced ones in a protected, well-managed reserve? Which is the best conservation plan: digging more ditches or planting more plants? The answer, it seems to me, might very well depend on your view of what 'wild' means, in the context of our unwild twenty-first-century landscape.

The Ice-cream Orchid

37
Early Marsh-orchid, cream-coloured form
Dactylorhiza incarnata subspecies *ochroleuca*

A robust marsh-orchid with creamy flowers with long, green
bracts and leaves that are hooded at the tips
A spring-fed fen in Suffolk
26th June
Helper: Richard Mabey

The Ice-cream Orchid was the only plant on my list that isn't
recognised, in Britain at least, as a full species. It is only a form,
albeit a very distinctive one, of an unusually variable species:
the Early Marsh-orchid. You can find this enticing plant in a
variety of wet places – damp meadows, boggy heaths, dune
slacks – with different colour forms that correspond to different
habitats. The standard pink-flowered kind, which supplies the

species name *incarnata* or 'flesh-coloured', grows in wet meadows and marshes. A few score of them flower annually in the water-meadow opposite my front window, little spurts of Rubens pink among the buttercups. A more compact, brick-red form specialises in the damp slacks between west-coast sand-dunes. A mauvy-purple one grows on wet heaths. You would assume them to be species, but they all seem to be expressions of the same entity, the Early Marsh-orchid. Its extraordinary genetic versatility enables the plant to colonise many different and contrasting habitats.

The rarest of all these varieties is one with cream-coloured flowers, known as 'variety' or subspecies *ochroleuca*. Close up, you notice that what seems to be a creamy shade is made up of a milky ground-colour and ochre-yellow spots. Its discoverer saw it as 'straw'-coloured. The writer and naturalist Richard Mabey, with more justice, has dubbed it the Ice-cream Orchid, for reasons I will come to in a minute. Like its fellow varieties, *ochroleuca* is a habitat specialist. In Britain it grows only in certain wet fens in East Anglia that are fed by underground springs. Upland moors and bogs are kept wet by the rain, but these fenny hollows rely on water pushed up from aquifers far below the ground: gin-clear water purified by a thick layer of chalk. The springs contain dissolved lime and feed a flower-rich meadow that is completely different from the acidic, rainwater bogs of the high moors. But their dependence on aquifers means that such places are vulnerable to abstraction. Even nature reserves are not proof against a bore-hole on the other side of the fence. Pristine, spring-fed fens are rare, and our incessant demand for cheap water is making them rarer still. As one of their signature flowers, *ochroleuca* has grown very rare indeed.

Mabey's Ice-cream Orchid has always been fickle in its flowering and hard to find, but recently it has been appearing more or less annually in a particular fen tucked away in the Suffolk countryside with no name on the map to give it away. Richard Mabey was one of the first to find it here, and I wanted him to take me there. Quite apart from anything else, I was determined to involve him in The Quest somehow, because he was, in part, unwittingly responsible for it. His own latest book was about plants. It focused not on botanical science so much as the extraordinarily manifold ways in which plants have played on our imaginations – or at least as they used to, when people felt closer to the natural world than we do now.

One of the more autobiographical segments of *The Cabaret of Plants* is about Mabey's own round-Britain botanical journey in the company of the photographer Tony Evans, which he wrote up as an earlier book, *The Flowering of Britain*. Both books are of the kind that open your eyes to the human responses to wild flowers and enable you to see the natural world differently. I had been educated as a scientific botanist, which allows you to identify stigmas and stamens and the likely pH of the soil, but blinds you to unscientific matters, such as beauty, as well as suppressing your innate sense of wonder (for the scientist sees wonder and sets about resolving it into measurements and facts). With the help of Tony Evans's brilliant photography, exploiting natural lighting instead of the flashgun, *The Flowering of Britain* reminded me that there was more to plants than botany; that they move us by their beauty and the way they settle into, and sometimes reflect, their surroundings. One of Evans's pictures lingered in my mind: the Bird's-eye Primrose, a tall, pink primrose with a yellow eye, on a misty, treeless hillside. I had become well acquainted with that primrose when I was studying plants in Durham for an abortive degree; too well acquainted in fact, for I had come to hate the tedious duty of clambering up hard, steep slopes to locate and count every last seedling, blown flower and leaf rosette. Now I saw what I had missed when I was slipping the metal quadrat frame round the accursed plants: the uncanny way the flower matches the 'pastel shades of the northern limestone', whose chalky leaves seemed to incorporate the very rocks of the dales. I saw Bird's-eye Primrose with new eyes and realised it was lovely. I was hoping to experience something of the same epiphany with another remarkable flower described in *The Cabaret*: the Ice-cream Orchid, but this time with the great man present in person.

Richard had been entranced by the orchid – not just by the thrill of finding such a rarity, but also by its unexpected beauty and resonance. Perhaps it was the silky, sensuous colour and texture of the flowers, which immediately turned his thoughts to food, to 'cream touched with citrus, lemon-meringue pie, cauliflower florets perhaps…' Or, as I now saw it, as buttermilk or, simply, dollops of rich vanilla ice-cream served on slivers of bright-green avocado, say. Richard's skin had prickled when he had found himself facing no fewer than twenty-five fine specimens of this almost impossibly rare orchid – more than had been seen for many a year (although in the best-ever year there were sixty). He was naturally 'hopping with delight at the possibility of having rediscovered a returned prodigal'. It seemed to be the ultimate find: a wild orchid, as little known and seen as the mysterious Ghost, and (unless you have a taste for Gothic things) a great deal more beautiful. As it transpired, the colony was in fact known about and was carefully watched, but had been kept as a great secret by a handful of local naturalists. They dutifully counted the flowers each year. Richard was lucky in finding twenty-five; a dozen or so is more normal. Perhaps the patient was responding well to treatment – for conservation volunteers were busy cutting scrub that threatened to invade the fen from the margins. They had put in a few cows, to keep the fen sufficiently short and open to allow the rare flowers space to breathe, and were also sealing in the wet by blocking ditches.

We were not quite as lucky. We found just three Ice-cream Orchids in flower. Richard had seen more in bud a week or two earlier, but they had disappeared, perhaps guzzled by deer, possibly by the very muntjac that we startled as we opened the gate. Our trio were all fine upstanding plants and they looked magnificent. I, too, without prompting, experienced a food fantasy: clotted cream and lemon curd, with the lattice-work of long green bracts only accentuating their lusciousness. Ice-cream Orchids are, in every sense, the *crème de la crème* – the cream of marsh-orchids. I took in their satin sheen, the stiff, unusually stout stems, the yellow-green leaves standing at an acute angle, hooded at their tips, and again the huge bracts. The flowers of *ochroleuca* are significantly larger than those of its relatives, and of a different shape: distinctly three-lobed with little notches on the sides. The plant is so distinct that you have to question whether a mere variety can stretch this far, and if we do not have instead an overlooked species. Certainly that is how most continental authorities, who are more familiar with the plant, see it. If they are right, this plant will need a proper English name. Perhaps they will name it after some animal, like the Frog, Lizard and Butterfly Orchids, or maybe, for consistency's sake, it will have to be the Pale

Marsh-orchid. But as far as I am concerned, the only possible name is the one that sets you drooling as you absorb the plant's delicious sensuality, exactly the same colour as full-fat Cornish vanilla ice-cream.

The Ice-cream Orchid is exquisite in its setting: the clear pools surrounded by moss with embedded sundews and butter-worts; the open fen coloured by pink Bog Pimpernel, Red Rattle and mauve marsh-orchids and, with a botanist's perception, the stunning variety of sedges and rushes. But it is the orchid that makes this place near unique, and the orchid that now attracts visitors by the score. Word had clearly got round. Two of our three flowers had served a lengthy queue of photographers, to judge from the trampled ground in front of them and the grassy path – deliberately cut to spare the fen from trampling feet – that led up to the spot. With their obscuring vegetation neatly pruned away, the orchids now seemed like actors, spotlit on a green stage. They had been photographed as eagerly as any starlet emerging from the curtains on the first night. From the right angle you could spot the plants from fifty yards away. Not that I was in any position to complain, for I too had contributed my mite to the trampled mess (Richard, I noticed, had stuck to the path).

As a plant with many admirers, *ochroleuca* isn't yet in quite the same trapped state as the Lady's Slipper orchid, cordoned off with plastic tape, like a crime scene, brindled with slug pellets and with its own warden to keep a wary eye on the fans. But people get very protective about wild orchids. At present the Ice-cream Orchid's photographers seem ready to strip the flower of its surrounding vegetation – indeed, of its innate wildness – for an image that will reveal its beauty at the expense of nature. We traduce the flower with our possessiveness.

36
Proliferous Pink
Petrorhagia prolifera

An annual pink, similar to the Childing Pink (see page 85),
but more divided, with a downy stem and growing on inland
sand in Norfolk
Cranwich Camp, near Thetford, Norfolk

35
Purple-stem Cat's-tail
Phleum phleoides

An attractive grass with tapering 'cat's-tail' heads and purple-
tinged stems
Borders of a sandy track near Icklingham, Suffolk
12th July

The Breckland of Norfolk and Suffolk is England's dry-land, a place of sand, whole dunes of the stuff once, more than twenty miles from the nearest beach. It is, or was, natural grassland, but of a peculiar kind that, leavened with a little lime from the underlying chalk, supports a variety of wild flowers rarely found elsewhere. It is home to treasured rarities with names like Fingered Speedwell, Field Wormwood, Perennial Knawel, Spanish Catchfly. There was a time when such plants could be found on sandy ground throughout the Breck, but today they have been pushed to the margins by the plough, tree-planting and housing. They bloom where they can: mainly in nature reserves, but also on strips of land that are still wild, on waysides, field margins, commons and even on waste ground within towns and industrial estates. I have seen Field Wormwood growing happily in the gutter, among fag butts and dog-shit. And one of the few refuges for Fingered Speedwell is among new houses in the beds dug for daffodils and young trees. Without this kind of versatility – the ability to find such unexpected nooks within an increasingly unfriendly landscape – the future of such plants would be bleak.

Although I have botanised in the Breck many times, there were still two plants I had missed. Both have rather silly names: Proliferous Pink and Purple-stem Cat's-tail, suggesting that they are plants distinguished only by botanists. Despite that, they are both, when viewed sympathetically, quite pretty and an adornment to the sandy scene, as well as natural curiosities. Proliferous Pink is closely related to Childing Pink, the plant I saw at the back of a pub in Shoreham, and indeed at one time they were thought to be one and the same. According to the floras, the differences are slight and technical. You can tell them apart by peering carefully at the coat of their seeds through a low-power binocular microscope: the Proliferous one has reticulate seeds (that is, seeds patterned like a net), while the Childing one has tuberculate seeds (that is, seeds studded with tiny tubercles). Otherwise they are both dainty annuals with stiff, narrow leaves that produce just one little rose-coloured mini-carnation at a time.

The differences sounded so slight that I wasn't minded at first to include Proliferous Pink among the Last Fifty. Moreover, its status is uncertain. It might be native or it might not be. The latest *Red Data Book* (or endangered list) of wild plants cannot decide, and so dubs the poor plant an 'intractable taxon', which is another way of saying 'we haven't the foggiest'. And, I thought, if it needs a microscope to identify it, then it shouldn't count.

What I was forgetting is that the descriptions you read in the academic floras are based on pressed flowers in a herbarium. So when I parked the car on the hard standing of a former army camp and nearly trod on a pink as I stepped out, I was pleasantly surprised. Proliferous Pink wasn't a lookalike of the Childing Pink at all. Its petals were more rounded and less notched. The stems were more branched, with more leaves running up them. Admittedly you did need a lens to make out the diagnostic downy hair on the stem, but I decided there and then to include this pretty little pink in my quest and thereupon gave it a number: Proliferous Pink, Plant 36; and, yes, I decided, almost certainly native. It is the kind of flower whose prettiness depends on a mass of flowers, so it was good to find it in comparative plenty, centred on a dry, sandy ditch, but also colonising the cracks between the concrete within yards of the road. It was a sweet little thing, a constellation of pink sequins borne on wiry stems, growing amid a medley of annuals, yellow and white bobble-heads of medicks and clovers, and the golden ribs of bright melilots.

It took a bit longer to track down the other one, Purple-stem Cat's-tail. Peter Stroh had told me it would be easy and that I would love it. 'It's a real beauty,' he said. Pete is, of course, an enthusiast. All the same, when I finally spotted it – after an hour or more of tramping down sandy tracks and peering along road verges – I discovered it in plenty and found myself agreeing. It's a nice, neat-'n'-tidy-looking grass with soft, fawn, slightly shaggy heads, like a guardsman's busby, attached to distinctive mauve stems. The shaggy look is created by the short spines ('awns') on each floret or glume. In certain lights the heads take on a pinkish tint. Once I had my eye in, I saw that this grass can be common enough to help define the locality – a track lined with the soft, low, pastel-hued grasses rooted in loose sand. Local people would surely have noticed it, and perhaps given it a better name than Purple-stemmed Cat's-tail (though, if so, they have kept it to themselves). I think I'd call it the Artist's Grass, for there is something rather brush-like about the heads, while the stems are stained with mauve, where the artist had been painting violets, perhaps. The grass has been doubly unfortunate, for its Latin name is even sillier: *Phleum phleoides*, 'the Phleum that is like a Phleum'. One way of telling it from other phleums is simply to bend the grass's 'cat's tail'. This one breaks up into distinct segments; the others don't.

Not far away I stumbled on another grass that even Peter Stroh wouldn't warm to. Here the name is definitely right: Ripgut Brome, a monster with a head like a harpoon, a grass that sticks in your trainers and stabs at your toes. I remember once walking through a whole hillside of it and having to throw my socks away afterwards. How much worse it must be for a furry animal, for the bone-hard seed-heads are covered in backward-pointing hairs like little barbs; you can feel them scratching against your skin if you run the grass-head between finger and thumb. Dagger-like, they work their way into an animal's paws, mouth, even eyes. To crown its evil nature, Ripgut Brome is capable of becoming a serious agricultural weed. It is a recent, accidental introduction to Britain and seems to be well on its way to becoming a worldwide pest, carried from airport to airport in socks, soft shoes, trousers, ruck-sacks… Unlike Purple-stem Cat's-tail, this grass has a great future ahead of it in an intercontinental, climatically changing, incredibly careless Britain.

34
Yarrow or Purple Broomrape
Orobanche purpurea

A parasite of yarrow, with purple flowers on a stout, leafless
stem
Cemetery at Lakenheath, Suffolk; grassy bank at Maryport,
Cumbria
27th June
Helper: Mike Porter

Broomrapes are the bad guys of British botany. They strangle
and they steal. They stand, stiff and upright in the grass, like
brown pokers, without leaves or any other green parts. They
are plants that have given up manufacturing their own food
by photosynthesis and have evolved to take up a new life
as marauders. They tap the roots of their host plants with

the help of a turnip-like organ below the soil – the 'rape' in broomrape. The small, lobed, delicately veined flowers are cross-pollinated and produce vast quantities of tiny seed, which can remain dormant in the soil for many years until stimulated to germinate by certain chemicals produced by their plant victims. Broomrapes flower unpredictably, in numbers one year and with next to none the year after. They are also anchored to ground where their host plants grow in quantity: ivy, knap-weed, thistle, wild carrot, according to the exact species. One lost species was a pest of hemp crops (*Cannabis*), used to manufacture ropes for naval yards. Only one broomrape actu-ally 'rapes' broom – the rather rare Greater Broomrape, *Orobanche rapum-genistae*. *Orobanche* means 'strangler'. You can't help loving them.

There are nine species of British broomrape, with dead-nettle-like flowers that vary in colour from white or yellow to red or blue. Some are rare, and there were two I had never set eyes on: the blue-flowered Yarrow Broomrape and the white-flowered Thistle Broomrape. Yarrow Broomrape is, arguably, the prettiest of the bunch. It parasitises common yarrow – that everyday lawn flower with a smell like crushed chrysanthe-mums. But clearly not just any old yarrow plant, for, unlike yarrow, Yarrow Broomrape is scarce and elusive. Warmth and space seem to be necessary, for in recent times it has been found mainly on the edges of sea-cliffs and banks in scattered places from the Isle of Wight to Cumbria. Keble Martin, who included just a tiny piece of the plant with three open flowers, claimed that it was common in the Channel Islands. In his Victorian boyhood maybe, but not now. Most British yarrow plants are perfectly safe.

This was a tricky plant to fit into my itinerary, for it has only a short flowering period around the end of June, the absolute peak time for flower-finding. I had heard that in some years it appears among the graves in the old cemetery at Lakenheath in Suffolk, and since I was down that way looking for Purple-stem Cat's-tails, I decided to drop by on the off-chance. I liked the idea of this highwayman of a plant flourishing on the graves, a wicked flash of blue by a lichen-encrusted headstone. So I wandered about 'God's acre' looking hard, and then I turned round and, retracing my steps, looked some more. Here the dead sleep among tall grass and wild flowers. There was enough yarrow to scent the cemetery, but no sign of the blue strangler.

On the way out I met the gardener.

'Are you looking for... the plant?' he asked.

I said I was and couldn't find it. Was I in the wrong place?

'It's gone.' He pronounced it 'gorn'.

'Gone?'

'Gorn. All gorn.'

It sounded as though the broomrape had packed its bags and wasn't coming back.

'What do you mean? Do you mean it's over? Over flowering?'

'There was a little bit at the far end. Now it's gorn.'

'So I'm too late, then?'

'Yes, yes. Too late. Gorn.'

That is the way with broomrapes. One year poking up from every tuft of yarrow, the next, and for no discernible reason, near absent. And that had grim implications for me, for to have any hope of seeing Yarrow Broomrape now, I would need to head for the Lake District, where it flowers a little later, and where my botanical friend Mike Porter knew a place where it occurs fairly regularly.

Ironically, the one place in northern Britain which the plant has made its own is an old slag-heap where the washings of coal were dumped unceremoniously close to the now-disused mineral line. Yarrow Broomrape grows among chunks of spoil and slag on open grassy ground that, as I noticed when I got there, was strewn with dog-shit. This is where people exercise and empty their dogs. But they have perhaps earned that right, for the same people campaigned hard to save the place from turning into just another housing estate.

The broomrape was easy to find. Mike and I counted seventy in good, fresh flower (a friend, who came here a week later, found ninety), mostly stumpy little plants with exotic pale-blue flowers streaked with dark purple and covered with a soft layer of hair that backlit each plant in its own halo of sunshine. Plant parasites normally treat their hosts with restraint; the Knapweed Broomrape, for instance, seems to encourage the growth of especially fit and healthy knapweeds by some as-yet-unravelled process of sharing. Not this one, though; its host yarrows looked wilted and sick. The broomrape was shorter, more dumpy than I'd expected, although, had we come a week or two later, we might have found taller, more poker-like plants, for broomrapes change shape as they grow, from cauliflower-heads to kniphofias, before the petals wither to a uniform brown. We found a few more on a wilder clifftop overlooking the nuclear power station and rival wind turbines at Workington. Tracking down Yarrow Broomrape had taken two full days and 500 miles in the peak of the season. And the Quest was about to get even harder.

Lipstick in the fern: The Wild Gladiolus

33
Wild Gladiolus
Gladiolus illyricus

A miniature gladiolus with bright-pink flowers that hide under
bracken in forest glades
Near Burley in the New Forest
10th July
Helpers: Clive Chatters and Jonathan Stokes

Back in my teens, when I was just starting to get interested in
wild plants, I read a piece about a couple who had been searching
for a wild gladiolus. They had devoted a couple of days every
summer to trying to track it down in the only place in Britain
where it grows: the New Forest. And every year they failed.
At last they spotted its 'cerise-pink' flowers, peeping shyly from
a knot of bracken, a surprisingly subdued presence, like a twist

of ribbon in a green shade. They had been looking for something much bolder, more like the 'glads' flourished by Dame Edna Everage.

As one Victorian botanist noted, the only way to find the wild British gladiolus is 'to stoop down and look through the leaf-stalks underneath the fronds of bracken'. Just two feet or so high, it is a graceful, even dainty plant, small enough to escape notice unless you are close by and looking hard. Moreover, it is shy. Perhaps only one plant in ten produces a flower and, without those pink bannerettes, its slender leaves would be lost among the soft grasses. Even when it does condescend to flower, the blooms seldom last much longer than a couple of weeks – less if the weather is warm. Hence our gladiolus is not as well known as you'd expect. You won't find its likeness on postcards in Lyndhurst. Even regular walkers in the New Forest seldom spot it. I certainly didn't, until a friend offered to show it to me. Unfortunately back then the plant was still in bud, a lipstick row of tight, rolled tubes. And, since that was the only time I had ever set eyes on a wild gladiolus, I decided it wasn't enough, and so included it in The Quest: a plant I could just about manage to squeeze in, between a tour of northern Scotland and another to the Norfolk Broads. Jonathan Stokes and Clive Chatters, who have probably seen more British gladioli than anyone else alive, kindly agreed to show it to me.

There is another reason why I had never seen it in good flower. Its habitat terrifies me. These days, bracken in the New Forest is full of horrible, clinging ticks, some of which carry Lyme disease. Though seldom fatal, this illness can be a life-changer. Victims of the tick suffer from varying degrees of headaches, joint-pains, flu-like spells and extreme tiredness. The symptoms come and go, but the damage to the body is irreversible, and cumulative. The ticks, most of which are nymphs no bigger than a pinhead, normally prey on deer and ponies, but they won't forgo the pleasure of plunging their jaws into our own softer parts whenever they get the chance. In my experience, ticks usually hang around unnoticed on your body until the small hours of the night when, as you dream, they creep out and bite. (Women are luckier; the things often cling to bra-straps and so can be located and removed.) The immediate sensation is an itch: intense, unwavering and wakeful. Unless you happen to be with a willing partner, you are reduced to blearily crawling out of bed and staggering into the bathroom to track down the horror with a shaving mirror and a pair of tweezers. They say – from experiments on dogs, apparently – that only 2.5 per cent of ticks carry Lyme disease. But that means you only need to be bitten an average of forty times to catch it. Jonathan Stokes, who studied gladioli when the disease was much less well known and recognised, was bitten hundreds of times. He came home crawling with ticks, some of them in his hair. And, yes, he has Lyme disease. In 1989 a quarter of all forestry workers in the New Forest tested positive for the disease. And between 2 and 4 per cent of the local inhabitants are also thought to have contracted it.

Lyme disease is now slowly killing off the nerves in Jonathan's feet; when the illness flares up, every step is painful. Flu-like symptoms are an annual affliction. The bug has also inflamed his liver, so that it cannot cope with alcohol. He is, in a sense, a martyr to botany. Clive Chatters has it, too, but he has got off more lightly. The disease's sudden eruptions can be knocked back with antibiotics, plus a week or two's abstinence from beer and wine. Tetracycline works best, but the disease always creeps back again through re-infection, for, as Clive points out, 'It is possible to have more than one generation [of the bacterium] working through you at the same time. We are its habitat.' Both men are remarkably insouciant about it. It's one of those things, they say, like being bitten by an adder or stung by a hornet. All in a day's work, when botanising in the Forest.

Jonathan had studied the distribution of wild gladiolus for a Masters course. In fact, 'study' understates the case. He was smitten, body and soul, by the plant's gorgeousness. He was the first, and quite possibly the last, to locate and assess the size of every colony in the Forest, enabling him to state with confidence that there are hundreds, rather than thousands, of flowers blooming in an average year, but also that they are surprisingly widespread, generally occurring in small groups on gentle, bracken-infested slopes by the edge of the woods. The trick, he told me, is to look for bluebells, for in the New Forest the two tend to go together, even though there are far more bluebell patches than gladioli. Patches of bluebell can be located from examining colour aerial photos taken in late April, before the bracken has grown up.

Another way to find gladioli is to search around the Forest's many natural hollows. These tend to hold pockets of frost in winter, and late frost helps to reduce the bracken's vigour, creating space for other shade plants to coexist.

I had taken the precaution of tucking my waterproof trousers into my socks and spraying both with Deet, as well as more liberal squirtings on my face, hands and neck. Jonathan and Clive were taking me to what was normally a good spot for gladdies in the Open Forest near Burley. We squelched all the way there. For a warm summer's day the ground was astonishingly wet. The New Forest is one big watercourse, said Clive. Here water flows over whole landscapes, forming temporary streams that push aside leaves and twigs, disappear underground and then bubble up again, seeping into quagmires, rippling into braided streamlets, stopping and starting with the rain. Perhaps that is why the gladiolus nearly always seems to grow on a slight rise, so that water can drain freely through its roots and its sausage-shaped corms, situated about three inches down in the clay-like earth.

Clive dived into the bracken, and after a minute or two his head surfaced above the ocean of fronds. 'Aha!' He had found a gladdie. I lay down to peer into the deep-green shadows and spied more – little spurts of pink among the stalks. One or two plants had flowered close to the path and had toppled over, perhaps from the weight of the flowers or maybe knocked over by a passing pony or deer. 'We've timed it right,' said Jonathan. It's hard to get the timing right, especially in a year like this one, when everything that wasn't late seemed to be early. Seeing the Wild Gladiolus now, I wondered why it took me so long to spot the plant, for the colour is a rich, sensuous pink with a pendant, fleshy lip on an open mouth. I couldn't take my eyes off it. I was pleased to see that a butterfly – a Large Skipper – felt the same way. It entered the beckoning blossom with a blur of fawn wings, probing the deep well of nectar, and emerged peppered with pollen. They say this butterfly is the plant's only regular, efficient pollinator and, if so, plant and butterfly must be locked into a mutual dependency. That is one reason why climate change is dangerous: for if circumstances forced the butterfly to emerge before the flower, or vice versa, then this beneficial partnership, which has presumably served both for thousands of years, would fall apart.

Clive is also worried that, as our winters grow milder, the frosts that keep the bracken low and sufficiently open may become a thing of the past. If the bracken grows too tall and vigorous, it will crush the plants beneath under a toxic mat of decaying fronds, robbing them of space and light. At that point the gladiolus's only hope of survival would be management, perhaps some kind of mowing regime designed to reduce the bracken's growth without eliminating it altogether. We ecologists are trained to worry about such things. We cannot see a beautiful plant simply for what it is without concerning ourselves with its safety, with the multiple things that could threaten it and which could, in time, wipe it out. We cannot enjoy tropical forests, despite the whooping monkeys and fantastical birds, because we suspect the trees will soon be gone, the land planted from coast to coast with oil-palms. The only answer to such ecological dudgeon, it seems to me, is 'Que sera sera'. Things will be as they will be. Enjoy things for what they are, not for what may happen to them. After all, we might all get blown up by a hydrogen bomb sooner or later. And it had been a delightful morning out in the forest, with wild England at its most bountiful, and a flower as sweet as a box of chocolates.

The Bison's Favourite

32
Holy-grass
Anthoxanthum nitens (or *Hierochloe odorata*)

A sweet-smelling grass with attractive bobble-heads, used to
flavour vodka in Poland, where it is known as 'bison grass'
The merse at Caerlaverock, on the Scottish bank of the
Solway Firth
27th June
Helper: Mike Porter

Holy-grass is a grass with a difference. You can't ignore its smell.
It is packed with the fragrant chemical coumarin, the scent of
new hay, redolent of drying grass in a midsummer meadow.
Chew a stem of Holy-grass and you will be surprised by a
taste-bomb somewhere between coconut and vanilla; it reminds

me of those sugar-coated 'Nice' biscuits. In northern Europe Holy-grass was strewn in church porches during religious festivals – hence the name. In Sweden it was also hung over beds to induce blessed sleep. But its best-known use today is in *Zubrowka*, 'bison-grass vodka', so called because Holy-grass is said to be a favourite of the herds of wild bison in the Forest of Białowieża on Poland's eastern border. *Zubrowka* is flavoured with the leaves only, but the grass's shiny, bobbly heads are also a delight, described in the handbook of British grasses, with unintended poetry, as 'pyramidal panicles of glistening spikelets'.

The only reason Holy-grass is not better known in Britain is that we have so little of it. All but one of its few, scattered sites are in Scotland (it just spills over into Northumberland). And the only place where it is not rare is Orkney. It might have been deliberately cultivated there, since most of its locations lie close to the sites of ancient churches. Fortunately I did not have to travel all the way to Orkney to find Holy-grass. There is a patch or two nearer to home on the shores of the Solway Firth, at Caerlaverock, a nature reserve noted for its winter passage of wild geese and croaking chorus of natterjack toads. Others come there to admire the sandstone castle, a fine moated ruin described as the last word in medieval fortification. Nobody goes there just to see Holy-grass, but I went all the same.

The instructions I was given by a kind local botanist were specific – or so I thought. 'The grass is just outside the fence separating the woodland walk from the back of the merse.' The merse is the local name for the cattle-grazed marshland by the sea. A hide was mentioned, and a gate, with a note that the grass grew 'beyond the gate'. There was, I'd been told, even a sign there with a picture of the grass, as if to say: '*Holy-grass grows here.*' Unfortunately, not knowing the area, I walked right past this 'woodland walk' and had parked my car at the wrong end of the merse, miles away. But the day was calm and sunny, and the sky was shrill with singing larks, and I thought I had plenty of time. So I set out on a long walk, following the track along the dry side of the merse, and after a couple of hours I located the sign and it did indeed have a picture of the elusive grass, though a completely useless one – it might have been any old grass – and, no, there was no sign of Holy-grass anywhere.

Looking for a particular grass in a large field full of grass can be challenging. Holy-grass is early-flowering, and a better time to search for it would have been six weeks earlier when the bluebells were out. But I'd been told the grass-heads persist most of the summer, even in a dry state. 'Keep sniffing,' they told me, 'that might help.' Mike Porter told me he knows when he's getting close to Holy-grass because he starts to splutter and sneeze. I wished he was with me now. I could have used him as a sneeze-hound.

Where was it? Somewhere here there was supposedly a big patch of Holy-grass. 'When you find the stile, work your way back carefully through the gorse patches and wet areas for about a hundred yards.' Yes, yes, but in which direction? And there was not one stile but two, and the gorse was all over the place. I tried to be rational. It pointed to the grass being close to the fence, but on which side – the one all churned up by cattle or the other, with dense, tall grass the cows couldn't reach? If I were a Solway cow, I thought, Holy-grass would be my number-one treat, my bovine biscuit. So I guessed that the grass would be on the landward side of the fence, and I guessed wrong.

I gave up. Feeling stupid, I trudged back along the sticky path. Skylarks sang merrily from a cloudless sky. 'Shut up.' I shouted. 'Just shut up!'

'You must have been quite close to it,' said Mike. I had in fact walked right past it. But there was no promised big patch, just a few tussocks, and it took Mike's GPS tracker to locate the Holy-grass close to the fence on the seaward side. The bobble-heads were still shiny and fresh, but not much like the pictures I had seen of it (Keble Martin didn't illustrate it). And the floras are too busy giving you the minute particulars of pressed plants to mention that Holy-grass grows in tall tussocks surrounded by squelch, that the leaves are not short but very long and narrow, and that they are fresh-green on one side and blue-green on the other. Moreover, these smelt only faintly of vanilla, and Mike didn't sneeze.

It was a relief to see the Holy-grass all the same. I took away a few leaves for an experiment I was planning with a hair-drier and a quarter-bottle of vodka (you dry the grass, add it to the vodka, then allow them to steep together for a few weeks). I felt I deserved a drink.

It is not often that one can use a rare plant as a flavouring, and although wild Holy-grass should not be picked in Britain, you can buy *Zubrowka*, Polish vodka flavoured and coloured pale green by a strand of the grass, from any supermarket. For a wonderfully wild cocktail, try this recipe from Amy Stewart's *The Drunken Botanist*: shake up one-and-a-half parts of *Zubrowka* with a half-part of Martini Bianco, a half-part of clear apple juice and plenty of ice. It looks lovely, tastes of Mummy's apple pie, makes you feel woozy extremely quickly and gives you the most wonderful, coloured dreams.

31
Crested Buckler-fern
Dryopteris cristata

An upright marshland fern with short, blunt-ended lobes
Woodbastwick Fen in the Norfolk Broads
12th August, morning
Helpers: Alex Prendergast, Patrick Barkham, Bob Gibbons
and Will West

There were five of us at Woodbastwick Fen, a wilderness of wet
inside a loop of the River Bure on the site of what used to be a
shallow lake: Bob Gibbons, last seen in this book at Stanner
Rocks photographing the Radnor Lily; Alex Prendergast, who
had shown me the Suffolk Lungwort; and Patrick Barkham, the
Guardian journalist and author, who was looking forward to

seeing some rare fenland flowers. Will West of Natural England was our guide.

When I started on my quest I was in two minds about whether to include ferns. Keble Martin hadn't. Nor had he included fern relatives, such as horsetails, clubmosses and quillworts. Some floras do and others don't. Ferns have much in common with flowers, in that they are advanced plants with a vascular system for transporting water and sugar manufactured by photosynthesis. However, ferns reproduce not by seed but by spores, which are released from little capsules. They have no flowers, only big leafy fronds that the Victorians found beautiful, but which the twenty-first century has largely ignored. I decided to include ferns in The Quest, partly because I like them, and partly because I had seen them all anyway, with one exception: and that was the reason I was in the Broads that warm August day.

For a minority of plant-lovers, ferns still have a strong allure. People enjoy the challenge of growing them, on a rockery or in a greenhouse, or even in customised tanks known as Wardian Cases. More than a century ago, when ferns were fashionable, collectors would uproot them from the wild without compunction. It became known as the Victorian Fern Craze, or pterid-omania, and it caused lasting damage, especially to species that reproduce slowly. Today a reduced band of enthusiasts still enjoy tracking down rare ferns and fern-allies, but nowadays they restrict themselves to recording and photography. Most of the desirable species can be bought from specialist nurseries. A year before my quest I went on a fern-hunt in Wales with two leading pteridologists, Fred Rumsey and Martin Rickard, and asked them what it is about fern-finding that they enjoy so much.

'Recording is a form of collecting,' reflected Martin. 'It's partly the fun of the hunt, but it's more than that. Unlike the Victorians, I don't collect the plants. I collect the memory. And I add the record in pencil in my copy of the local flora.'

The challenge of finding the really rare ones is part of the attraction. Ferns often grow in remote and rocky places. At the heart of the hunt, said Fred, 'is our desire to see things that are hard to track down – like the miniature mountain *Woodsia* ferns. They are small and inconspicuous, and grow in some recess within a vast natural landscape. If they happen to be attractive or have interesting back-stories, that is a bonus. But the real challenge lies in hunting them down: using your knowledge and your wits to find the likely places, and the fern's small niche within them. And there's the enormous satisfaction it gives you when you get it right.'

'Which we don't always,' added Martin. 'You get information from all directions. Sometimes it falls into place, and sometimes it doesn't.'

When it does, fern-folk seldom celebrate loudly. Fred and Martin talked about one of the great fern-finders of the recent past, Derek Ratcliffe, and his fabled rediscovery of the Killarney Fern in the Vale of Ffestiniog. 'I had a celebratory cup of tea,' Ratcliffe had written in his diary. 'And then I went home.'

Though I'm not a fern-finder on that epic scale, I too enjoy searching for ferns, especially in good company. On that trip with Martin and Fred, we too managed to track down Killarney Fern inside a dark, damp hole in the rock no bigger than a microwave oven. We found and duly counted the equally rare Oblong Woodsia among a wilderness of rocks, including cliffs that I would not have approached, were it not for fern-gold. We even found a very rare fern hybrid, called *Asplenium* x *alternifolium*, which looked nothing like either of its parents – a reminder that, with ferns, hybrids are quite as exciting as pure species, as are 'sports': ferns with frilly edges or some other oddity, which can be grown on in cultivation.

The one fern I had never set eyes on is one of Fred's favourites, Crested Buckler-fern, *Dryopteris cristata*. Unlike most ferns, which prefer rocky places or humid forests, this one likes wet fens and is usually found tucked away among sedges and reeds. Crested Buckler is one of our few bog-ferns and, growing where it does, it is also one of the hardest to find.

Its elusiveness is a quality that Fred admires. He goes after it in places where few of us would care to tread (and would damage the habitat if we did). To make it even worse, some of its remaining sites are in the middle of military training grounds. Fred remembers a particularly stressful search on a Surrey heath, with a full-scale training exercise going on just beyond the bushes, 'with gunfire, thunder-flashes, the works'.

It's the fern's unusual ecology, he says, that really grabs him. Crested Buckler-fern is often to be found in spring-fed fens, but there is more to it than that, for it doesn't seem to like alkalinity, the abiding feature of such places. Rather, it tends to be found on islands of acidic peat within the fen. 'I see it floating on its little islands of sphagnum [bog-moss],' said Fred, 'with its feet in contact with – and presumably somehow reliant on – the calcareous [lime-rich] waters below. You can't help wondering what it's up to, why it's there.' A good way of finding the fern, he says, is to look not for the plant itself but for a more visible marker: a dying birch tree. Why Crested Buckler-ferns like to grow near dying birch trees is just another mystery. No one knows why. It just does.

And so, with Will West's help, we tracked down a sick birch tree out in the marsh, and there, sure enough, was our fern: a circle of fronds growing in a big green shuttlecock, more or less bolt upright among the sedges and reeds. You could recognise it right way from the slightly lopsided shape of the fronds, with their short, blunt-ended pinnules (the smallest division of a fern frond), with the lowest pair larger than the others and also lopsided. It is a paler, more yellowy green than most ferns. Many plants surprise you when you see them for the first time. They might be bigger, or smaller, than expected, or more intensely coloured, or with something or other that a mere drawing cannot capture. Crested Buckler-fern was different. It looked exactly as I expected. It was like meeting someone famous and saying, 'I'd recognise you anywhere!'

There wasn't much of it. Just a dozen or so plants over an area the size of a tennis court. Times are hard for the Crested Buckler-fern. It seems to be vulnerable to drying, and its required pristine, mossy fens are in short supply. It is considered to be 'near-threatened', having disappeared from much of its former range. Without nature reserves and army ranges, it would stand little chance of survival; and even nature reserves are dependent on sufficient resources to maintain them, and are vulnerable to whatever is happening on the other side of the fence. I found a perfect example to photograph, with some shiny, leathery fertile fronds, their lower surface covered by beautiful kidney-shaped spore-bearing structures ('sori'). It was in good light. I went over to tell Bob, but when we retraced my steps, I couldn't find it again. 'That often happens,' he mumbled.

I like to think that, millions of years from now, the Crested Buckler will be preserved as the one British fern in a layer of coal that marks the one-time existence of the Norfolk Broads. Future paleobotanists will suppose it to have been a common fern, one that everyone would have known. They will consider it the bracken of the early Holocene.

30
Holly-leaved Naiad
Najas marina

An underwater plant with opposite pairs of prickly leaves and
no discernible flowers
Hickling Broad, Norfolk
12th August, afternoon
Helpers: Alex Prendergast, Patrick Barkham

My other target plant that day was even less easy to find. For it
grows underwater – and such is the state of the Broads that it is
hard to make out plants growing deep down in the murky depths.
One way to locate deep-water plants is with a grapnel. Like an
angler, you cast your line into a likely stretch of water, chivvy it
about a bit and then haul it in. With luck, an uprooted fragment
of the plant you are looking for will trail from one of the tines.
You also need a boat. Patrick was an experienced canoeist; so was
Alex; and I had at least done a bit of paddling on holiday in Florida.

So, after lunch, we headed for a boatyard called Whispering Reeds, by Hickling Broad, and hired a three-man canoe.

Alex was our grapnel man and lookout; since I had last seen him several months previously, his green Mohican hair had faded to yellowish. Patrick took up the steering position at the stern. And I clambered in amidships. Off we paddled into the Broad, at what seemed to me a most surprising speed.

It was hard to see Alex, lean and tanned, watching the water for signs of life beneath, and not think of a noble savage in his birch-bark canoe. Specifically he reminded me of Hiawatha, the hero of Longfellow's saga of the Old West, before the coming of the white man. He had become Alexwatha, paddling across the big-water in search of a trailing weed with a poetic name: Holly-leaved Naiad, *Najas marina*. A naiad, as classically inclined readers will need no reminding, is a female spirit or nymph that presides over water, whether it is a fountain, a spring, an underwater cavern or even a pond. By analogy, our plant was the resident spirit of Hickling Broad, its signature species – the one that makes this place different from all the others.

Reader, indulge me here. It might be just the talk of water spirits, but I feel that the mantle of Longfellow has fallen on my unworthy shoulders:

Then did Alexwatha, sturdy, carefree Alexwatha
Cast the rope with iron weed-drag, hurled his trusty iron grapnel,
Far into the waters Hickling, choppy, chilly, windy Hickling,
Pulled from deep below the water, muddy, cloudy, greenish water,
Several different kinds of stoneworts,
Gritty, smelly, baffling stoneworts,
Stoneworts rare as Mysore rubies, special to the waters Hickling,

Far below the waters trickling,
Lay the stoneworts, small plants prickling,
Prickling, trickling, Hickling stoneworts,
Stoneworts loved of Alexwatha.

In other words, Alex had not found a naiad to show us and was instead fishing up examples of primitive plants called stoneworts – which, it must be said, thrilled him more than it did his fellow paddlers. Alex explained their salient points. This one was darker, that one had more robust spines, and most of them smelt a bit like onions with a hint of raw fish thrown in. Alex said the fishermen call it 'onionweed'.

We were edging close to the reedbed when a cheery cry came from the prow. Alex had spotted what looked like a broken bit of naiad floating in the water, a foot or so of trailing weed. Holly-leaved Naiad is a singular plant, distinguished from all other aquatics by bunches of long, prickly-looking leaves. They are not deep-green, like holly, as Keble Martin had portrayed them, but pale and translucent, and nor are they sharp. They are closer to the texture of soft plastic. The flowers, such as they are, are tucked inside the leaf axils and could be mistaken for tiny buds. Holly-leaved Naiad is said to be dioecious – that is, the plants are either male or female. Every British plant examined so far has turned out to be female, which would suggest that sexual reproduction rarely happens. Yet Alex has found plenty of ripe naiad seed, and has indeed collected some for the seed bank at Kew.

Peering down, we found the naiad to be reasonably plentiful in places, more so than we had feared. But a friend who had known the plant when these waters were much less disturbed by boat traffic told me that the naiads then grew much larger, to the size of a small bush. Ours were more attenuated, adapted perhaps to life in the gloom. All the same, we were now a cheery crew:

Happy then was Alexwatha, happy, too, his crew of two-mates,
Happy at the sight of naiads, frilly, greeny, prickly naiads.
Forth they came from deep-lake waters, murky, soupy, turbid waters,
Trailing, broken on the waters, hung the nymphal, lustrous naiad,
Rarest of the weeds of water, famous flower of waters Hickling.
Praise they made of Alexwatha, mid-mate Peter, steersman Patrick,
Sang the skills of Alexwatha, naiad-finder, stonewort-fisher,
Alex with his bristling haircut, hair of yellow, Alexwatha.

Alex asks me to point out that Holly-leaved Naiad is a protected species under Schedule 8 of the Wildlife & Countryside Act, and that we were therefore not using a grapnel to find it, but were merely using our eyes. When planning this encounter the previous winter, I had imagined jumping overboard at this point to swim among streamers of naiad in a sensuous communion with the aquatic world. But it is easier to jump out of a canoe than to crawl back in again. And now we had come to the point, it was cool and breezy, and I suddenly remembered that Hickling Broad is apt to produce blooms of plankton, including a nasty little critter called *Prymnesium*, which is toxic enough to kill fish. So I satisfied myself with running my arm through the water, stroking the tips of naiads just below the surface. No point in killing myself for botany.

We paddled back to Whispering Reeds feeling like the Famous Five, though, of course, we were only Three.

The Gingerbread Sedge

29
Elongated Sedge
Carex elongata

A distinctive sedge with spiky, gingerbread-coloured heads
springing from an elegant fountain of fine leaves
A marsh in Roudsea Wood, near Grange-over-Sands, Cumbria
28th June, morning
Helper: Mike Porter

I had to face it. A great many of the remaining flowers on my
list were northerners, and a large proportion of them flowered
at about the same time, around midsummer. My plan was to bag
as many as possible in a great looping journey to the far north.
I would head first to the Lake District, where Mike Porter had
offered to put me in touch with certain elusive wild flowers of

Cumbria. Then I planned to head north into Scotland, to Pitlochry, and then on to Lochaber and a hoped-for meeting with a rare and lovely alpine. The last stage would take me further north still, with several mountains to climb: to Skye, to Assynt and so on to the far north coast. A dozen plants later, I would take the road home for an appointment at the other end of Britain. It would end up being the longest drive of my life.

The devil factor was the weather. So far I had been lucky and had been able to enjoy most of the first twenty plants in sunshine. The Quest had not been a doddle exactly, but it had been fun. But some of these northern flowers were going to need long walks, and even some scrambling, whatever the weather. I was reasonably confident about my level of fitness, but less so about wandering on my own through mizzle and mist. I packed my best waterproof crag-hoppers and waterproofed my boots and backpack. I gave the car a new tyre and charged the battery. I relearned how to use a mobile phone (one keeps forgetting) and bought some more OS maps. I briefly considered buying a GPS personal tracking device, but decided against it. It wasn't that I thought it was cheating. It was more that I doubted whether I could get my head round its use, and that it would therefore be more of a hindrance than a help. I took a compass instead. And instead of an iPad, I took a notebook and a pencil. I would do my botany the Keble Martin way.

Mike Porter is a retired schoolteacher and one of our leading authorities on sedges. He is also, along with two others, Cumbria's official plant recorder. He is a great fell walker, like his hero, Alfred Wainwright. He has climbed most of the Lake District's fells and crags and pikes, recording their special plants as he went. He and his wife Julie had kindly offered me a bed for my stay. I had planned to meet Mike at the first of our plant hotspots, Roudsea Wood by Morecambe Bay.

Roudsea Wood is a place of wonder. I don't know anywhere quite like it. It lies by the sea, but you wouldn't know it; there is neither the sound of waves nor the faintest tang of weed or salt. The wood rides on a double platform of rock above the sea, one half limestone and the other half slate, with a marshy dip in the middle. Because of the contrasting rocks, lime-rich and lime-poor, as well as the alternation between wet and dry, Roudsea Wood has a wealth of plant habitats. Being an ancient wood, it also possesses some remarkable trees. It is, for instance, a northern outpost for our native Small-leaved Lime, whose mighty roots writhe and twist over bare rock like frozen pythons. There are also some huge natural yews, some with leaves covering the flaking bark like feathers on a chicken. And right in front of us, growing from a cleft in the rock, was its most special tree, Roudsea's own whitebeam, *Sorbus lancastriensis*, a beautiful flowering tree confined to Morecambe Bay. So that was a good start to our walk: a bonus whitebeam.

A minor snag was that part of the wood had been fenced off to protect a pair of nesting ospreys. For miles around, road signs pointed the way to the birds, called with comic familiarity 'The Ospreys' ('The Ospreys Are At Home'). Those who followed the signs might have been disappointed to get only a distant view of the nest at the top of a pine tree, and not the intimate spectacle implied. I was more worried that the birds might injure our chances of seeing Plant 29, Elongated Sedge – also known, to its intimates, as the Gingerbread Sedge. I remembered the annual Bird Fair at Rutland Water, sited next to a marshy corner noted for rare docks and mudworts. I had been tempted to check them out. But the best place is right in front of the bird hide and, if I had, I'd probably have been lynched.

'Don't worry,' said Mike, 'we needn't bother the ospreys.' The Gingerbread Sedge lies deep inside the wood, in a marshy valley that few would be able to locate without an intimate knowledge of local geography. *Carex elongata* is a peculiarly difficult species to pin down. It is widespread, occurring here and there in shaded, boggy ground from Hampshire to Loch Lomond, but nearly always in small numbers, and almost always well hidden. It is a plant of strange preferences. In one place it is rooted on the drowned wooden gates of a sluice. In another it grows in flooded woodland, on mossy branches buried in the peat. And although it is a good-sized sedge, with stems a couple of feet tall rising from a fountain of floppy leaves, it can be hard to spot in the dappled light and deep shadows of its bosky habitat. That is probably why I had never seen it.

The first thing I noticed as we drew near the swamp was a cluster of overlapping brownish 'spikelets' – the sedge's nut-like fruits. Only then did I spot the fountains of leaves, half-lost in the murk. 'Now,' said Mike, 'you'll need your hand lens.' To admire sedges you must become an apostle of minute particulars. 'Do you see how it's exactly the colour of ginger-bread? And look at those red stripes on the utricles and the little forked beak at the tip' (utricles are the individual 'nuts' that cluster together to form the spikelet). 'And the pink leaf-sheaths. Isn't it a beauty? A bit past its best, of course, but still nice.' And 'elongated'? 'Well, it's just a translation of the scientific name. It refers to the long shape of the head. Not a very good name. I prefer "Gingerbread Sedge", though of course I couldn't use it in a journal.'

We saw many other interesting plants, especially sedges, but time was pressing. The next plant was waiting by the beckside of a distant fell.

28
Leafless Hawk's-beard
Crepis praemorsa

A 'yellow composite' with bunches of shaggy, dandelion-like
flowers held on stiff, knee-high, leafless stalks
The banks of a beck near Orton, Cumbria
28th June, afternoon
Helper: Mike Porter

Our second stop was a beck that tumbles down from a rocky
hillside in a mixture of sheep-bitten grass and pale limestone
crags above the pretty village of Orton in the Upper Lune Valley.
It has been a classic site for wild flowers ever since John Ray
passed this way more than 300 years ago. He discovered a new
British plant, Alpine Bartsia, which still occurs here, perhaps

close to the place he found it. Three centuries later, in 1988, another visiting botanist, Geoffrey Halliday, spotted something else that was new. He was the first person to set eyes on the Leafless Hawk's-beard, *Crepis praemorsa*, in Britain – my missing Plant 28.

Leafless Hawk's-beard is one of the 'yellow composites' – plants with flowers like dandelions that come in a wild confusion of names, many with 'hawk' in them. As well as hawk's-beards, we have hawkweeds and hawkbits. According to the ancient philosopher Dioscorides, plants like these were used to make a decoction dispensed as eye-drops to hawks to improve their eyesight, and hence their hunting prowess. The curly bits beneath the flower are supposed to resemble the hackle-feathers of a bird of prey, its 'beard'. Leafless Hawk's-beard differs from other, similar-looking hawk's-beards in a number of subtle characters: above all its largely leafless stem, but also its sparse 'pubescent' hairs (short and stiff) and its loose clusters ('corymbose cymes') of shaggy yellow flowers, an inch in diameter. Most of the plant's lance-shaped leaves are confined to a rosette at the base of the stem, and each ends in a sharp nip that provides the species with its name *praemorsa*, meaning 'nibbled at the tip', as if by mice.

We spotted one, and then several, then lots of Leafless Hawk's-beards on the bank by the babbling brook. It was lucky the sun was out, for the flowers close up in dull weather. Perhaps we were lucky to see it at all, as the plant is a shy-flowerer in Britain and there are always more of those nibbled leaf rosettes than of flowering stems. 'Lovely, isn't it?' said Mike. 'Well, it's certainly different. How did the Lakeland botanists miss it?' 'Probably because they didn't know it was there,' said Mike.

Further up the beck we found more of them, about a hundred plants in flower, mainly on the moist terraced bank between the beck and a stone field wall. There were none at all in the nearby meadow cut for hay, even though, according to some books, that is supposed to be its habitat.

Is it really a native plant? 'Of course it is,' said Mike. Its discoverer, Geoffrey Halliday, agrees: 'The undisturbed nature of the site and its remoteness, coupled with the presence not far away of indisputably native species... strongly suggest that it too is native... Despite scepticism,' he added, pointedly. The grounds for this 'scepticism' are that the nearest site to Britain lies in eastern France. On the other hand, the plant occurs in very similar streamside locations, and among the same kind of vegetation, in Scandinavia. It seems easier to accept that Leafless Hawk's-beard is a native flower that the botanists managed to miss, rather than attempt to explain how it reached this lonely beckside in the North Pennines by other means. It is not the sort of plant that appeals to gardeners.

That evening in the garden, after an excellent dinner cooked by Julie, and under a cloudless sky screaming with swifts, I asked Mike why sedges appeal to him so much. Botanists often get hooked on particular families, sometimes rather unlikely ones. Tim Rich has a thing about hawkweeds. David Pearman is mad about medicks. Chris Preston cannot pass a pond without checking it for pondweeds. But because botanical writing is focused on plants, not people, you rarely hear an explanation of how these strange passions began (though Pearman admitted to me that what he liked about Mediterranean medicks was that they often grew near tavernas). Earlier that day we had stopped by a patch of wet where Mike had shown me, with obvious love and pride, a tiny, rhapsodically dull little plant called *Carex pauciflora*, Few-flowered Sedge. It consisted mostly of a short stalk with a few straw-coloured, bristly bits at the top – a minimalist plant, even by sedge standards.

Mike sipped his glass of Pineau des Charentes and considered my question. 'Well,' he said at last, 'I like their subtle charms. Take *Carex pauciflora*. It's a quiet plant.' You can say that again. 'It's not all on the surface, it's not "in-your-face". But when you get really close, down on your hands and knees' – down in the bog, with midges whining at your ears – 'you begin to appreciate it more. There's the backdrop, for a start, with Carrock Fell rearing above you and, often, peregrines calling from the crag. And here they are, the little sedges, with four to five spikelets each, yellowy-green and distinctive, looking good. I love to see them anywhere, any time. I think they…' He took another sip. A swift screamed past at roof height. 'Well,' he tried on a different tack, 'if you're keen on a certain group of plants, you tend to like them, don't you?' Actually, he admitted, *Carex pauciflora* was not his *favourite* sedge. But it was still a sedge and, like most sedges, decidedly fussy about where it grows. 'To love sedges,' he said, 'you have to love habitats.' Good sedge-country, especially in the uplands, is often beautiful, lakes and marshes surrounded by hills. Sedges are an expression of cool northern wilderness. It helps that they come in all shapes and sizes, from *Carex pauciflora* to leafy plants three feet or more tall. All right, they don't have colourful flowers, but in their way they are graceful, even beautiful. *Carex*: plants we should care about, perhaps, although that name is Greek for 'cutter'. Try picking a sharp-stemmed sedge and you will realise what the Greeks were getting at.

Mike's love of sedges was catching. However, our next plant was not a sedge, but a rush.

27
Thread Rush
Juncus filiformis

A miniature rush with a pompom head halfway along a
thread-like stem
On the shingle shore of Derwentwater, Cumbria

26
Alpine Enchanter's Nightshade
Circaea alpina

A rock plant with a modest cluster of white flowers and little
drumstick fruits above a nest of toothed, heart-shaped leaves
Falcon Crag, Borrowdale, Cumbria
29th June
Helper: Mike Porter

Our destination the next day was Borrowdale, in the heart of the Lakes, the craggiest, cloudiest, rainiest corner of England. We knew we had reached the right place because the road-sign said: 'Borrowdale Valley'. 'I hate that sign,' said Mike. 'Surely everyone knows that a dale *is* a valley.' 'Would they say "Derwentwater Lake"?' Or the "South Down Hills"?' I suggested, egging him on. 'Almost certainly.'

There was more of the same when we reached the car park. A noticeboard attached to the spacious toilet block informed us of the many exciting things we could do to 'go wild' in the Lakes. For instance, it seemed we were in the middle of 'Squirrel Awareness Week'. Among the fun-themed activities on offer were 'story time' – readings from squirrel-themed tales – and various 'worksheets' and 'interactive games', none of which sounded as though they involved the outdoors. There was also a course in owl-hooting. 'If you are lucky, an owl will answer your call.' But, reading on, I learned that it works best only in the dead of winter. Otherwise it is a complete waste of time and only annoys the owls. 'They mean well,' said a tolerant Mike. 'It's better than computer games.'

We had come to Borrowdale to nail the Thread Rush, *Juncus filiformis*. I thought Few-flowered Sedge was a minimalist plant but, compared to the Thread Rush, it is a rose. Imagine a sliver of rush just four inches high, consisting of a stem literally no broader than a bristle, with a tiny pompom of reddish-green florets about two-thirds of the way up. And nothing else. If Thread Rush grew among grass, it would be invisible. Fortunately it grows on bare ground, among pebbles on the edge of lakes where the water draws down in summer. And, despite appearances, it is a tough little plant. When they turned

Thirlmere into a reservoir years ago, local botanists thought that would be the end of its colony of Thread Rushes. But they came bouncing back at the water's edge, as before, just several yards further upslope. It is one of the few rare native plants that seem to be increasing.

What I noticed first were the little pompoms, seemingly suspended in the air. It was only when the plant was right under my nose that I could make out the 'thread' stem. What it lacks in glamour, the little rush makes up for by its setting. Across Derwentwater, dark blue beneath the sky, marched the hills of Borrowdale: High Spy, Maiden Moor, Cat Bields, Causey Pike, Sail Fell, Eel Crag, Grisedale Pike, Hopegill Head. Washed by wavelets, thrashed by a yearly twelve feet of rain, the little rush clings to its patch of stony lakeshore, year on year. Perhaps it has been there almost as long as the lake. The great thing about threads is that they bend with the wind and tide. A more rigid plant would be broken and washed away in no time.

Our other Borrowdale plant was one I had long wanted to see. Alpine Enchanter's Nightshade, *Circaea alpina*, is another species that is hard to spot, even in the shrinking number of places that retain it. Its close relation, the Common Enchanter's Nightshade, *Circaea lutetiana*, is larger and much more vigorous, and seems to be increasing at its smaller sibling's expense. They appear to be meeting more and more often and, when they do, they hybridise, producing a host of halfway plants called *Circaea* x *intermedia*. Our path up the hillside was in fact lined with the hybrid, which, though sterile, multiplies rapidly by throwing out creeping stems. And so, by degrees, pure-bred Alpine Enchanter's Nightshade is being replaced by these crosses, these evolutionary dead-ends. It is as though the gods of botany had taken their cue from its name and placed the plant under a dark enchantment. Its best hope now is to lie low in places still beyond the range of the common species. Luckily, the Alpine Enchanter's Nightshade flowers earlier than its larger relative. Without that temporal gap, it would probably not have survived at all.

Alpine Enchanter's Nightshade is tiny. In Keble Martin's drawing, tucked away at the bottom of a plate of willowherbs, it also seems dull and weedy, all leaf and burr-like seed, with only the tiniest cluster of white flowers. As I was to find, it is prettier in reality, but it is hard to know exactly where to look. The plant seems to have a hazy range of habitats. It might grow in a shady gully on the hillside, or in a woodland seepage, or tucked away among stones on a fan of scree. Anywhere open and damp enough, in fact – and everywhere in Borrowdale is damp.

Our plant was in fact right by the path, but out of sight under the bracken. It was just as well that Mike had brought along his trusty GPS tracker, which turns plant-finding into a game of countdown. 'Only twenty yards now... ten... it must be close now; three, two, one – bingo! Where is it?' We looked and looked again. 'It's here somewhere. It must be.' He parted the bracken and whistled with relief. 'Phew, it's still here! Look there. Isn't it a beauty?'

'Yes, Mike.' Compared with its blowsy relative, the Alpine Enchanter's Nightshade is crisp and compact, as befits a flower with 'alpine' in its name (though actually it is misnamed, and is rarely found above 1,200 feet). Raindrops nestled in the cup of its dainty notched leaves. The tiny flowers had a kind of crystal purity, almost a sparkle. It would have looked better in moss by a waterfall, but you can't have everything. 'Lovely, isn't it?' whispered Mike.

There is no doubt that GPS is a valuable tool for the surveying botanist. No professional would be without one now. Instead of wrestling with maps, grid references and a compass, as in the old days, the modern flower-finder simply loads up a 12-figure grid reference and follows the beeps. It doesn't work so well on vertical cliffs, of course, but in general GPS has rendered traditional map-reading redundant. All the same, as I say, I had decided to stick to my compass and pencil. It is really a matter of not wishing to go too far down the path of technology-dependence. Since I love nature, I prefer to use what nature has given me – eyes, a brain, a sense of direction. Advanced technology, it seems to me, is a one-way street: once you take the digital route, there's no way back. Working with devices that compute far more quickly and accurately than the human mind, you become addicted. You are no longer at one with the sun and wind; you've become Wiki-man on his trail of beeps. I didn't want to make things more difficult for myself than they already were. And I accepted gladly every offer of help. But I also wanted to feel free. I wanted, among other things, for my quest to be an escape from the quotidian realities of keyboard and gadget.

We returned from the misty hills to another of Julie's splendid suppers and a bottle of Mike's favourite Pouilly-Fuissé. The post had brought another bag of mystery sedges for identification. Mike pulled out a leafy specimen and peered closely at its leaf-sheaths and utricles. It looked like being another late night with the microscope.

soil level

25
Creeping Spearwort
Ranunculus reptans

An exquisite miniature buttercup with creeping stems that bind
together the stones on which it sits
On the shingly shore of Ullswater, Cumbria
30th June
Helper: Mike Porter

The next day we drove over a hill with a majestic view and down
to Ullswater, where we hoped to find a miniature buttercup called
Creeping Spearwort, *Ranunculus reptans*. Keble Martin had drawn
its portrait on Plate 3 of the *Flora*, a dainty little flower that dances
up the page through of a series of arching stolons (creeping stems)
and culminating in a tiny golden flower. 'Sandy lake margins in
the north,' noted Keble. 'Very rare.' It has been recorded from just

a few Scottish lochs and Cumbrian lakes, but there has always been doubt about what the British plant actually is – whether it is the true *reptans* or a hybrid. It seems that Creeping Spearwort is always swamped by greater numbers of its relative, the Lesser Spearwort, *Ranunculus flammula* – a larger, coarser plant, despite its English name. They say you would have to go all the way to Norway to see true Creeping Spearwort. The hybrid is called *Ranunculus* x *levenensis*, after Loch Leven, one of its sites. It has been suggested that the hybrid, being more variable than the pure-bred species, is better attuned to British conditions. It is partly fertile and so is capable of back-crossing and producing all kinds of intermediates, from nearly *reptans* to nearly *flammula*.

Creeping Spearwort, or a hybrid very like it, has been known at some Lakeland sites for up to 200 years. Mike was as keen as I to see how it was getting on at Ullswater. We free-parked with the National Trust again and strolled down a newish, surfaced path (Mike helplessly spotting a hybrid sedge on the way). It was a pleasant place to be on another sunny day, with Chimney Sweeper moths dancing in the tall grass, foxgloves peeping though the bracken. We arrived at a gravel shore in a perfect half-moon bay, and then we saw the reason for the new path. A recently constructed jetty projected hideously into one of the finest views in England. In his *A Flora of Cumbria*, Geoffrey Halliday had feared that 'tourist pressure' would one day threaten the survival of this rare buttercup. It seemed he was right.

However, the little buttercup was still present in quantity: squibs of golden yellow glinting in the bare gravel. It had even survived under the slats of the jetty. I could understand now the purpose of those arching stolons in Keble's drawing. They not only allow the flower to spread rapidly over the bare surface, but also help to anchor it to the stones: a necessary anchor-cable in a place buffeted by waves. The flexible stems lasso and wind themselves round the pebbles like balls of string, creating a labyrinth of interconnections, with occasional little whips of narrow leaves. And then, in a final spurt, they throw up those tiny, glittering buttercups.

Our plant had the bay more or less to itself, apart from the usual opportunistic docks and willowherbs. But it didn't look like a hybrid. We did find plants with characters intermediate between the two parents, but they were a little further inland, where damp hollows met the gravel shore. The little buttercup that was so perfectly attuned to survival in a hard place looked very much like the real thing. But, Mike pointed out, the onus would be on us to prove it, and that would demand lab work far beyond the resources of amateur botanists. In the meantime, all we could do was nurture the conviction that the experts have got it wrong, and that Ullswater's little buttercup is your actual *Ranunculus reptans*, as English as Cumberland ham, as homely and rooted as Lakeland pencils. I gave it a big tick with my best crayon and went off for lunch.

The Plummeting Botanist

24
Alpine Catchfly
Silene suecica (or *Lychnis alpina*)

A pretty, pink-flowered rock plant with narrow, pink-tinged
leaves; noted for growing in dangerous places
Hobcarton Crag, Whinlatter Pass, Cumbria
30th June
Helper: Graham Tomlinson

My last flower of the Lakes was a true alpine. To find it, I faced
a clamber up a gully between cliff faces usually described as
'rotten' – not because the place is unpleasant to look at, but
because the rocks tend to crumble the moment you trust them
with your weight. This is what Alfred Wainwright, that connois-
seur of craggy places, had to say about Hobcarton Crag:

The crag is a place of quiet solitude... In summer there is pleasant colour, the bilberry – greenest of greens – making a luxuriant patchwork among the grey and silver rocks. In shadow the scene is sombre and forbidding. The silence is interrupted only by the croaking of the resident ravens – and the occasional thud of falling botanists.

This is a place to look at and leave alone.

The reason plummeting botanists come here is to see the Alpine Catchfly. This is a rare and famous flower confined to just two places in Britain, one in the Scottish Highlands and the other here in the Lake District. During its short season in early summer, its shocking-pink flowers form splashes of bright colour in the dark fissure that splits the crag. The reason it is rare is that it can survive only on rocks rich in heavy metals, which are toxic to other, more competitive plants. It is also why the rocks fall apart so easily; they are riddled with mineral veins that make them pretty toxic to climbers, too.

It was probably not a good idea to attempt this climb on my own. But the recent fine weather was holding and it felt good to be stretching my legs on a long walk. I navigated my way through a conifer plantation – with some difficulty, for there were no waymarks – and soon I was on the open fell, in the great green, bilberry-covered bowl described by Wainwright, with pipits singing and the occasional cronk from a distant raven. The conical mass of Hobcarton Crag loomed ahead. I recognised the cleft in the rocks from Wainwright's drawing: a deep gully of loose slate. It is a well-known winter climb when the rocks are bound by ice and snow, but is usually avoided in the summer. It looked scary.

I felt suddenly anxious. The catchfly season is short and hard to predict exactly. Doubt grew as I laboured up the defile. It was steep, and slippery with loose slabs of slate. I wished I had done more homework on where the catchfly grew. Much of the cliff beetling above me was not only out of reach, but out of sight. With a flush of excitement and relief, I spied a patch of pink, but it was only wild thyme, not wild catchfly. Any plants within reach would, I reasoned, have been dug up yonks ago – for there was once a brisk trade in Cumbrian catchflies. I was already halfway up. Where was it?

Ah, there the Alpine Catchfly was, right down by my feet. A tuft, nearly over-flower, was sprouting from a boulder that had at some point detached itself from the cliff, taking the catchfly with it. Then I saw another, fresher one high up on the rocks, and then another and another, catching the sun in Sweet William-like clusters – pink butterflies in hell. Some looked weather-beaten and were already ripening papery capsules of seed. I counted about thirty clumps, though more daring climbers in better years have managed sixty. Carefully I edged along a cleft to photograph a particularly attractive tuft, though it was shaking almost as much as I was. The cronks of ravens were closer now. They say that the raven's rather limited vocabulary – basically a cronk followed by another cronk – expresses all manner of avian emotion, from tenderness or joy all the way to rage. I guessed I was hearing a mixture of surprise and anger. I wondered, suddenly, what the raven would do if I slipped and fell, like one of Wainwright's thudding botanists. Would that be my last glimpse of the world, as I lay there with a broken back: a raven approaching cautiously, head cocked, black eyes glittering, licking its beak?

Then I heard a different sound, a trickle of falling stones, and spotted someone coming up. I could tell he was looking for my flower. Naturalists have a keenness of gaze that is unmistakable. We made contact. His name was Graham Tomlinson and he was a retired physics teacher. In fact he had taught at the same school as Mike Porter and knew him well. He was on his way to the top and suggested that I come with him. 'There's a stunning view from up there,' he said, 'and the gully goes all the way up.' Since he was older than me, he took it for granted that I was fit and fearless. In fact, he confessed he feared he might hold me up.

Thankful for a companion in the wilderness, I agreed and upwards we clambered. The gully grew narrower, and also wetter and more oppressive. Soon it was possible to touch both cliffs at once, which helped the climbing, but brought on a nasty sense of claustrophobia. Graham stopped and had a rethink. 'This is worse than I'd expected. Let's climb up the ridge instead. It's an easy climb, if a bit exposed. *You* won't have any trouble. Don't worry if you want to go on ahead. I'll catch you up.'

Fifty feet further on, in a vertical direction, I was frozen to a ledge and looking down at the view of the valley between my legs. 'Hang on,' shouted Graham, now a good distance above me. 'Not much further. You're doing well. Just a few more feet. Look, there's a good hold there.'

I dragged myself up, hands and face blotched with sheep-shit, up and over the last rock-band and onto the top, a stony roof under an enormous sky. I lay on my back gasping like a landed carp. 'It's easier going down,' Graham reassured me, looking as fresh as a daisy. When I found the strength to sit up, I had to agree that it was one of the finest views in England: the beckoning swell of the plateau, a vista of perfect walking across short grass, over the ridge to Grisedale Pike and out towards the hills of Skiddaw, the world at my feet. I accepted a glass of wonderfully cool water from Graham's Thermos (what a good idea – why don't I get good ideas like that?).

So, with mission accomplished, we strolled back over the hump of Hobcarton. Graham talked about his ornithologist son, based in Oregon, whose ambition was to see every species of owl in the world: all 300 of them. It would probably take him the rest of his life, but to him it was worth it. It was his way of taking a love of owls to its extreme limit. That was reassuring to me, because I was starting to wonder whether all this questing after flowers was really a good idea. What was gained, apart from a certain inner satisfaction? Who would care? I would return to that thought increasingly over the next stormy week. I think the only thing that kept me going was the conviction that it was too late to stop now.

Interlude

Many years ago I stood barefoot in a cold mountain stream looking at possibly the dimmest, and certainly one of the rarest, flowers found in Britain. It was Teesdale Sandwort, a distant relative of garden chickweeds, with tiny green spikes for leaves and peppercorn flowers on straight wispy two-inch stems, whose white petals were almost lost inside cup-shaped sepals. You cannot see it without getting wet. The plant grows on moss and gravel by the sides of a shallow, fast-flowing stream on a hillside – just one hillside in the whole of Britain. I was tempted now to drive over the hump of the North Pennines to see it again for old times' sake, before continuing my journey north.

Thoughts of Teesdale took me back to the days when I visited that cold fell nearly every day in pursuit of a doctorate in botany, back in the days when I wanted to be a proper botanist. I thought, when I started, that Upper Teesdale is possibly the most exciting place in England: the meeting place of plants from north and south, with more plant rarities than you can shake a stick at, including two with Teesdale in their name, the sandwort and the Teesdale Violet (but not *Teesdalia*, the Shepherd's Cress, which was named after a botanist called Robert Teesdale). When I got the chance to study the dale's wonderful wild flowers, I thought my dream had come true.

In fact it was about the worst decision I ever made. My work formed part of a long-running project to try and understand how these special plants manage to survive. On the face of it, the odds seem stacked against them. To begin with, Upper Teesdale is grazed to within an inch of its life by that unnatural beast, the sheep (for there never was a wild British sheep). Sheep act like lawnmowers, nipping the vegetation tight and more or less ensuring that few flowers get a chance to ripen and set seed. In the 1960s a sizeable section of the best hill in the dale was drowned by a new reservoir at Cow Green, the broad valley where the infant Tees used to wind. Some of the precious plants were rescued by volunteers and cultivated in pots at the university, with a view to re-establishing them one day. Unfortunately that never happened, for they were lost; and besides, as I was to discover, it is not easy to grow Teesdale rarities in pots.

My research topic was called 'population dynamics'. Scientists had been studying the ebb and flow of animal 'populations' for years, but until recently no one had used similar techniques to study the lives of plants. I was given a basket of plants to investigate, among them Teesdale Violet, Spring Gentian, Bird's-eye Primrose and a few others – but not, funnily enough, Teesdale Sandwort. The plan was to record the plants year by year using that favourite tool of botanists, the quadrat, a metre-square metal frame within which the exact position of every individual can be plotted. Sunk in the turf, out of reach of the scratchy little hooves of sheep, were the markers for our quadrats – dozens of them. My job was to record all the plants, three times a year, noting whether they were flowering, fruiting, putting forth runners or just sitting there, minding their own business. If there were flowers or seed capsules I was to count them, too. I even took soil samples to see how many seeds were down there, waiting to turn into plants. Back in the lab, we used statistical methods to plot how each population was doing, which in turn would form an estimate of how long individual plants lived, whether or not each population was stable, and whether or not it mattered if they didn't set seed (of course it would matter, you might think, but actually it didn't).

Take the Spring Gentian, the most intensely coloured of all alpine flowers – I loved its bright-blue stars, but taste is a personal thing. Sarah Raven described it as a plant resembling a cigarette-holder with a blue flower stuffed down one end. On these cold fells, spring can be as late as June, and the gentian continues to grow after flowering, so that the seedpods stick out from the turf. This becomes their undoing, because the pods are promptly nibbled off by the oblivious sheep. And so, if they are to ripen seed, the gentians need to find places where the sheep cannot get at them. But the sheep get everywhere. The surprise for us was that it doesn't matter a bit. Spring Gentians have a fall-back measure in the form of vegetative runners, like those of strawberries. Each patch of gentians, it seems, is a genetic entity, and so these patches can survive indefinitely without setting any seed at all. We worked out that some of them were hundreds of years old. Hence you could say that, however unlikely it seems, the sheep actually contribute to the gentian's survival by keeping the turf short and relatively open. In thicker, taller turf, the gentians would quickly run out of space and light. Sheep are not ideal; perhaps cattle and ponies would make better agents of gentian conservation. But those who dismiss our (admittedly overgrazed) hillsides as 'sheep-wrecks', as little more than green-baize tabletops, should spare a thought for the Spring Gentian.

Work like this is slow and ponderous, and it takes a long time to achieve results. For every eureka-moment, when you think you are getting somewhere, there are weeks and weeks of recording and measuring that could be done by any O-level school kid with enough patience and mental stamina. After nearly a whole summer of it, I was no closer to producing work of sufficient originality to satisfy the examiner than when I started. For the first and only time in my life, I lost my love of nature. I began to hate the dale, with its mists and cold rain, its insufferable midges, the daily trudges up and down the fell. Even the piping of dunlin and plover began to sound as miserable as I felt. At low moments I would have been quite happy for them to build another reservoir and flood some more of it. The space in my life that was always filled by nature – my heart's space, I like to think – became shadowed and desolate. I began to drink too much. I fell out bitterly with my supervisor, a woman who had dedicated her life to the study and defence of the dale and its wildlife. She expected 100 per cent effort from her students and, once mine had fallen to below, say, a quarter of that, there were words. She became the scolding mistress of my nightmares, glaring eyes behind magnifying spectacles. The year that started in hope ended in hell.

Forty years later, I was once again on that familiar road across the High Pennines from Penrith to Barnard Castle. I stopped by the hotel at Langdon Beck and got out. A lapwing was calling, but where were all the flowers? These verges used to be rich in wild flowers, with blue and yellow mountain pansies and fan-leaved lady's-mantles. What had happened to them? And where were the golden globeflowers that used to brighten the meadows in early summer? The place was still much the same in its broad contours: the same line of the hills, the stone walls and the whitewashed farmhouses, the same old crags of whinstone, the waterfalls and, of course, the reservoir and its dam. But much of the wild colour I remembered seemed to have drained away. The memory of my summer on the fell still felt oddly raw. I could have walked on and searched for the last few, late-flowering gentians, and the sandwort in its little beck, but suddenly I didn't want to. I felt a strong urge to be somewhere else.

Back then, I did the only sensible thing and resigned. Three months later I was working full time for the Nature Conservancy in north-east Scotland, and nature was suddenly wonderful again. It felt like falling in love again after a tiff.

23
Whorled Solomon's-seal
Polygonatum verticillatum

A lily relative with clusters of small white flowers tucked
under spreading whorls of narrow leaves
A wooded ravine near Pitlochry, Perthshire
1st July
Helpers: Martin Robinson and Iain MacDonald

I had gone all the way to Pitlochry to see a lily. Whorled
Solomon's-seal is a splay-leaved relative of the more familiar
garden plant, with tight 'whorls' of pale-green, cupped flowers
rather than single lines of them. It is rare, and hard to spot in
the dim light of wooded ravines that are its main habitat in
Britain. Luckily, two Scottish botanists had offered to show me

a patch of Whorled Solomon's-seal in a steep wooded glen. Martin Robinson is the local plant recorder, and Iain MacDonald works for Scottish Natural Heritage in Inverness. 'There's never very much of it,' they told me, 'and what there is tends to get bashed about.' It's a very unlucky plant. One of its sites had been smothered by a landslip; a tree fell on another little colony. You would waste your time, Martin told me, trying to find it on your own. He was right about that, because I had – the previous year – and had found nothing.

After a squelch through a muddy wood, followed by a scramble up a slithery bank, we found it. Martin knew the place from a certain configuration of trees, one of them leaning towards the lily as if trying to protect it. Even when you are practically on top of it, Whorled Solomon's-seal is hard to spot in the murk and tangle, especially when, as here, the best plants are obscured by bracken. Yet it is quite attractive and is even occasionally grown in gardens, not so much for the flowers as for the purple berries and its transformation in autumn to a pleasant russet shade. But you rarely see those tints in the wild plant, Martin told me, for in these dank glens it tends to sag and look sorry for itself. Ripe seed is seldom set, and 'all colonies are threatened', notes the *Red Data Book*, concluding with a list of the griefs that have afflicted this most unfortunate of plants: erosion of stream banks, bank slippage, wind-throw, deer-browsing, agricultural run-off, trampling, summer drought, winter floods...

I thanked Martin and Iain and set off on the long, twisting road across the Highlands to Glenfinnan. The next plant in my quest was going to be tougher.

22
Diapensia
Diapensia lapponica

A beautiful, early-flowering alpine with shiny white flowers
embedded in a cushion of copper-green leaves; one of the
world's most rugged plants
On a windy hilltop near Glenfinnan, Lochaber, Scottish
Highlands
3rd July
Helper: Ian Strachan

My B&B was on a crag overlooking the wooded valley and
its bubbling burn. The lonely house had been requisitioned
by the army during the war and used to interrogate prisoners.
There had been dark goings-on, thought my landlady, down
there in the cellar. She showed me her wild garden on a terrace

at the front of the house. There was a damp hollow with flowering iris and ragged robin, or rather, 'that yellow one and those pink ones with raggedy flowers'. '*I'm* here to see a flower,' I said, perhaps unwisely. She asked me its name and wanted to write it down. '*Diapensia*? How do you spell that?' It would be another thing for her visitors to do, to go and see Diapensia. 'They always ask me what else there is to do here,' she said, 'once they have seen the monument and the railway viaduct.'

When, I wondered, did we lose our former intimacy with wild flowers? My mother was no botanist, but she and her village-school friends knew the names of the corn marigolds in the fields, and the 'keck' by the wayside, and the little bobbing 'quaker grass' on the common. She knew that docks could soothe a nettle sting and that the sharp taste of sorrel leaves relieved your thirst. That these berries are good to eat, while those are poisonous. Wild flowers were familiar things, which you saw every day on your way to school or work and sometimes picked, and knew the names of, without consciously learning them, just as you knew the names of the flowers in your garden. Are we losing our natural curiosity about wild flowers? My brother has a patch where ragged robin appears every spring, like pink mist over the grass. He likes it enough to delay mowing until the flowers are over, but always needs reminding of its name (I wouldn't offer him its Latin name, though it's a good one: *Lychnis flos-cuculi*, the cuckoo-flower – the plant that blooms when the cuckoo sings). As far as the media is concerned, wild flowers are hardly on the radar at all. When I used to write natural-history pieces for the papers, I asked to include wild flowers from time to time, but was always told to go away and have a word with the gardening editor. As an established principle, flowers are about the garden. There has been a loss to language, too – those homely but poetic names that have been part of everyday discourse since the Tudors: speedwell, willowherb, tansy, butterbur, comfrey, forget-me-not. Some say that names don't matter; that it is much more important that we *care*. But imagine someone professing to love football, but not knowing the rules of the game, or the names of the players, or anything about it really.

Diapensia does not score highly as a name, but in other respects this flower ticks the boxes. It is known from just a single hill at the back of beyond. It is pretty: very pretty at its brief peak, a mass of pearly white flowers resting on a glossy, deep-green cushion of compressed leafage. But it is hard to time it right for, unlike most alpine flowers, Diapensia flowers early in the year. I had originally planned a special trip to see it at the end of May, but this year it wasn't yet in flower. Now, in the first week of July, I feared I might have left it too late. Of all the plants on my list, Diapensia is perhaps the most romantic. Its remote ridge is rocky and blasted by gales, a bare place where other plants struggle to gain a roothold. It blooms alone, out of sight, and often above the clouds.

It is not surprising that Diapensia wasn't discovered until 1951, even though botanists and nurserymen had been combing the Highlands for 200 years. It was discovered not by a flower-seeker but by a retired businessman who was looking for birds. Charles Frederick Tebbutt, an amateur archaeologist from St Neots, was spending a summer day walking in the hills. Near the top of the ridge he spotted a pretty flower that he didn't know, picked a bit and posted samples to the botanic gardens in Kew and Edinburgh. The experts had no trouble identifying it. To wanderers in Lapland or the highest hills of New England, Diapensia is well known. The surprise was that it should occur in Scotland, way south of its known range in Europe. Word got round, and among the new plant's first visitors was Robert Moyes Adam (1885–1967), a flower artist and keen amateur photographer. He had used the same heavy, half-plate field camera all his life, an instrument that he had made to his own specifications back in 1908. 'I never take a photograph,' he used to say. 'What I do is expose a plate.' His images were always monochrome, but the big plates lent them a definition and atmosphere beyond that of contemporary cameras. Adam's panoramas of the Highlands were always in demand. They are now regarded as classics of their era.

Adam sweated up to Diapensia's ridge with all his kit on a rare clear day. But, like so many others since, he found he had left it too late. The flowers were already over and, in their place, pinkish seed capsules sprouted from the coppery-green cushions. He took his picture anyway, one that became the defining image of Diapensia country. And what a shot it is! Adam makes it look like the barest, loneliest hill in Britain. Ridge after ridge rolls away into the distance, all seemingly scraped clean of soil, except in the deep gullies that score the hillsides. In the foreground lies only shattered rock and gravel. But peer carefully and you can just make out the cushions and seed-heads of Diapensia.

It is a famous photograph and I have always longed to stand on that very spot, with Diapensia at my feet. My opportunity came when Ian Strachan, the plant recorder for Westerness, kindly volunteered to guide me up the secret hill. We met in the National Trust's car park, opposite the monument to Bonnie Prince Charlie's ill-fated bid for the throne. I read the notice: After soaking up the battles and the slaughter, '*Why not sample our delicious home baking?*' It reminded me of the café at another iconic location, called 'Jak-o'Bite'. Why not, indeed? Don't let our bloody history spoil your appetite: that seems to be the wholesome message.

There are two ways up Diapensia's hill: steep or very steep. Ian chose the slightly less steep one. It was misty on the tops, but a cool, damp breeze kept the midges away. But what began as a firm path soon disappeared into a bog, and the rest of the walk was a long slop through bog-moss and cotton-grass, and then a clamber through shattered pale-grey rocks half a billion years old. We ascended through what I call a mizzle – halfway between mist and drizzle – climbing steadily, one boot forward and the next sliding back. From my raised hood and steamed-up specs, all I remember is a blurry moving carpet of green and grey, grey and green. At length, rock overtook boggy grass, the air grew chillier and I sensed we were nearing the top.

'Diapensia,' said Ian, suddenly. Why didn't he shout it? Why didn't he yell? He had spotted tight packs of leaves in a tongue of gravel between two fangs of rock. Yes, it certainly was our plant, but where were the flowers, those brilliant pearls of the Arctic? We were soon finding more cushions – scores of them – many of them battered and torn by Lochaber's frightful winds. But only the last few flowers of the season. Like Robert Adam, I had missed the spectacle by a whisker.

I found a relatively fresh flower and looked at it for a bit. 'I thought they'd be bigger.' Noticing the silence that followed my tactless remark, I added quickly, 'But it's very nice all the same. Not at all disappointing.' Actually it was very disappointing. In fact I was broken-hearted. But even so, the fading blooms repaid examination. Artists have always had trouble conveying Diapensia's cold beauty: the pellucid texture of the flowers, with their intricately arranged stamens and stigmas. It is a flower that Fabergé might have wrought in white enamel and gold. Within each cup of pure-white petals lies an inner ring of yellow, twin-lobed anthers with the rigid pin of the stigma in the middle, like a dart in a bull's-eye. The flowers emerge from their bulge of glossy leaves on short, pinkish stems. By unceremoniously tipping a loose cushion sideways, Ian showed me how the plant is in fact a little tree pushed flat against the ground, with its trunk buried deep in a cleft. Some patches had died back in the middle, 'like old rock-roses in a garden', in the phrase of John Raven, classical scholar and veteran alpine botanist. From one sprang a cheeky seedling rowan – for hope springs eternal.

Diapensia was the queen of its ridge, sharing it with only the odd scrap of crowberry or clubmoss or hardy grass, or (slightly more interesting) Trailing Azalea, with its little pink star-flowers. Someone described this top as being possibly 'the least nutritious piece of rock in Scotland'. Why Diapensia is here, but – as far as we know – nowhere else in Britain is a mystery. Perhaps it has something to do with the abundant white veins of crystal quartzite, which weather to produce the coarse sand that Diapensia seems to depend on.

There are 1,200 Diapensias, Ian told me. Someone counted them all. They stay the same, year in, year out. In Diapensia-land, nothing happens quickly; the plants are long-lived; the growing season is short, but nature is in no hurry.

Most alpine flowers grow in gentler places than this, with at least a skin of soil to retain moisture and provide basic sustenance. Most, too, rely on a covering of snow to blanket them from the frosts and biting wind. Diapensia demonstrates just how tough a plant can be. In one of its arctic retreats the temperature can fall to an impressive -58° Celsius. A layer of wax insulates it against the cold. The compressed leaves absorb heat, so that the middle of Diapensia's cushion is warmer than the ambient temperature. Its deep, thick root anchors the plant so securely that it can withstand the world's most powerful winds. For example, it abounds on the top of Mount Washington in New Hampshire, where wind-speeds of up to 234 miles an hour have been recorded.

Without soil, where does Diapensia find the trace elements necessary for the health of any plant? Some think the waxy flowers trap dust in the wind, like crag-dwelling sea anemones, and then somehow convey it to the roots. Another possibility is that Diapensia survives by the intercession of fungi. Some of the rootlets, I noticed, are yellowish and plump – a sure sign of mycorrhizal fungi within (that is, helpful fungi inhabiting the plant's roots, in the manner of the Ghost Orchid). Fungi, unlike plants, can work on gravel, breaking it down with blisteringly powerful acids and releasing the poor modicum of salts within. As for the pretty flowers, they have not evolved to delight the artist's eye. Diapensia needs conspicuous flowers of the right colour and wavelength to attract whichever pollinators make it to these rugged tops.

While we lingered taking pictures, the sun broke through the mist. It was like a curtain lifting on a play. There, all of a sudden, was the famous view, little changed except for one thing. I saw now how misleading monochrome photography can be. What seemed in Robert Adam's picture to be bare rock is in fact green and vegetated: the moist green hills of Lochaber. And I also saw what his lens had been careful to avoid: the distant road in plain view. From the arctic home of Diapensia, I watched a bus go by. I could even catch the distant clackety-clack of the West Highland railway.

We descended in afternoon sunshine. Ian didn't think much of the theory that Diapensia had been accidentally introduced by Norwegian soldiers training nearby in the 1940s. For one thing, some of the plants are clearly very old. You can tell their age, he told me, by counting growth rings on the tap-root. No one has actually done this on the precious Scottish plants, but specimens of comparable size in Canada have invariably been upwards of 100 years old. Ian is in no doubt that Diapensia is a native species. One day he hopes to find another patch as he tramps some of the remotest hills in Britain, recording plants.

The Ice Age Plant

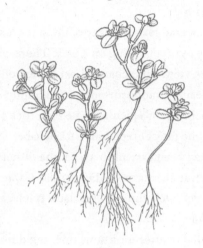

21
Iceland Purslane
Koenigia islandica

A tiny arctic sorrel with circular green leaves smaller than a
pea and a bright-red stem
Wet gravel near the summit of The Storr, Isle of Skye
4th July

I had never been to Skye, though I have longed to go there ever
since hearing the Skye Boat Song as a boy: '*Speed, bonnie boat,
like a bird on the wing... Over the sea to Skye.*' When I was very
young I thought the bonnie boat had actually flown up out of
the sea into the sky, like a bird.

Driving over the bridge that now connects the island to the
mainland really did feel like taking off. The arch is so steep that

for a wonderful and slightly scary moment all you can see is sky and cloud. Two things hit you when you land on the far side. First, the realisation that Skye is quite a big island. It is about the size of Buckinghamshire, and it takes a couple of hours to drive from one end to the other. Second, the visitor notes that not all of Skye is brooding mountain and romantic sea-loch. The road to Broadford is dull, and so is the town.

I was there to see two remote plants. Alpine Rock-cress is found nowhere else in Britain, though you can find it growing happily by the road in the Alps. Iceland Purslane, also known by its scientific name of *Koenigia*, is an arctic plant at the southern limit of its range in Britain. Neither plant is conspicuous. *Koenigia* is one of the smallest in the flora; most plants could fit on a 50p coin. Its flowers are no more than pale pinpricks between tiny, succulent circles of leaves. Its most distinctive aspect is its bright-red stem.

I followed the crowd up the steep track leading to the Old Man of Storr. Eventually the slope eased and the Old Man's dunce's cap rose above us, and the view ceased to be spectacular and became stupendous. The Storr is a strange mountain. The landward side is a smooth, almost featureless half-dome, but the side facing the sea has long ago split and tumbled down, leaving numberless broken rocks and soaring pinnacles of basalt. We walkers looked like pygmies in a valley of trolls. Behind rises a sheer curtain of rock. I had to find my way around it somehow, and so on, up on to the plateau where I hoped that *Koenigia* was waiting for me.

Those who had made the walk in sandals were now nursing their feet. Just a few hardy souls were continuing up the cliff path. A little girl was running down a slope of short, springy grass with outstretched arms, pretending to be a bird. 'You'll break the other one!' shouted her mother. Through binoculars I could glimpse lush vegetation thronging the rock ledges: little spurts of yellow, pink and blue against black rock. My way was blocked by a fence, presumably for safety reasons. I hopped over and carried on walking, conscious that the noise was receding and that I was suddenly on my own. I entered a vast scoop in the hill, an enormous green bowl that seemed to offer a way up. There was no path now, but the slope was moderate and the intervening rocky terraces an easy scramble. Up I crawled, stared at blankly by about a million sheep. The sun beat down and soon I was at the top, sweating profusely, on the roof of Trotternish, looking down on the bald pates of the Old Man and his craggy friends.

What a view! The summit of The Storr is a primal wilderness, with not so much as a bush for shelter, just swells of gravel and grass rising and falling above the sea: Britain before the trees, a vision of the Ice Age. You could play cricket on the sheep-mown grass (though a six would send the ball spinning over the cliff, to fall among the crowd 1,000 feet below). Here and there were hollows with shoots of bare, reddish gravel, some with surface water flowing from hidden springs. I had map references for *Koenigia*, but they weren't necessary. All I had to do was wander over to the nearest hollow of wet gravel and there it was: our little Iceland Purslane, just visible from head height as little points of pink and green. Crouching down in the icy trickle, I confirmed the diagnostic red stem. The plants were not well grown. The growing season is short here, and many of the little purslanes had not developed much beyond the seedling stage. With my lens I could make out some pinpricks of flower buds on the more developed plants, enough anyway for a tick. Come early autumn, these plants would turn russet-pink and be visible from whole yards away. Still, I had been to the Ice Age and seen *Koenigia*. Now for the Alpine Rock-cress. Another easy twitch, I hoped. Another doddle.

20
Alpine Rock-cress
Arabis alpina

A white-flowered cress, similar to Garden Arabis with
toothed, hairy leaves and long, thin pods
The Black Cuillin, Isle of Skye
5th July
Helpers: Michael and Sue Scott

A kind, local botanist had given me directions to find it. There
was so little of this plant, he told me, and it is so inconspicuous,
that even a detailed map would not be enough. Instead he sent
me a photograph of the cliff face with some markers highlighted:
a particular cleft, a line of slightly paler strata, a certain patch
of green on the dark rock. To reach it meant another slog up a

treeless glen followed by a lengthy clamber over loose scree and rock bands. It was not, he warned, a journey to make in mist or rain. And that was a pity, because the hot spell was finally breaking and more usual Highland weather was on the way.

Alpine Rock-cress was discovered about a hundred years ago by a keen walker, naturalist and all-round show-off called Henry Chichester Hart. No one but a botanist would have spotted it. No great beauty, this plant could easily be mistaken for the kind of weedy, white-flowered cresses that invade newly-dug gardens in the spring. Its distinguishing features are not the bland, white, four-petal flowers so much as the densely hairy, grey-green, wavy-toothed leaves and long, slightly curving pods. I have seen it in European mountain ranges quite commonly, even growing by the road and looking crisp and neat. But in the Black Cuillin of Skye it generally looks as tired and wet as its few human visitors, as if longing for a bright hillside in Switzerland. It was appropriate that it should have been discovered late and by a super-fit walker and climber. Hart's style of botanising was to march over the hills at what he termed 'a steady 5 to 6 miles an hour'. If you couldn't keep up – and hardly anybody could – that was hard luck, for he 'would not dally for a slowcoach'. He once bet a friend fifty guineas that he could walk from the middle of Dublin to the summit of Lugnaquilla in County Wicklow and back again within twenty-four hours – a round journey of 112 miles. He won his bet, with ten minutes to spare. Today admirers attempt to emulate that feat in a yearly Hart Walk. When he married, in 1887, aged forty, Hart naturally chose the Black Cuillin for their honeymoon: nothing like the hardest hills in Britain for nourishing love. Whether or not his lady was with him when he discovered the Alpine Rock-cress, history does not relate. I suspect she was some miles back at the time, nursing a sprained ankle. All we know for sure is that Hart found it, and then carried on at his usual speed to make the first recorded ascent of Sgurr a' Mhadaidh.

One person who headed in Hart's footsteps into those grim black crags was the botanist Peter Jepson, who described the place as 'the most hostile environment anyone could contrive for a plant'. It took him three attempts to find it. The first was a washout: a sudden storm 'that turned the cliff faces into waterfalls'. There was, he discovered, 'only so much water one can get down the back of one's neck before becoming thoroughly despondent and depressed'. The second attempt was a two-day rock scramble, but it, too, ended in failure. But on the third try he not only found the plant, but also discovered it in a new place in a neighbouring corrie. Another who trod the same path, the classical scholar John Raven, remembered a 'stiff and gloomy walk' and a clamber over 'an apparently endless scree'. I wasn't looking forward to it much.

I had arranged to do the walk with my old friend Michael Scott, the Scottish naturalist and broadcaster, and his wife Sue, an accomplished marine biologist and photographer. Mike gallantly volunteered to drive. The forecast was not encouraging. A warm front had arrived in the night and it was raining lightly as we set off, though with some hope of easing up later on. The low cloud matched my spirits. I would not have chosen such a day for the toughest walk of the quest and I considered our chances of success close to zero. But I felt I had no choice: the timetable I had set myself was tight, and this was the only available day. I had to try.

One thing at least had changed since Peter Jepson and John Raven had trudged up to those ferocious cliffs. The walk might still be 'stiff' but it could no longer be described as 'gloomy'. The car park was full, and cars and campervans were lined up along the narrow road. The path, which was now broad and well-maintained, was busy with walkers eager to see the island's newest tourist attraction, the 'Fairy Pools'. From its rise among the black crags, the stream tumbles down the hillside, swirling its way through natural weirs and waterfalls, a thread of clear-blue glen water, pausing here and there in deep, rocky pools with shores of pale gravel, before plunging on again. The Pools looked very pretty even under lowering, unsmiling cloud. A noticeably multinational set of anoraked walkers were peering into the boiling waters and posing for the Facebook shot, smiles and laughter in the mist.

We passed them and continued upwards to the waiting rocks. We are not letting you up here easily, the crags seemed to whisper. This is hard country. Are you sure you're hard enough, you three, one of you with a limp, we notice, one with white hair, and all of you getting on a bit? The rocks, which now hemmed in the stream and blocked our way, coincided with the arrival of the cloud-base. We were entering a world of vapour, a white zone of mist that still showed no sign of lifting. Mike decided this was the right place to turn back; his knee was hurting. Sue and I forced ourselves on, seeking a way through a half-seen wilderness of rock, some of it loose, some of it like tumbledown walls, threaded by countless trickles and streamlets treacherous with slime. Fortunately the rock was gabbro, as rough as emery paper, offering a good grip and plenty of holds. On we struggled.

Despite my conviction that our walk would be fruitless, I quite enjoyed the climb, feeling little spurts of youth in my aching limbs as we clambered up one outcrop and slithered down the other side, just as one had done as a boy on wet cliffs by the seaside. We knew we were somewhere within a semi-circle of unclimbable cliff that encloses the upper corrie. There was now a smudgy greyness within the mist that suggested approaching rock walls. We were in the land of the rock-cress. 'Give it an hour?' suggested Sue.

We got out our charts and notes and photographs. Without a clear view of the corrie, identifying the telltale sliver of cliff that held the only patch of Alpine Rock-cress within reach was impossible. A particular line of rocks was supposed to lead straight to it, but which line? There were lots of rocks tumbled beneath the cliff and strewn about the surprisingly fresh and springy grass of the corrie. The compass was no good either: these rocks contain iron; they are magnetic, and, as far as I could see, proper north was currently facing west.

'It's clearing up a bit.' We could make out bits of the cliffs now, but not the battlemented tops. The flora was as sparse as I've ever seen. Where the sheep could reach, it was just tufts of grass, but mostly there was nothing much at all, just naked rock lightly plastered with moss and lichen. Suddenly Sue's sharp eyes spotted some white flowers about twenty feet up at the edge of a gully. The light was twilight dim, and even binoculars could make out no more than a fuzzy patch of indeterminate shape. Sue took a few camera snaps and then enlarged them. Glory be, it was a rock-cress! We had found a rock-cress! That was the nearest we came to a big triumphant tick, a victory of hope over sanity. Yes, it was a rock-cress, but it was the wrong one. We had found Northern Rock-cress, *Arabis patraea*, also something of a rarity, but not nearly as rare as the elusive Alpine Rock-cress. In these conditions, it might have taken us hours, maybe days, to locate the tiny patch. 'Well, we can say we tried,' I said. But I could see Sue would be back to continue the search when the weather cleared, if the weather cleared. I know when I'm licked, but Sue is made of sterner stuff.

Hours later we were drinking coffee in the sun with wonderful clear views all along the island coast – all wrapped in sunlight apart from the Black Cuillin whose stubborn peaks were still covered in cloud and rain. 'These hills make their own weather,' observed Mike. It's as if they have a mind of their own; as if they love rain; love the dim, grey light, and the silver lines of water streaming from every gully. *Arabis alpina* had eluded us. The quest was getting harder, more desperate, by the day and there was worse to come.

19
Norwegian Mugwort
Artemisia norvegica

A rock plant with yellow button flowers suspended above a
tuft of hairy, divided leaves
In gravel on a high, bare ridge, Cul Mor, Scottish Highlands
6th July
On my own, rather unwisely

Distances are deceptive in the far north. You can see Cul Mor
from miles away, but it took three hours to reach it from the
Kyle of Lochalsh. The scenic but dreadfully slow narrow road
wound round every corner of that fretted coastline, past inlets
and sea-lochs, rivers and waterfalls, the scenery becoming ever
rockier and more waterlogged. On this quiet morning some lochs
were mirrors, while others nursed their own private cloud of

mist. I should have been walking, not driving, in this oasis of fair weather. After refuelling at Ullapool, I entered a new and strange landscape where the rolling hills turned into isolated giant hats, perched on an elemental plain of rock, water and bog. The hills now had Viking-sounding names: Suilven, Quinag, Stac Polly, Canisp.

Cul Mor means 'large back' or, in a perhaps truer interpretation, 'large hind-part'. From a distance it looks like a bare, bony bottom, the big bum of a giant, perhaps on his hands and knees looking for a rare flower. Like other hills hereabouts, it is an inselberg (an isolated mountain) of Torridonian sandstone sitting on a platform of Lewisian gneiss. Geologists used to puzzle over that, because the oldest rocks sit on top of younger rocks, and that seemed impossible; the geology was back-to-front. The eventual solution came to the Victorian geologist Charles Lapworth – by his own account, in a dream. He was doubtless still thinking about rocks and strata as he dozed off in his bedroom at Inchnadamph. A huge mass of rock was on the move, grinding westwards, colliding with the younger rocks in its path, first crushing them and then crumpling them forward in its terrible onward motion. The cliff seemed to be coming at Lapworth, too, threatening to flatten the dreamer in his bed. He woke with the idea of a 'thrust fault' clear in his head. But, like Darwin and his theory of evolution by natural selection, Lapworth was fearful of its implications. Rock strata were supposed to be static. The idea of continental masses drifting and colliding and turning upside down needed a bolder spirit to champion it. But he was to be proved right. When land masses collide, stupendous things happen: mountains rise, earthquakes shake the planet, and volcanoes pour liquid magma all over the place. It was all discovered right here, close to the car park where I prepared myself for another long, wet walk.

The only way to Cul Mor is from the east. All other ways are blocked by water, by lochs the shape of spilt milk that circle the hill like a moat. Although the top of Cul Mor is only 2,785 feet – and so the hill is a mere Corbett, and not a Munro – it looked impressive enough in its isolation, as well as a long way off. Clouds were already building from the east, and in these parts the weather can change from sunshine to pelting rain almost before you can whip your anorak out of the backpack. I had to go through with it, to find another recently discovered alpine plant, Norwegian Mugwort. How I wished, at that moment, that people would stop discovering them. Who was the real mug here? I thought.

Mugworts are, in the main, untidy-looking weeds with divided leaves and undistinguished flowers, resembling failed daisies with all the petals pulled off. Compared with its lowland cousins, Norwegian Mugwort is a prince, with yellow button-flowers held on a short hairy stem above stiff, silvery leaves. It is a plant of world rarity, being otherwise found only in Norway and the Urals (a similar plant that may or may not be the same species is found in North America, where it is known either as Boreal Sagewort or Spruce Wormwood). Our plant is regarded as a distinct endemic subspecies *scotica*: so Scottish Norwegian Mugwort. Only three sites are known. It is a late species, so I was not expecting to find it in full flower, but it was the only chance I had.

The walk began with a well-made stalker's track, but all too soon it veered off in the wrong direction and I was reduced to following a line of cairns. Then they too gave out, and thereafter

I had to pick my way by eye in weather that was turning sour and grey. The first mile was bright with flowers: yellow butter-cups, pink louseworts, milkworts as piercingly blue as garden lobelia. Abruptly the sweet pasture gave way to barren deergrass, sedge and moss, and then to shelves of silvery-grey gneiss. The bony buttocks of Cul Mor were hidden in low cloud. At its foot, on a shoulder called Meallan Diomhain or 'lazy lump', I met three men coming down. Bad weather on the way, they advised; take care now.

It was soon mizzling with that soft rain of the west, the sort that noiselessly flannels your face, dapples your specs and gently feels its way down your collar. The gloomy shades of neigh-bouring hills deepened the sense of claustrophobia. I pulled up my hood and trudged on. In the fading light I found myself among a maze of rocks. I must, I reasoned, be on the saddle between the tops, in the cleft between Cul Mor's twin peaks.

The actual top was guarded by angular boulders. Some were firm, but others wobbled underfoot, and all were now wet and slippery. Rain was coming on hard. From beyond, in the direc-tion of the hill's nearest neighbour Cul Beag ('little bum'), came a rumble of thunder. I still had some way to go, down the bare western ridge, whose name translates as 'rough nose'. Flattish brown rocks appeared out of the cloud like monstrous cheeses. In good weather this might have been a walk to cherish, a high narrow way over an awesome wasteland of rock and water. As it was, in the half-light, with the rumble and bang of the approaching storm, it was fearful. With my hood toggled tight, I could see only what lay directly ahead, swimming in and out of my ken through the mask of my specs. All I wanted was to meet my mugwort and then hare off back to civilisation.

I stumbled over a series of shelving rocks. Between a jumble of low boulders I glimpsed what the plant's original discoverer called a 'sideways slipping basin'. Among the clitter of sandstone chips were little clumps of divided leaves: mugwort! They are supposed to have a bitter smell, like fir needles, but not today. I couldn't see any flowers. Where were the flowers? Were those knot-like things its buds? Yes! Tick! But the rain was pelting down so hard I could hardly make them out. I felt rather than saw them.

Then there was the most almighty bang, followed by a flash. The storm had arrived. In terror, I splashed back up the slope as fast as my clunky boots could carry me. The right thing to do was to find shelter among the rocks well below the ridgeline and wait out the storm. But both sides plunged down steeply, and my only thought was to get off the hill as quickly as possible. Another flash burst over Cul Mor, a blast of white light, mighty close, horribly assertive. I swear I smelt electricity. If I live, I thought, I might find this quite funny – the terrified, fleeing figure with the thunder god hurling bolts after him.

It was pelting with *hail* now. I bumped and slithered over the dripping scree. The track I'd missed coming up was now a torrent. As I followed it down, I began to talk to myself. And then shout. I did the storm scene from *King Lear*: '*Blow, winds, and crack your cheeks! rage! blow!*' In a funny way, shouting seemed to help. Lear's storm, we are told, reflected his psychological state, for there was a worse storm raging in his mind. But shouting is also therapeutic; it takes your mind off your aching back and tired feet, and the horribly near bangs and flashes. The heavens rumbled, the hail pelted down and, Lear-

like, I raged. '*Rumble your bellyfull! Spit, fire! spout, rain!...
Strike flat the thick rotundity o' the world! Crack nature's moulds!*'
Defiance makes you feel less helpless. Shakespeare must have
known that. An hour or two later I was back at the car park,
soaking wet and shivering, but feeling brave again.

18
Purple Oxytropis
Oxytropis halleri

A beautiful member of the pea family, with clusters of blue
flowers held on hairy stems above a tuft of ladder-like leaves
On a sea cliff at Bettyhill, Sutherland
7th July

Breakfast in the Highlands is not a perfunctory thing. The 'full
Scottish' at my B&B included options of black pudding or haggis,
on top of the already laden plate of bacon, eggs, mushrooms
and tomatoes. I opened the paper and then nearly dropped it on
the toast and marmalade. 'Lightning strike kills hikers,' I read.
It had been a different storm, hundreds of miles away in the
Brecon Beacons, but on the same day as my own brush with
destiny. Two walkers on an exposed ridge near the top of Pen y

Fan had been hit by a stray bolt. They were found and airlifted to hospital, but never regained consciousness.

It was raining again by the time I was back on the road, still heading north. On and on wound the narrow road, through bands of mist and islets of pearly, occluded light. On past brooding peaks, their quartz-frosted shoulders shrouded in low cloud. Some were scored by rills, as though scratched by a giant cat. Finally there was nothing ahead but the pale-blue sea. I had reached the furthest north. From the top of a peak here, on midsummer's day, they say the sun never sets.

It took all morning to reach Bettyhill. There was no danger of taking a wrong turning because there was only one road, and I was on it. I had come all this way to see a plant that symbolises the end of Britain: an elegant member of the vetch family with clusters of purple flowers that, as befits a flower of the near-Arctic, are covered in shaggy hair, a kind of woolly blanket to keep the plant warm and prevent water loss from the sharp coastal winds. If it were not so rare, it might have earned a more imaginative name than Purple Oxytropis.

I did not know exactly where to look for it. I had seen pictures of the plant growing quite profusely on what looked like blown sand – though not necessarily by the sea, for sand blows a long way in these parts. I stopped at a Klondike-like cabin that served as the village shop; it boasted a good selection of maps, fishing gear and malt whiskies, but not much else. I asked the way to the nearest beach. 'You want Farr Bay,' said the lady. 'It's lovely down there, and you'll probably have it all to yourself.'

It was, but there wasn't any Purple Oxytropis on it, and I wasn't quite alone. Two children, probably locals, were splashing in a puddle of seawater. I walked past the beach and over the dunes, which in turn backed onto sweet, sandy grassland bright with flowers: thyme, milkwort, fairy flax, eyebrights. Finally I walked up to some cliffs and cautiously peered over the edge. Ah, *there* you are! About ten feet down, on a spur of rock, was a patch of purple. Intense blooms on ladder-leaves, outlined in silver, caught in a halo of northern light. The flowers were a little past their best, and pods were forming on some of the heads. I longed to clamber down to touch them, but the cliff edge was loose and the beach was a long way down. For a moment, though, I was caught between safety and desire. Falling is an occupational hazard of botanists, for in the presence of the beautiful and the rare, we temporarily lose our fear. One of the few people to have seen all the British wild flowers was David McClintock, author of the famous *Collins Pocket Guide to Wild Flowers*. Late in life he reached out to a rare heather on a beetling cliff, slipped and fell headlong onto the rocks. He dismissed the incident as a mere 'contretemps', but he walked with a stoop for his remaining years. I gave my flower one last, lingering gaze through binoculars and called it a day. I still had another twenty flowers to go, and I wouldn't succeed with a broken leg.

I was packing the car at the hotel the next morning when a young man came running up. His name was Trevor and he had spotted my name in the guest book. He was a conservationist, busy surveying birds on the estate, and he wanted to tell me about some new developments. Dropping my heavy bag in the boot, I turned towards him and, at that moment, something twisted in my back. I gasped in pain. I was dreading this – some sprain, a slip of a disc, out here at the furthest point from home. 'Go on,' I panted. 'Just a spot of back trouble.'

Trevor hadn't noticed. He wanted to tell me about a clothing store billionaire called Anders Povlsen, who had bought a 49,000-acre slice of northern Scotland on the Ben Loyal and Kinloch estates – land once owned by that notorious evictor, the Duke of Sutherland. Povlsen was the man, well known in Scotland, who had made a success of Glen Feshie in the Cairngorms, the place where Landseer painted *The Monarch of the Glen*. Until Povlsen arrived, the Monarch and his mates had been truly in charge of the local ecology. They browsed the heather and young trees and made sure that natural regeneration took place only where deer were excluded by high, ugly fences. The whole glen had been blitzed by deer and, in winter, some of the animals used to die of starvation. Yet now, inside ten years, and aided by a progressive estate factor, this outsider from Sweden had managed to reduce the marauding herds to something like sustainable levels, while the apparently dying woods were springing back into life. Pine, birch, juniper and rowan are regenerating well, and all of a sudden the glen looks healthy and vibrant again, even though it has local wiseacres shaking their head at the growth of 'jungle'.

'It could happen here too,' said Trevor. 'Oh, are you all right? You winced just then. As I was saying, we could have salmon back in the rivers, new woods springing up along the burns...'

I wanted to stop him there. I really was in horrible pain.

'Greenshank, golden plover, wading birds. Redwing, maybe...'

'Sorry, it's my back. I think I might have twisted it.'

'Phalaropes, pine marten, wildlife tours, the local economy...'

'It sounds great. I'm going to have to sit down.'

'Isn't it weird how it takes an outsider to bring this about? He's now the second-largest landowner in Scotland, you know.

He loves Scotland. But he's not hidebound by history. He's got this basic idea...'

Yes, yes, and good luck to it. I found that if I pulled the driving seat forward and used it to brace my back upright, I could drive without too much discomfort. But I could probably forget about clambering up more rocks or wading through another mile of bog. I thought I could manage just one more plant, before setting off for home and entering the final round of The Quest.

The Nightmare Sedge

17
Estuarine Sedge
Carex recta

A tall, fine-leaved sedge confined to river estuaries in the far
north-east of Scotland, differing from its nearest relatives in
habitat and various minor botanical characters, mostly to do
with the glumes (the nutty bits held on a stalk)
A salt-marsh near Bonar Bridge, Sutherland
8th July

Estuarine Sedge is a tall, leafy sedge, distinguished from its
nearest relatives chiefly by a bristle on the glumes of the
female flower. That may not sound much, but the accumula-
tive effect of these bristles gives the plant a definite prickly
('aristate') look. The best way to find it is to follow a tidal
river right down to the sea. But it needs to be a river in the

far north of Scotland between Thurso and Inverness, because this particular sedge isn't found anywhere else. It is thought to be a 'stabilised hybrid' that evolved here relatively recently, although, curiously enough, one of its putative parents, *Carex paleacea*, is a Scandinavian species that has never been recorded from Britain. Estuarine Sedge is considered to be 'vulnerable'.

I parked by the river at Bonar Bridge and followed the path to a seawall. Thereafter it was a painful limp through long grass, but after a quarter-hour of stumbling, I found it. What I saw wasn't an individual plant so much as a whole landscape of sedge, a couple of acres of salty swamp dominated by *Carex recta*. It was a worthy setting, too: calm, reflecting waters enclosed by low hills. Having absorbed a little of Mike Porter's love of sedges, I found myself viewing this one with sympathy. About three feet tall, it had graceful, slender leaves and long bracts that overtopped the ponytail spikes. But what I remember most is that many of the plants were crawling with aphids, bugs with a pale, waxy skin that seemed to have taken on the very texture of the plant whose life-juices they were sucking. For several nights afterwards, between wakeful bouts of back pain, those bugs entered my dreams, crawling over impossible meadows and swamps like a plague of lice. Whenever you touched them, they left a nasty corrosive wax on your fingers. The Quest had begun to generate nightmares; I remember dream Diapensias and Oxytropis turning shrivelled and brown under a hail of insect pests, or morphing into horrid shapes under a blistering Highland rain. Meanwhile, back in the real world, a cloud of midges was gathering. I faced a fourteen-hour drive, bolstered from extreme pain by straps and a cushion. I was quietly losing the will to live, and The Quest still had three months to run.

Interlude

At close to midnight, I crawled out of the car and, bent double, tottered to my back door. I thought I might have slipped a disc. I also feared a recurrence of sciatica – those, to me, familiar shooting pangs running down one leg, usually the right one, bad enough to need a pill to sleep. But, it seemed, it was only a sprain, presumably the result of driving too far on twisting Highland roads in a small car. A heated pad pressed to the hurt worked wonders; I could live with the diminished pain. All the same, I wasn't feeling well; nothing that could be located, more a vague sense of being below par, of feeling tired half the time, with nil appetite and a lowered sense of *joie de vivre*. At the time I put it down to the pressure of having to find another flower when I would rather be, say, peeling a potato with a toothpick.

An advance copy of my new book, *Rainbow Dust*, was waiting in the boiler house. As usual there was plenty to do before the launch. The *Daily Express* wanted an op ed on 'the Butterfly Effect', the *Independent* a full-length essay on 'People and Butterflies'. I had to appear on *Saturday Live* with Julian Clary and a couple who travelled everywhere on a tandem bike ('What's it like, watching his bum all day long?' Julian had asked). The worst of it was a ten-minute live interview on Irish radio. 'Tell us about de mats,' the radio man had said. Mats? What did he mean? Maps? Why was he asking me about maps? 'Mats – de mats!' He meant 'moths'. I really wasn't well.

Fortunately, perhaps, the next few plants did not involve much trekking in the rain. I was losing faith in my ability to find flowers on my own. And that was another thing: at moments my vision would suddenly turn blurry. After blinking a few times, things would usually snap back into focus, but it was unsettling. As was my voice, for whenever it was necessary to say something on air, it often came out as a hoarse croak. Was it just another of the little surprises nature has in store as we approach old age, I wondered? (For, after all, none of us have direct experience of being old until we are.) Or were there more proximate causes? I put it out of my mind, but woke in the night and worried about it.

16
Upright or Tintern Spurge
Euphorbia serrulata (or *E. stricta*)

A dainty annual with small leaves, often tinted pink, with
tiny spurts of yellow florets and seeds covered in tall,
cylindrical warts
A wooded ravine in the Wye Valley near St Briavels,
Gloucestershire
20th July
Helper: George Peterken

George Peterken had agreed to show me Tintern Spurge. It is
also known more correctly as Upright Spurge, but that is only
a translation of its scientific name, *Euphorbia stricta*. It doesn't
say much about a plant, really, to assert that it is upright. George

lives in the spurge's British heartland, in the lower Wye Valley. It is usually a plant of ancient woodland, and George is our greatest living authority on the subject; indeed, he practically discovered the concept of ancientness and of plants that need settled conditions and tend to disappear if a wood is clear-felled. For much of his life he has followed the changing fortunes of one particular place, Lady Park Wood, to find out exactly what happens when a wood is left alone to develop naturally. It may be surprising, but no one had the foggiest idea what British woods do when left to nature, for the understandable reason that there is not a single, wholly natural wood left. Lady Park Wood, which has deliberately been left unmanaged for the past fifty years, is the nearest we have to primeval conditions. And what it seems to be showing us is that ecologists had got it wrong. According to theory, a natural wood should carry on indefinitely in more or less its present mature state. Occasionally an old tree will die and a host of sprightly young saplings will compete for the space. But in general a natural wood is supposed to be as permanent as stone: high, stately, serene – and predictable.

What actually happened in the past half-century at Lady Park Wood is wholly unpredictable damage and disaster. Some trees survived, but many were trashed by squirrels or by drought or late snow. The elms died of disease. Regenerating saplings were chewed up by deer, and no clear winner has emerged among the competing trees. What we see is formed by the 'chance impacts of various disturbances'. George has written a scholarly book about it.

He knew a site for Tintern Spurge deep in the woods a couple of miles from his house, and about ten miles from Lady

Park Wood, though he warned me that the spurge is not as frequent as it used to be. A short walk through a field and then along a wooded stream, and there it was by the track, in small quantity but in attractive company: wood vetch, yellow-wort, hedge parsley. I surprised myself saying, 'What a pretty little thing!' – for, after all, it is only a spurge. George agreed that it was 'dainty', with little pricks of startling yellow set in a pointillist mosaic of pink and green, leaves and bracts. Dainty and, unfortunately, endangered. Most of its former woods have grown too shady. There are only around twenty sites left in the whole valley.

This might seem surprising because, as an annual, Tintern Spurge produces masses of fertile seed, and a well-grown plant can go on splurging them out for weeks on end. The seeds are dispersed with the help of ants, which are attracted by droplets of natural plant oil clinging to them. The spurge often grows close to water or on tracks that turn into temporary streams whenever it rains, and so some of the light seeds probably float away, bobbing like little corks as they are taken downhill. The plant's essential weakness lies in the seeds' limited viability; they don't seem to last long. George knows woods that haven't been coppiced for decades in which the entire seed-bank has probably rotted away, leaving no way back for the plant unless we step in and help it.

Although it is, as I say, quite an attractive spurge, it is hard to imagine anyone getting hot under the collar about it. And yet botanists have disagreed about this plant with surprising warmth. The argument is over its status – that is, where the plant came from. The *New Atlas of the British & Irish Flora* sits on the fence: it is either 'native or alien'. But one of the authors, David Pearman, included Tintern Spurge among his 'doubtfully native species' in a recent paper, on the grounds that its discovery came late, in 1773, and because it is confined to disturbed ground, such as our woodland track. Besides, say the sceptics, why should a mid-European species like this be confined to Gloucestershire? It doesn't make sense. If it is native anywhere, it ought to be Kent.

George Peterken disagrees. He points out that the Wye Valley was virtually unknown to botanists before the late 1700s, and the record of Tintern Spurge actually precedes that of the bluebell. Yes, it needs open ground to germinate and set seed, but that is because it is an annual, and annuals need bare soil. It is associated with some of the oldest and richest woods of the valley and usually grows among natural vegetation. George considers the plant to be a 'gap-phase' species that appears from buried seed after the trees are coppiced or felled, only to disappear again once the canopy shades over. For instance, it appeared in vast numbers at a wood called Coed Wen, after the soil was disturbed by lorries removing fallen elms. Besides, asks George, if it is introduced, who introduced it? Why should anyone want to? He believes it is more logical to accept it as a native species, unless and until convincing evidence suggests otherwise.

The broader argument is over what constitutes native-ness, and why it matters. When the first plant atlas was published in the 1960s, all British wild flowers were considered to be either 'native' or 'introduced' – one or the other. But its successor, the *New Atlas*, published in 2002, found it necessary to distinguish between ancient 'introductions' and modern ones. Poppies, for example, have been with us for thousands of years (we know this because their pollen survives in archaeological deposits), but they are nonetheless believed to be non-native because they lack a wild habitat; they are always to found in arable fields or on disturbed ground. Such plants are now called 'archaeophytes' or 'old plants'. For those whose origin is thought to be much more recent, another term has been invented: 'neophytes' or 'new plants'. If Pearman is right, then Tintern Spurge would be classed as a neophyte. And that would mean an end to conservation efforts, because the limited resources available have to be channelled to help disappearing native species. Neophytes as a class need no such help. Dozens of new plants establish themselves in the wild every year.

On my way home I stopped off at another site for Tintern Spurge, at Highnam Wood near Gloucester, a well-known, open-access place popular with birdwatchers and dog-walkers. To my surprise, the gate to the car park was locked with a distinctly unwelcoming notice warning me not to block the entranceway. I parked further down the busy road and walked back, climbing over the gate. The bird hide, too, was locked. It would in future be opened, I read, 'only when staff are present'. The bird-feeders had been removed, and so had the back wall of the hide. All very mysterious. The place was deserted, but I felt as though I was being watched by hidden eyes, perhaps by a CCTV camera in the bushes.

The sign that hadn't been removed told me that Tintern Spurge can be seen all along the main path, but I couldn't find a single one. Returning to the car park, I took another look at the sign, and then looked down. There it was, growing profusely, inches from my feet. On a nearby mound of earth and gravel there was more, this time big, blowsy plants in full sun, and not at all dainty, with longer branches, glossy red stems and the coin-like leaves already turning gold and coral-pink.

The mystery of the locked gate and warning notices was revealed in the online local paper. There had been sordid goings-on in that hide. Someone walking their dog had interrupted activity that, although also canine in name, is not fit for family viewing. The police had been made aware of 'certain activities taking place' and, the warning continued, 'those involved will be dealt with appropriately'. And there, I thought, lies yet another hazard for the roving botanist in modern Britain. Nothing is ever quite what it seems.

A Pick of Peppers

15
Tasteless Water-pepper
Persicaria mitis (or *Polygonum mite*)

An annual bistort-relative with trailing spikes of pink flowers
A river bank at Upper Lode, near Tewkesbury,
Gloucestershire
15th August
Helper: Brett Westwood

I have always loved Tewkesbury, that flood-prone town on the confluence of the Avon and the Severn. A place of mills, bridges and half-timbered high streets, crowned by the Romanesque gem of Tewkesbury Abbey, it has somehow escaped the planning blight that ruined Worcester, Gloucester, Exeter and other West Country towns. Years ago I walked every inch of the countryside around Tewkesbury in an attempt to reconstruct the landscape as it was 500 years ago, ahead of a public inquiry over the fate of the battlefield of Tewkesbury, fought in 1471. The town was firmly against the development. So was English Heritage, which regarded it as a test case for its new 'Battlefields Register'. In short, we won, and the heart of the old battlefield, with its higgledy-piggledy meadows, hedgerows and streams, was saved.

I returned to Tewkesbury one fine August day with an old friend, Brett Westwood. Brett presents Radio 4 nature programmes, including the very successful *Tweet of the Day*. Generous-spirited, with a lovely broadcasting voice, he is also an extremely well-informed naturalist, as adept at identifying tiny weeds as he is at spotting flies, spiders and other small beasties. It was thanks to Brett that I was able to tick off one of my bogey-plants: the not-so-rare, but impossible-to-find Pale Willowherb, *Epilobium roseum*. There it was, growing in quantity along the suburban street close to Brett's garden wall.

We had agreed a *quid pro quo*. I would perform on ladybirds for Brett's current radio series, and in return he would show me the next plant on my list: Tasteless Water-pepper. He knew a site near Tewkesbury, although he hadn't been there for years and was unsure whether it was still there. The brief entry in the *Flora of Gloucestershire* was no help: '*Banks near Tewkesbury ... This needs confirmation... Local and rare.*'

Tasteless Water-pepper is another of those made-up English names that makes very little sense unless you know a bit about the plant. Its species name *mitis* doesn't mean 'mite' or 'mighty' but 'mild' or 'bland' − in other words, 'tasteless'. This is to contrast the plant with its nearest, and much commoner, relative, the Common Water-pepper, *Persicaria hydropiper*. That, as its name implies, tastes fiery hot. But you don't need to wander the river bank chewing vegetation to identify the rare one. Tasteless Water-pepper has pinker flowers that are without glands. Its seeds are more glossy and, in another of those faintly silly botanical terms, it grows 'suberect', meaning not quite erect, but not flat on the ground, either. Tasteless Water-pepper is a rather in-between sort of plant.

The only reason it was on my list is that I had never bothered looking for it. Though rare and getting more so, Tasteless Water-pepper is still fairly widespread across England, Wales and Northern Ireland. It crops up in disturbed places by ponds and rivers, in old peat diggings, in mud trampled by cattle, even by gates. As an annual, it persists only in permanently wet, open places without too much competition from more aggressive plants. Such conditions are found naturally where water draws down in the summer, leaving a band of mud on which fast-growing plants can stake a claim. Unfortunately these conditions are becoming hard to find. Fences separate cattle from river banks, so there is no trampled mud. Rivers, lakes, even the pond on the village green tend to be regulated to minimise draw-down in summer – for people, like ducks, prefer to have water in their ponds all year round. No one except the naturalist loves bare mud.

At Tewkesbury there is still a place where the water level rises and falls with the seasons. It lies in a backwater of the Severn at Upper Lode. Back in the 1850s an enormous concrete lock was built here to improve the river navigation and open it up to the latest steam tugboats pulling their long trains of barges

– an expensive scheme that was soon rendered redundant by the railway network. The works cut off a bend in the river, which has since become a quiet backwater, popular with fishermen. The mud exposed by the river in summer has been colonised by an impressive list of uncommon plants that flower when the water is at its lowest, in August. They have earned this stretch of the old channel the status of a Site of Special Scientific Interest.

In this summer of downpours the water was higher than usual. We donned wellies and squelched down the track leading from the lock. Almost immediately I was in the realm of persicarias. Their pretty pink and pale-green plantain-like heads dominated the lower bank. The task was to sort out which of them was *my* persicaria. I was fully prepared to do some serious nibbling, but in fact Tasteless Water-pepper turned out to be unexpectedly distinctive. It was in perfect flower and most of the trailing heads were bright coral-pink, speckled with green (technically speaking, the colour is a compound of tiny *white* petals and more prominent reddish bracts). To my eye, Tasteless Water-pepper has a crisp elegance that is lacking in its blowsier relatives. Brett found in it something 'Japanese-y', as pink and sweet as almond blossom. In cases of doubt, we could check the nodes, those segments at the base of each flowering branch, which in our species have frilly ends. Tasteless Water-pepper is another underrated and, perhaps, overlooked flower. It grows in colourful company too; the bank was a natural garden of pink persicarias, yellow bur-marigolds, pink and orange balsams. Oblivious fishermen had beaten paths through it, to find places to cast their lines.

We also made a discovery, or thought we had. As we got our eye in, we found plants that seemed to be halfway between the tasteless and the hot-tasting water-peppers, with looser, greener heads. They even tasted in-between, which is to say, only mildly peppery. The hybrid between *Persicaria mitis* and *P. hydropiper* is currently unrecorded from Britain. For our apparent discovery to become an authenticated record, I would need to collect material and get it analysed. I suspect someone will beat me to it. They usually do.

Meanwhile Brett was diverted by the insects visiting the flowers. He spotted a fiery red bug sitting on a leaf. '*Corizus hyoscyami*,' cried Brett. 'Isn't it gorgeous? Look, its orange-and-black pattern makes a face, like a tribal mask. They say it smells of cinnamon.' When he had the time, he said, he was going to come back here and search for Lesne's Earwig. The habitat looked just right. I felt an unexpected twinge of envy. How exciting life must be, when you can take a short walk down the river bank and find small wonders in every bush or basking on a flower head, or making themselves comfortable under a pebble. Why don't we take more notice of the small things? Why don't more of us look for Lesne's Earwigs instead of playing golf or washing the BMW?

While Brett poked around for more bugs, I admired the view. Across the floodplain the light of late afternoon had caught the stones of the distant abbey. It was the peace of old England, a view without TV masts or high-rises or parked cars, just the play of mellow light on tall grass, on stone and water. Wild flowers were continually taking me to places like this and to such islands of calm and tranquillity – glimpses of old England full of heart-yearning beauty. No more than a mile away, vehicles were queuing on the motorway, after an articulated lorry had jack-knifed across two lanes and hit a small family saloon. Lengthy delays were likely. We wandered back along the bank, happy with what we had found.

The Bogey-plant

14
Copse Bindweed
Fallopia dumetorum

A climbing plant with arrow-shaped leaves, tough, liana-like
stems and tendrils of white flowers
A hedgerow at Sandy Balls, Hampshire
28th August
Helpers: Martin Rand, Brett Westwood

I have mentioned 'bogey-plants' before. They are the ones
that, according to the books, should be easy enough to find,
but which are actually incredibly hard, bordering on impossible. Funnily enough, Brett Westwood and I shared the same
ultimate bogey-plant: the Copse Bindweed. In fact Brett was
inclined to doubt its existence; he thought the whole thing
might be a not-very-funny joke, thought up by Darwin or

someone like that. Copse Bindweed does sound rather unlikely. It is a native version of Russian Vine, with similar tendrils of white flowers and the ability to scramble over the hedgerow, sometimes to treetop height, with the aid of woody, liana-like stems. But, unlike Russian Vine, it is not a success. Copse Bindweed has always been difficult to pin down as it tends to appear and then disappear, and in recent times the disappearances have greatly outnumbered the appearances. I have looked for it in places where it had previously been unmissable, sprawling over the periphery of woods and decorating the hedge banks with its festoons of white – but found nothing, not so much as a dead liana. Perhaps most woods today have grown too shady for a plant that depends on periodic surges of light for its growth. Some of the places it has recently been found sound distinctly second-best: churchyards, shady lanes, timber yards.

Martin Rand, the plant recorder for South Hampshire, thought he might be able to show us a few plants, but warned that Copse Bindweed was experiencing yet another poor year. I told him just one would do, so long as it had managed to produce a flower and convinced us it really does exist. Martin, who I had not met before, could stand as an archetypal British field botanist. Retired but still active, he is lean with a neatly trimmed white beard and a precise manner. He used to be a digital programmer for the Ordnance Survey. He devotes around forty hours a week, unpaid, to the Hampshire flora, chairing committees, logging records and organising courses, surveys and projects. He reminded me once again of how lucky we are that there always seems to be a fund of people like Martin to keep field botany on the road. In past times, people like him were usually country curates or doctors or schoolmasters. Now they are often men and women who have worked with numbers, in computing and programming, or in university science. What unites them, then and now, is a strong rootedness to their particular patch, combined with a love of identifying and recording wild plants. Field botany has a long history in Britain, dating back to the seventeenth century. Though it was never in all that time as popular as bird-watching, it still surges on, in ebbs and floods, adapting and shedding ideas, and always with the same focus: 'the study, understanding and enjoyment of British botany'. Like Tennyson's brook, 'men may come and men may go, but I go on forever'.

We walked down the narrow lane to the point where the hedge was crossed by a line of pylons. 'There it is,' said Martin. Where? 'Down there.' I was looking up. Glancing at my feet and then crouching in the lane to get a better look, I spotted just two little plants at the bottom of the hedge, clearly Copse Bindweed with its distinctive arrow-head leaves, but not quite the sturdy climber I had hoped for. They had put out a few tentative tendrils and, given a few more weeks of warm weather, might grow up to reach the middling parts of the hedge. The bunched white flowers on their short pedicels were already ripening into the distinctive winged fruits, more broadly winged than the bindweed's near relative, Black Bindweed, and running further down the stalk. 'I may have a better one to show you,' said Martin hopefully.

He did, just one, in an overgrown hedgerow at a place called Sandy Balls. Here, at least, was a Copse Bindweed that was really trying. Its twisting, rope-like stems had been given a bunk-up by bracken and a holly bush and were now reaching far above our heads towards the canopy, putting out little bunches of winged seeds in the process. We looked, and groped for words. 'A river of leaves flowing upwards,' suggested Brett. 'Self-effacing.' 'A vegetable delta fed by braided channels,' offered Martin, getting into the spirit. 'It's quite a charming plant really,' concluded Brett after a pause, perhaps impressed by the singularity of those sharp-pointed leaves, and the jungle-vine, perhaps strong enough to support a lightweight Tarzan. He was pleased that, at last, he could believe in it.

These may have been the only three Copse Bindweed plants in the whole of Hampshire that year. Let us hope it was just the dull weather.

A Pot of Strapwort

13
Strapwort
Corrigiola litoralis

An annual with small greyish leaves and even smaller white,
red-tipped flowers growing as flat as a strap
On the gravel shore of Slapton Ley, South Devon
20th August, morning
Helpers: Andy Byfield, Brett Westwood and Clive Chatters

There were four of us now, standing on the shore of Slapton
Ley in South Devon, a large lake separated from the sea by a
bank of shingle. I was feeling knackered. A dinner at London's
oldest French restaurant to celebrate *Rainbow Dust* had left me
with the worst hangover of my recent life. After an equally
bibulous barbecue weekend for chums – an annual tradition –
I was a wreck. I stared at the water as dull-eyed as a stranded

porpoise. With me were Brett, once again, and Andy Byfield, our host, a genial gardener-cum-conservationist and nature writer. And Clive Chatters, doyen of the New Forest and a lead player in the Hampshire Wildlife Trust. All old friends who have managed to do some good in the world.

I wondered whether their achievements have something to do with rootedness. All three have a patch of England they can call their own. As well as his home turf, in South Devon, Andy is at home in the Isle of Purbeck, in Dorset, and the Lizard in Cornwall. Clive's bailiwick is Hampshire and, above all, the New Forest. Brett's best place is the Wyre Forest in Worcestershire, on which he has written and edited a wonderful book, *The Nature of Wyre*. Every naturalist should have a place they know intimately and can watch through the seasons; where every great tree is a friend and songbirds are not just 'nature', but neighbours. Compared with them, I am a wanderer on the earth, but, after twenty years, the Upper Kennet Valley is starting to feel like home.

We were looking for Strapwort, a plant unlucky enough to have earned my number 13. I was dreading another search on hands and knees (it was hard enough staying upright), for Strapwort is an inconspicuous plant consisting of a flattened mass of greyish-green spatula-shaped leaves and tiny clusters of white flowers, faintly dotted with crimson. The key to finding it is to look not for the plant itself, but for promising patches of its natural habitat, bare gravel close to the lake shore. There were once gravel shores all around Slapton Ley, but today most of it has turned into dense reedbeds. The only places you find the gravel now are where the shore has been disturbed – for example, where boats have been drawn up.

Sure enough, it was right by a boat that we found it. Strapwort, to my surprise, is quite nice. The little cup-shaped flowers had crimson bracts and their inner reproductive arrangements were like little green stars. The stems were tinged with red, the greyish leaves smooth and succulent. It is a noticeably *flat* plant, hence 'strap'. The largest of twenty-three plants briskly counted by Clive covered about thirty square inches. Since it was rooted only at the central point, and bound together by the jumble of stems, you could lift half of the plant from the ground like the page of a book. This is another endangered species. Our small colony contained perhaps a quarter of all the naturally occurring Strapworts in Britain today. You could fit the entire population on a kitchen table and still leave room for the plates.

The next patch of gravel had Strapworts too, some of them flowering underwater. The lake, swollen by rain, was green with plankton. Blanket weed smothered parts of the shoreline. There was a definite pong of decay. 'God, what a stink! Has something died?' 'I think it's the lake that's dying.' 'What a sad place.' 'Death, death,' cried Andy, histrionically.

It wasn't sewage or a corpse. Slapton Ley has become a sink for the excess fertiliser that is removed from the surrounding fields by rain, and eventually runs into the lake. This surge of artificial nitrates creates plankton blooms. The lake turns green; and then, under the hot August sun, the plankton dies and starts to stink.

But so long as you like flies, there's always a bright side. Brett spotted a dark insect buzzing over flocculent blobs of green slime. '*Eristalinus aeneus*,' he said happily. 'It loves rotting gunk. Look at its spotty eyes.'

An attempt by Kew Gardens to boost the natural population by introducing potted Strapworts on the far bank has been pronounced a success, though it seems a bit early to be celebrating. Grown from seed collected from the surviving plants, the tender seedlings were dug into specially prepared plots of mud and gravel. The introduction has boosted the total number of Strapworts to about 400, ten times as many as when the plant was at its lowest ebb.

Clive, for one, was not impressed: 'It's so sad that the solution has to be gardening in pots.' It seemed obvious to us that what the Strapwort needs is not pots, but natural habitat. 'What I'd like to see here,' said Clive, 'is cattle wandering about the lake shore, keeping the vegetation open, like it used to be, and the reeds down. And I'd also set about clearing some of those overhanging willows. Even where there's still gravel, there's danger from too much shade.' But he might run into opposition if he tried cutting down trees in such a well-known beauty spot. And the cattle might trouble the walkers' dogs. All the same, you wonder why those entrusted with saving our rarest plants prefer to act as gardeners and not ecologists. This kind of direct intervention is in fashion, because it gets immediate results and also provides possibilities for experimental science, and so for funding and students' diplomas. But it seems to me that cultivation techniques deny the plant its natural birthright: its wildness. We are enslaving it to our own agenda, to our plans and rules and priorities. There has to be a better way – one that leaves the gardening to nature.

Andy had a surprise for us before our hoped-for encounter with a second, even rarer plant. He led the way onto the nearby beach, crowded with families. Here and there, among the wind-breaks and tents, are islands of natural vegetation, and in one of these was something rare and precious: a Sea Daffodil, a large white, fragrant lily with fleshy, grey-green leaves. It would be another week or so before it flowered, but one of the plants had produced a fat bud. When it finally does flower, those nearby will notice a rich, heavy fragrance, one that Gerald Durrell described in *My Family and Other Animals* as 'the distilled essence of summer', a 'warm sweetness that made you breathe deeply time and again in an effort to retain it within you'. Unknown to our cold shores before 1990, the Sea Daffodil has become established in a few places on the south-west coast, although how or from where, no one knows. Perhaps it was brought back as seed from someone's Mediterranean holiday. Or possibly it is a new category of plant, a 'neo-native', borne northwards to England on a current of warm water. If Strapwort is on the way out, Sea Daffodils may be on the way in. The sun-warmed shore of future Britain may have an alluring scent.

A Green Bayonet

12
Triangular Club-rush
Schoenoplectus triqueter (or *Scirpus triqueter*)

A modest rush-like plant with a stiff stem, triangular in cross-
section, ending in a sharp point and a cluster of florets two-
thirds of the way up
On river mud in the Tamar Valley near Cotehele, Cornwall
20th August, afternoon
Helpers: Andy Byfield, Brett Westwood and Clive Chatters

My other plant was Triangular Club-rush. I would offer its scientific name, but it keeps changing. For most of my life it has been
Scirpus triqueter, simple and memorable. More recently it was
renamed *Schoenoplectus triqueter*, but then some authority had a
closer look and decided its true name is *Bulboschoenus triqueter*.
Many British plants, particularly among the grasses, sedges and

rushes, have been through a bewildering merry-go-round of names. The onset of molecular taxonomy accelerated the game, by proving that things are not always what they seem, and that two very dissimilar plants might nevertheless be closely related. Yellow Bird's-nest, for example, turns out to be a relative of heather that has given up on chlorophyll. But under any name Triangular Club-rush is one of our rarest and most elusive plants; indeed, it may even be extinct in the wild. The rush's problems are twofold (but probably linked): loss of habitat and hybridisa-tion. When it comes into contact with one of its two club-rush relatives, the triangular species seems only too ready to exchange genes. Unfortunately the hybrid is sterile; it is a genetic trap. Triangular Club-rush could not have survived the centuries intact unless something had isolated it from its relations. It is probably habitat degradation that has forced them together. Our Club-rush is a plant of tidal mud on the banks of broad rivers where seawater meets fresh water. Its rivers are, or were, the Tamar, the Arun, the Medway and, long ago, the Thames. But in recent years the species has been found only on the Tamar and, in Ireland, on the Shannon.

Despite its eagerness to hybridise, Triangular Club-rush is a distinctive plant with a three-cornered stem and a cluster of drab flowers that are rounded in shape rather than pointed – where you can find a flower, that is, for the plant is often found in a solely vegetative state. One of the problems is the lack of good illustrations. The only good one I know of is in an out-of-print field guide.

So how do you set about finding an extinct species? As with Interrupted Brome two months back, my solution was to look for a *reintroduced* plant. But even that is hard enough. Most of the seed used for attempts at re-establishment came from dried-up herbarium specimens, some of whose seeds, remarkably, were found to be still viable. Young plants cultivated in pots had been dug into the mud in various places along the lower river, but with mixed success: '*Twelve plants introduced on the river bank at Site A. Five still there in August,*' ran one report. '*Plants introduced by Environment Agency at Site B. Only a few crumpled stalks seen on return visit,*' said another. '*Eleven plants introduced at Site C; only one remains.*' '*Site D: one clump, none in flower. Looks vulnerable as sediment seems to be subsiding.*' So this is not yet a success story.

Our original plan, to hire a canoe and paddle out to inspect the banks, was defeated by the tides. Instead we tracked down the site of the most recent introduction attempt in a backwater near Cotehele on the Cornish bank. We caught sight of the characteristically slender, blue-green leaves of non-flowering plants from the road-bridge. I slithered down the bank and found myself in a wet, muddy hollow. And right in the middle, glory be, was a Triangular Club-rush in flower – possibly the only one in the whole of Britain.

It is not, hand on heart, spectacular, except in its rarity. Imagine a single stem, as erect as a guardsman's sword, broad, sharply triangular and narrowing to a point. At the base are a few narrow leaves half-buried in the mud. At the other end, just below the top, a cluster of small, pale-reddish-brown florets breaks through the stem. Clive was onto it with his lens, checking whether each glume ended in a *mucronate* point and whether they were sufficiently *notched* at the tip. Satisfied on these points, he pronounced it 'good *Scirpus triqueter*' (he can't be bothered with the new name). It had a certain scimitar-like elegance lacking in its coarser relatives. And a kind of tragic glamour from the near certainty that it is doomed: for these transplanted club-rushes do not seem to produce seed. They need to do that rather urgently, because their muddy habitat is unstable, constantly slopped on by the tide or removed by the current as the water dictates. Bank erosion the previous winter had already reduced its limited habitat by one-third. It has been pushed to the margins and beyond by the relentless march of the reeds.

'Birders think reeds are always a good thing,' commented Andy. 'But they are not a good thing here. Along the Tamar they are not even particularly good for birds, and they are an absolute disaster for plants.'

We went for a celebratory cup of tea in the National Trust shop. Old framed photos on the walls showed us what the river used to be like: bare-banked with wandering geese and without a reed in sight. Perhaps most visitors compare this with the view from the window and consider the latter an improvement. But reeds are a plant monoculture, compared with the diversity of plants that were there before. Triangular Club-rush is only one plant victim among many others.

We were a merry party that night, over a drawn-out supper in Andy's greenhouse. We had all brought a stash of wine and managed to get through a lot of it. Brett and I ended up singing a botanically themed ditty by Gilbert and Sullivan:

Then a sentimental passion of a vegetable fashion must excite your languid spleen,
An attachment à la Plato for a bashful young potato, or a not-too-French French bean!

Though the Philistines may jostle, you will rank as an apostle
in the high aesthetic band,
If you walk down Piccadilly with a poppy or a lily in your medi-
eval hand.

Does any pleasure exceed that of drinking wine with friends on a warm summer evening in a walled Victorian garden? I didn't know it, but this was the last real binge I was going to enjoy for a long time. The root cause of my rumbling malaise, almost forgotten on that balmy day in South Devon, was about to make itself known. The next flower lay more than 500 miles away by land and sea. And yes, Andy, I *will* have another glass of that.

Interlude

I was due a second trip north, this time to the island of Coll to search for more missing plants, an orchid and a trio of water-weeds. But then something happened that cast doubt over whether I would make the journey after all. For several weeks my mother had been unwell with a chest infection that, ominously, was resisting the usual quick-fix of antibiotics. Mum was ninety-three and frail. But, as usual, she seemed cheerful when I came in, insisting that it would soon blow over, as all her ailments did, and that I shouldn't change my plans on her account. Then, four days before my planned departure, she was admitted to hospital for 'tests'. I found her asleep in the corner bed of a small top-floor ward overlooking the downs where the writer Richard Jefferies, as 'Bevis', had played as a boy. I was horrified at the change in her appearance. 'Your own mother wouldn't recognise you,' they say, but for a moment I didn't recognise my own mother. They had apparently administered a strong drug and, as far as I could see, it wasn't working. They snatched away my posy of sweet peas. Mother opened her eyes. She insisted on getting out of bed and sitting up in her gown and slippers. 'Fetch me a stool for my leg,' she said. 'Don't they have a stool? Well, fetch me a cushion or something. Don't look at my hair,' she added, turning to me. 'I'm a mess. But don't you worry – you go on your trip. I'll be all right.' Mum was of the wartime generation that doesn't make a fuss. She'd been ill before and had got over it. 'You go to see your flower,' she said. 'What was it called? I'll be thinking of you. I'll see you when you get back.'

Damn the flower, I thought. But I would be away only four or five days – perhaps less, if we cut it short. The nurse, with whom I held a whispered consultation behind the door, wouldn't go beyond the obvious fact that Mother was 'poorly' and that they were trying out a different drug, an antibiotic. She mentioned its name, but it meant nothing to me. I began to feel more hopeful a day later when Jane, my brother's ex-wife, who is a nurse, dropped in to see her and told me Mum seemed 'quite chirpy' now and reasonably comfortable.

The day before my departure I looked in again. Mum had been transferred to a wing in the hospital proper. The wards there are named after birds, perhaps for added chirpiness. Hers was 'Kingfisher'. She was sitting up in bed, with an oxygen mask close by for emergencies. She looked, I thought, much better (she'd had a bath with eucalyptus oil and sighed with pleasure – 'I can breathe again'). We even managed to complete the crossword. 'You can't keep a good woman down!' cried the ward nurse. Funnily enough, this airy commonplace seemed to lift a burden from my shoulders. I would go to Coll, and by the time I returned Mum would be well on the way to recovery, and perhaps even discharged. She was expecting to be discharged that very night. 'Don't worry about me,' she repeated. 'I can cope.'

'Don't worry.' In fact both of my parents were chronic worriers. Mother worried about everything and everybody, except herself. She worried about me whenever I went away, thinking I might have forgotten something, or gone to the wrong airport or boarded the wrong plane. Worry, it seems to me now, is a form of possessiveness, inseparable in a mother's case from love. By pretending to worry about me, she kept alive the parent–child bond that began at my birth. It was her way of hanging on to motherhood long after she had been unable to do much for me in practical terms. It was no use telling her not to worry. Worry was her right. Worry was what she felt to be necessary.

11
Irish Lady's-tresses
Spiranthes romanzoffiana

A small orchid with clusters of white flowers arranged in a
threefold spiral among green leafy bracts
Wet flushes among grass on the island of Coll, Inner Hebrides
4th September
Helpers: David Pearman, Bob Gibbons and Ben Jones

It was a long way to *Spiranthes*, the Irish Lady's-tresses: about
500 miles by land and sea. It is called 'Irish' because that was
where it was first discovered, at Bantry Bay in County Cork back
in 1810. But it is really a displaced North American plant (where
they call it the Hooded Lady's-tresses) that somehow gained a
toehold in the far west of Europe. In Scotland you might find
Irish Lady's-tresses on Colonsay, or Barra, or Benbecula, but the

best chance is on the island of Coll in the Inner Hebrides, where it occurs in a score or more places, mostly where water-flushed grass meets the parent rock, the ancient, pale-grey Lewisian gneiss of the Isles.

Even so, it can be quite a challenge to find. You could roam all over Coll in the right season and still not see it. The flowering time is short and unpredictable. In an early season the orchid might appear in July, but in a late one not until late August. Its numbers vary, and recently the trend has been firmly downwards. Twenty flowers would constitute a strong colony nowadays. And it is inconspicuous: creamy-white blooms the size of a clover-head; a threefold spiral on a lattice of green. You need a weather eye for the places it likes: open wet ground where the grass is not too thick, where surface water trickles down a gentle slope. Without flowers it is impossible to find, for the slender leaves are lost in the grass.

A factor in choosing Coll to make the search was that my old friends David and Anita ('Sammy') Pearman were staying on the island. David just happens to be the co-author of *A Flora of Tiree, Gunna and Coll*. Coll is his favourite island. And, as more luck would have it, Bob Gibbons was keen to come too and offered to give me a lift in his campervan. It had all come together nicely, I thought.

We soon tracked it down. In fact it was close to being an anticlimax. David had asked Ben Jones, the resident RSPB warden, to find us a plant and he duly spotted a patch of Irish Lady's-tresses not a hundred yards from his back garden. Despite the lateness of the season, the orchid was in perfect bloom. Ben's dog, a long-haired collie called Ash, led the way: we found seven pale spikes wagging on three-inch stalks in a boggy garden of water mint, spearwort, ragged robin and miniature marsh mari-golds. The cream frilly-tipped flowers peeped this way and that as though they had been pleated onto the stalk. *Spiranthes* means 'spiral' and refers to the characteristic twist of florets, like an over-the-shoulder tress of hair, braided with white ribbon. The flowers are said to have a pleasant vanilla-like scent, though not in the present cold breeze and mizzling rain. The plants were shaking too much for photography, so we just admired the seven blooms and let their image soak into our minds. On the way back Ash jumped over the wall to land in Ben's arms. It was a trick they had worked out together.

Ben told us that past efforts to conserve the orchid had often ended in disaster. Botanists are good at spotting, counting and mapping flowers, but not always very good at conserving them. One once-large colony had been, on the advice of the surveyor, fenced against cattle, in the hope that this would allow them to flower freely and set seed. But instead the orchids promptly disappeared. One year there were eighty flowers, then twenty, then none. This was not what had been predicted. Another large colony collapsed after the RSPB accepted advice to remove live-stock during its flowering time. What they had all failed to realise is that Irish Lady's-tresses is a poor competitor. It actually *needs* the muddy spaces provided by pounding and puddling hooves. All right, the animals will eat some of the flowers, but the plant can cope with that. Besides, it hardly ever seeds anyway.

After a coffee at the Jones' croft house, we had a quick poke around his garden for interesting weeds. One of the delights of Coll is that even garden weeds can be interesting. I was confident we would find Northern Dead-nettle, *Lamium confertum*, a plant I had never seen well. Unfortunately Ben had been weeding his vegetable plot shortly before we arrived, perhaps to have it looking clean and tidy for his guests. Hence there were no dead-nettles among his neat rows of marrows and beans. But there was a large pile of them on the compost heap. I had missed seeing the living plant by about ten minutes. Does a freshly dug-up plant still count as a tick? Under Ben's bemused gaze, I removed a couple from the reeking pile and gently replanted them among the broad beans.

10

Slender Naiad

Najas flexilis

A delicate underwater plant with short translucent leaves
arranged in whorls along the stem
A loch at Ballyhaugh, Coll, Inner Hebrides

9

Pipewort

Eriocaulon aquaticum

A strange aquatic plant with flowering stems like six-inch nails
erupting from underwater clusters of leaves
In shallow water, Loch a Mhill Aird, Coll, Inner Hebrides

8

Slender-leaved Pondweed
Potamogeton filiformis

Another underwater plant with narrow, blunt-tipped leaves
arranged in tufts, with clusters of minute florets at the tip of
long, spreading stems
A brackish rockpool near Calgary Point, Coll, Inner Hebrides
4th–5th September
Helpers: Bob Gibbons, David and Anita Pearman

With the Lady's-tresses out of the way, we turned to the water-
weeds. We were almost at the countdown stage now. Just ten
more plants to go; The Quest suddenly felt achievable. Had it
been too easy? The next species, I knew, was going to be a test.
Slender Naiad, *Najas flexilis*, is a cousin of the Holly-leaved
Naiad that we had fished out of the water at Hickling Broad. It
has the same whorls of translucent leaves and near non-existent
flowers, but is a more graceful plant, with narrow leaves whose

tiny prickles you need a lens to see. It is a plant of clear, deep waters, mainly in western Scotland. The only person to have surveyed Slender Naiad recently (perhaps ever) had donned a wetsuit and snorkelling gear. A less efficient, but more usual, means of detecting it is to wander along the lake shore, turning over any washed-up vegetation on the off-chance that it will contain a naiad or two. Chris Preston, the expert on underwater plants, told me he looks for plants snagged on barbed wire by the waterside. Otherwise, there is almost no chance of spotting it from the shore.

David had a plan. He knew a small loch with a wooden jetty from which you could cast a weed-drag into the depths or, if I had a mind to, jump in. With that in mind, I had brought along a small grapnel and my old wetsuit top that, too late, I realised was now a couple of sizes too small. There was another shock when we pulled in by the loch. The jetty was no longer there. Exposed to Coll's Atlantic gales, it had rotted and fallen to pieces. A few planks bobbed on the water.

Before we go on, I should explain that I wasn't feeling well. I'd tossed and turned all night long in our comfortable hotel in Oban. After a splendid dinner with the Pearmans, washed down by David's favourite Galician wine, plus a nightcap or two at the bar, I would normally have slept like a top. Then during the ferry crossing, in a choppy sea, I felt sick and had to go up on deck to gulp cool, reviving air. Since I don't usually get seasick, I wondered whether it was a sympathetic illness born from worrying about my mother. Seasickness normally ends abruptly the moment you set foot on dry land. It doesn't turn into land-sickness. I thought a good breakfast might help. It was a good breakfast, but it didn't.

The wetsuit added to my sense of breathlessness. It had stopped raining by now, but the air was cold and breezy. David suggested we took things slowly and by stages. The first stage, he counselled, was lunch. Then we should take a recce. But I couldn't wait. I wanted to see whether there was any way into the loch, short of swimming. The near side was effectively sealed off by a broad bed of bogbean, glossy trefoil leaves above a slippery network of stems and roots. Grimly I stripped down and waded in. The water was freezing. In no time at all, one leg was gripped by a noose of bogbean – and over I went with a splosh. 'Try slithering across on your belly,' shouted David, waving a sandwich. 'Like a seal.' It was no use. The bogbean guarded the water as effectively as a minefield. It was impassable.

My grapnel was no good, either. The line was too short to reach the deep water and I managed to cut my finger open on the sharp tines. Dejectedly I slopped out of the water and sat down heavily. All that way for this.

'Have something to eat,' suggested David. Sammy's picnics are always abundant and delicious, but my interior plumbing was grumbling mutinously. A brisk Atlantic breeze stirred the bogbean and sent wavelets rippling over towards the far shore. 'The far shore,' said David, suddenly. 'There's a chance what you are looking for might have been blown ashore. It's worth a try.'

We did try, but without success. There were no broken naiads on this hard shore. The only remaining option was to swim. '*I* would,' said David, in an encouraging way. 'With a top like yours, I'd be off like a shot.' ('I wouldn't,' I was glad to hear Bob mumble.) 'You *can* swim, can't you?' David added, as if suddenly anxious. Yeah, yeah, I can swim. Though generally crap at sports, I could sometimes win a swimming race. I considered. First, my insides were hurting. The place where David thought the naiads might be was about forty yards off, against the wind. It was safely swimmable, even without flippers (why hadn't I brought flippers?). But, I reasoned, the waves had disturbed the sediment and it would be hard to spot any weeds in the depths without a face-mask (why hadn't I brought a mask?). I'd be diving blind. Besides, I would have liked some sort of guarantee the plant was actually there. 'Try again tomorrow?' I suggested, weakly. I reasoned that I would probably feel better tomorrow, on the grounds that I couldn't possibly feel any worse. Trudging back, we passed a boat hauled up on its limbers. It was only later that it occurred to me that we might have made good use of it.

It was easier to find Plant 9, Pipewort, a strange thing resembling a six-inch nail sticking out of the water from a tuft of submerged leaves. Close up, its nail-head or pipe-bowl is soft, with the consistency of a cushion, its minute florets embedded in wefts of grey wool. Bob gamely lined up his tripod, elbows and knees immersed in freezing water, waiting patiently for the moment of stillness that never came. I felt curiously disconnected. It was another plant; that was all.

We found Plant 8, the Slender-leaved Pondweed, *Potamogeton filiformis*, at the far end of a six-mile hike. The west side of Coll is wild and uninhabited, with crescents of white sand unmarked by human footprints. From a rugged headland we watched a pair of basking sharks swim close in, their triangular fins nosing through dark-blue water. The neighbouring isles were bathed in the pearly light of the north, in subtle, misty colours: grey, green, blue. David was soon busy at his hobby of picking cast-up cowrie shells, pink and grey, delicate as fingerprints. It has become a kind of pilgrimage for him, pacing the shore like a wading bird, peering intently and then, with a sudden motion, ducking down to pick up the barely visible titbit. Perhaps there is something feral in it. It's his way of communing with the island he loves. But he also loves the fact that the cowrie's Latin name is *Trivia*. It's his trivial pursuit.

We found the pondweed in a large, clear, flat-bottomed pool kept fresh at the landward end by the trickle of a spring. It is the wispiest of weeds, as fine as green wire. Pull a piece from its sandy bed and the fine leaves cling together like the hairs of a paintbrush. I waded in, cool fine silt clouding between my toes. While the Slender Naiad had led me to the waters of hell, this felt closer to paradise. The world with its follies and troubles lay behind, and all around was only nature, the call of a lonely shore-bird, the wash of sea on clean, white sand. I could build a cabin here, I thought. Plant a few rows of beans. Maybe a hive of bees... Suddenly Bob's mobile phone began to bleep. Modern technology has a way of shattering your dreams.

We were returning down one of the island's narrow roads with grass growing up the middle, when Bob's sharp eyes spotted something: a tiny creeping plant with blue-green oval leaves growing up through cracks in the surface. We got out and lay down in the road for a closer look – there is never much traffic to worry about on Coll. 'Wow!' I said. 'I think it's Northern Knotgrass!' Perhaps I should explain. Northern Knotgrass, *Polygonum boreale*, lives up to its name in being more or less confined to the Hebrides and Orkney. It had never been recorded from Coll – no doubt because not many people bother to peer at plants in the middle of the road, for obvious reasons, and especially when there are miles and miles of moors, rocks and clear waters to explore.

'It can't be.' David looked nonplussed. He examined the modest weed with his lens for a long time. 'I think it must be,' he concluded, reluctantly. 'See how the petioles are well *exserted* from the stipules.' I racked my brains to remember what 'exserted' meant. I knew what it was, not from technical botanical characters but from a memory of a picture in a book – though not in Keble Martin, for this is another plant he hadn't bothered to illustrate. It was a new species for me, but not one I'd decided to count, unless I could call it Plant 8a. It was what is known in the trade as a 'tart's tick' – a late addition of a not-uncommon species. Could I use it as a serendipitous substitute for the wretched naiad? I'd like to have done, but unfortunately there were too many witnesses.

Supper that night should have been festive – the island hotel is noted for the excellence of its cooking – but I found myself unable to keep down anything solid. Soup was what I ate, very slowly. 'Off to bed with you, sir,' ordered the sensible Pearman. The pillows were soft and deep. Lulled by the island air and the wash of the tide, I was drifting off when there was a tap on the door. It was Bob. My brother Chris had just texted him. Our mother had taken a turn for the worse. She had developed pneumonia. She was breathing with the help of oxygen. Chris and Jane were with her, by her bedside.

The next flight from the island's airstrip was two days hence. It would take at least thirty-six hours to get home by ferry and train. 'Stay where you are,' advised Chris. 'There's nothing you can do. Just come home as soon as you can.' I gratefully accepted another lift from Bob. It meant abandoning my second go at the Slender Naiad and, with it, any hope of completing The Quest. But that did not seem important now. The lure of island flowers, I reflected bitterly, had been a siren's wail. It had led this traveller onto the rocks. I had chosen a flower above my own mother.

'It's sad news. Mum passed away at six this morning.' The message was on my answerphone. 'I don't think she suffered,' said Chris, later. 'She just went to sleep and didn't wake up.' The boys – my nephews – had been there the night before and both of them had held her hand. The fourth-floor wing where she died was named Saturn, the bringer of old age. She must have been only a few paces from the room where her husband, and my father, had died three years before. It was on her birthday, celebrated with us in Ramsbury, that she had first caught that fatal, final chill.

Jane told me that, near the end, Mum knew she had to go. 'I've never been as bad as this,' she whispered. 'It's not like me, is it?' 'No.' 'This may not end well.' 'It's frightening, isn't it?' 'Yes, it's frightening.'

But soon old man Saturn gathers us in his arms and, it seems, we just let go. Pneumonia, they say, is the dying person's friend. It's what they call a natural death. You stop breathing, your heart stops ticking, and that's that. You've made it to the end; the journey's over and you can rest. We should be so lucky.

Mother had been my first wild-flower mentor and companion. Although she was not a botanist, she was familiar with the wild flowers of her village and knew their country names: the roadside 'kecks', the 'arrowheads' by the river, 'quakers' on the common, and wild garlic up at Swithland Wood. She bought me my first flower book, *The Observer's Book of Wild Flowers*, with its classic, 200-year-old illustrations by James Sowerby. Together we ticked off each flower as we found them: White Bryony, Field Scabious, Germander Speedwell. We were puzzled, I remember, that we couldn't find Corn Cockle, for, the book assured us, we were practically bound to see the bright-pink flowers as we wandered through the corn (this information, I learned later, was badly out of date; for the Corn Cockle was, in fact, practically extinct). Mother was there again when I found my first *rare* plant, Early Spider Orchid – Plant 700, or thereabouts – and she took a picture of the teenage me, grinning at it. In her sitting room was a watercolour of another orchid, the Burnt-tip, that I had commissioned after we discovered it on a walk along the downs. We once even climbed Ben Lawers together, and she sat on a rug admiring the view as I explored the corrie. I would probably have learned the wild flowers sooner or later, perhaps through university or a field course. But thanks to my mother, it was sooner, and sweeter, rising from the springhead of childhood and simple shared memories.

As Robert Browning said, 'All love begins and ends' when your mother dies. It's not grief you feel, or not right away. Just numbness and a strangely shocking realisation that, at last, you are alone.

Interlude

Bob and I had left Coll on the morning ferry. It was as we joined the M6 that the ache under my ribs ceased merely to hurt and became unbearable. It felt as though my insides were being compressed by some external force, with a malignancy that suggested the cause was something worse than my original suspicion, an ill-digested breakfast. I panted for breath. At the next service station Bob bought me some Rennies; I chewed my way through two whole packets and they seemed to help a little. As in homeopathy, faith is nine parts of the cure. It gives you something to focus on. Keep sucking those mints. Hang on to the mint. When I finally threw up, it was the gentlest puke ever – a soft, relieving foam of mint-flavoured alkalinity, as quiet as milk.

It wasn't food poisoning. Or seasickness. It took Nurse Tracy one prick of a needle to get to the heart of my mysterious malady. She glanced at the reading, widened her eyes and said, 'Wow!' ('Wow', I knew, is not a word you want to hear in a doctor's surgery.) 'That's quite an impressive glucose reading. Five is normal; anything over eleven is grossly abnormal. Want to know what yours is?' 'Tell me.' It was nineteen, some considerable distance past grossly abnormal. What did that mean exactly? 'It means you have diabetes,' she answered gaily. '*Type 2*.'

'I hope you don't have a sweet tooth,' laughed the doctor. Why do they think it's funny? Existence is sweet. Love is sweet. Chasing wild flowers on a summer afternoon is sweet. A craving for sweet things is hard-wired into our genes. To deny sweetness is to deny life itself. 'No, no,' I said, thinking of the lemon-drizzle cake I had been guzzling the day before. 'I can live without sugar.' Was life about to turn sour?

They gave me a DVD that teaches you how a sugar-free life can still be fun. There was a clip of a happy middle-aged man on a surfboard and a slightly older woman, maybe his wife, in the garden trimming the roses. Both looked deliriously happy. Perhaps they were looking forward to their supper: another salad, with a glass of water to wash down the pills.

Could I starve it out? Could I get normal again? Tracy shook her head. 'I don't recommend that just now.' At this point, a different doctor came in. Not my usual smiling GP with his 'Another clean bill, Mr Marren!', but the top doc, the head honcho, the one who dealt with the more impressive sickies, the determined no-hopers. And he had more exciting news. I was about to be told why my insides hurt.

They had analysed my blood for signs of bodily meltdown. They can tell the state of your liver by expressive hormones called gamma GTs. Like Nurse Tracy, he seemed impressed, but not, as they say, in a good way. 'Gosh,' she said. '*Phoo-ee.*'

'I expect you've been feeling tired,' observed the top doc. 'Well, yes, a bit. Life has got rather hectic lately.' 'A healthy liver has a reading of less than fifty,' he told me. 'More than a hundred can mean liver disease, or perhaps problems with your bile duct.' He paused. Medical people are taught to be non-judgemental. 'Is it alcohol-related?' I asked. 'Yes. Your reading was 425.' 'What?' 'It has probably been building up for some time.'

Looks can be more eloquent than words. And the glance that doctor and nurse exchanged seemed, to me, to make one simple proposition: *You're ours now.*

It defined the moment when, almost for the first time, health professionals took an interest in me. There would be the start-up course for the novice diabetic. They would keep a dossier on my liver and kidney function. Pills should keep my obviously damaged pancreas ticking over, for now. They would note the drugs I'd been prescribed and their effectiveness, and all the scans (they had booked me in for a liver scan, right away) and all the check-ups. For every medical problem there's a drug. By the end, my poor mother was taking a shelf of pills, each one adding to the cocktail swirling through her arteries, defying nature, keeping her alive and in tolerable comfort, though never in full health. She died only when one pharmaceutical declared war on another. She died in the cross-fire.

Having enjoyed good health since gaining man's estate, I had never taken much interest in medical matters. As far as I was concerned, illness was something that happened to other people. But although you don't realise it right away, by the time we reach our sixties we are embarking on the leaky ship of mortality. The body no longer works with its accustomed ease and efficiency. It seems that I had lived with a mild and undiagnosed form of diabetes for months, possibly years. Things had reached a sudden crisis when my liver started diabetically malfunctioning, after a lifetime of heedless, if usually fairly moderate, drinking. I'd always assumed I had a good liver. Hitherto it had held up well to intermittent storms of beer, wine and spirits. I could drink all night without getting pissed; or, at least, not incapably so. I'd hardly suffered a hangover in the past twenty years. On the other hand, I had been drinking more than the usual amount lately: that vinous bash with the lads in Devon, for instance. And so my liver had screamed for help. It had screamed blue murder. It had had enough. It wasn't going to put up with this level of abuse any longer. But it wasn't just the juice. It couldn't have been. 'If it was just the booze,' a friend told me, 'at that level you would have been a non-functioning, whacked-out alco. Your friends would have carted you to detox yonks ago.' You have had a lucky escape, my friend.

7

Hartwort
Tordylium maximum

An annual umbellifer (the parsley family) with large, bristly,
heart-shaped fruits
Disturbed ground near bushes at Benfleet Downs, Southend,
Essex
23rd September, morning
Helper: Fred Rumsey

I had been advised to take things easy for a bit, but The Quest
still had another stage to run. It was not one, thank God, that
required any more climbing or swimming. It involved nothing
more stressful than a drive around the county of Essex to knock
off a few more plants that flower towards the end of the season.
With a twice-daily dose of gliclazide and a low-sugar diet, and

no alcohol at all, the pain had subsided and I had lost some weight. But my body had one more trick to play. My eyesight was affected. My vision would suddenly blur, then snap back into focus. It was eerie, frightening. The optician advised me to drive only in daylight, preferably only in bright sunshine. And not to drive long distances. 'In fact, unless you have to, don't drive.' She would not prescribe new specs because, she told me, my sight would change from day to day, according to my blood-sugar levels. The lens in the eye absorbs glucose. Where there is too much of it, the lens changes shape: it expands, like a cake-guzzler's waistline. 'Your eyes will recover,' she said, but it would take some weeks yet. 'You always know when your sugar level is too high,' they told me. 'Your legs will itch.'

I made it as far as Aldershot, where Fred Rumsey and his wife Sue have a cosy, timber-framed cottage much like my own, crammed with botany books. They share the house with an ancient and obviously much-loved cat, which offered more proof that my eyesight was bad when I nearly sat on it. I thought it was a cushion.

Kind Fred offered to drive. It took two-and-a-half hours in the crawl of morning traffic to reach Southend. Our destination was Benfleet Downs, a place Fred had known since boyhood; it was the patch of ground that inspired him to take up a botanical career, latterly at the Natural History Museum. Benfleet's downs are not made of chalk, but of heavy, lime-rich clay. They roll down to Benfleet Creek, a side-channel of the Thames, thronged with small boats and boatyards. In one corner stands a ruined castle. It's a pleasant enough patch of wild, managed by the local council as a country park, but, at first sight at least, it does not look botanically exciting, with its mixture of scrub and grass kept well clipped by mowing machines. Yet, despite appearances, it is a botanical hotspot, one of the first to be discovered, and known to London botanists since the seventeenth century. It is the only place in Britain where one can reliably see one of the plants in my Last Ten: Hartwort, *Tordylium maximum*.

Hartwort is an umbellifer, like a small version of cow parsley, distinguished by lop-sided flowers with large outer petals and small inner ones and, later, by big, brown, coin-like seeds. As an annual, it needs disturbed ground. The scraping of rabbits provides one refuge for it at Benfleet, but we found its fading stems on a bonfire site where conservation volunteers had been burning cut scrub. There was quite a lot of it, too, though by now the flowers were over and the heads were shedding seed. Fred was pleased. Hartwort has had a chequered existence here since being found in 'considerable quantity' back in 1950. By 1970 it seemed to be in danger from a combination of scrub encroachment and over-zealous mowing. All one visiting botanist could find was cut stems in a pile of grass. Fortunately the seeds were still viable. He had shaken them loose, some to grow on in his garden (where Hartwort quickly became a weed) and the rest dispersed to friends. Some of this stock was sown or planted out on the down, and so today it is impossible to know whether the plants are natural or introduced. Fred thinks it is probably a bit of both.

Some doubt whether Hartwort is a native species at all. But, as Fred points out, Benfleet Downs is exactly the sort of place that a southern species like Hartwort would choose. And there are plenty of undoubtedly native Hartworts on the opposite side of the Channel. The wonder is that it has not managed to spread beyond the few remaining scraps of natural grassland along the Thames estuary. With climate change behind it, it just might.

The Hopeless Case

6
Sickle-leaved Hare's-ear
Bupleurum falcatum

A small annual plant with fluffy yellow flowers and curved,
sickle-like leaves
A roadside bank near Ongar, Essex
23rd September, afternoon
Helper: Fred Rumsey

The Sickle-leaved Hare's-ear was never common. Its sole British
site is, or was, near Ongar in Essex, formerly the last station of
the Central Line. Where this attractive annual plant with frothy,
bright-yellow flowers came from, no one knows. It might be
native – Fred certainly thinks so – or it might be a fairly ancient
'introduction'. All we know is that it was first found in 1831 and
that it persisted on the same roadside spot for the next 130 years.

Then, in 1962, the diminished colony was casually destroyed when workmen cleared its ditch, cut back its hedge and then lit a bonfire.

In 1979 a small patch of the plant was rediscovered close to the original site. Whether these were descended from the original colony, or had sprung up from seed scattered there by botanists, again no one knows (Fred: 'a bit of both, probably'). Unfortunately, once again workmen were on to it. More scrub was cut and burnt and, as before, they chose the exact site of Sickle-leaved Hare's-ear for their bonfire. And then, as if to make absolutely sure, the whole verge was sprayed with herbicide all the way from Epping to Chipping Ongar.

That made the plant 'extinct in the wild'. But not completely lost, for a local botanist, Stan Jermyn, had collected seed from the last plants and sown it in his garden. The Hare's-ear had also been introduced to a couple of nature reserves in Essex, and to the botanic gardens in Cambridge and Kew. And that might have been that, but for one more chance event. In 1985 the Hare's-ear's former patch was bypassed in a road-straightening scheme. This made it possible to construct a new bespoke habitat from a bank of local chalky clay now running parallel with the road, but separated from it by a broad verge. This might have seemed a forlorn hope, for the artificial bank measures only about 130 by 25 feet, a matchbox nature reserve even smaller than the one at Badgeworth, Gloucestershire, famed as the world's smallest, in *Guinness World Records* (it, too, protects a rare flower – the Adderstongue Spearwort); 360 square yards is not much to hold the entire British population of a wild plant, but, it seems, it is all that could be spared. 'Unlikely to persist' was the gloomy prognosis of the *Red Data Book*.

It did persist, though. Fred parked the car in a nearby lane and we made our way to the bank on foot. The Hare's-ear had obviously had a busy year. Only a few plants still bore small umbels of yellow froth, and most were now in seed, pinging out the small black specks at a touch. From a mere three plants noted in 1996, the colony has gone from strength to strength, pushing up hundreds of plants, visible in late summer as a foam of yellow. Against expectations, the Hare's-ear had been given a helping hand by a plant thought to be a problem: thistle. The prickly leaves acted as a nurse crop, protecting the seedlings from rabbits and sheltering the tender plants as they began their rapid spurt of growth. We could see now what pictures cannot adequately show, and could appreciate what an odd little plant it is, with its little yellow button-flowers and its fleshy, spindle-shaped leaves that sometimes curl into the shape of a sickle, or fork into a pair of asymmetric bunny ears, apparently as a result of the bud being nibbled by froghoppers. Whoever named it the Sickle-leaved Hare's-ear was trying to pack in as many of these characters as possible.

I was glad we had come to this bleak and noisy spot. This is plant conservation at its most extreme. Even our rarest plants usually have a habitat to call their own. But the Hare's-ear has lost its natural home altogether. Its artificial bank depends on maintenance, on weeding and pruning, as in a garden. And the result is not so much natural vegetation as a crop of Sickle-leaved Hare's-ear. Indeed, the difference between this nature reserve and a garden is more a matter of location than technique. Whether *Bupleurum falcatum* can still be called a wild plant in Britain is a matter of interpretation. But in the circumstances it is probably the best that anyone can do. At any rate it had fulfilled its duty as my Plant 6 and, in its quirky presence, teetering on the very brink of loss, I felt it deserved its place in the final few.

5

Pedunculate Sea-purslane
Atriplex (Halimione) pedunculata

A small annual purslane with stalked greyish-green pods
A creek on the coast near Southend, Essex
23rd September, late afternoon
Helpers: Fred Rumsey and Tim Pyner

And now for something completely obscure. We ended the day
on the marshes of the Essex coast: a ragged line of grass, creek
and mudbank and, beyond it, nothing but the slow, heavy ripples
of the grey North Sea. We had come here, to a place that is
still a secret, to see another plant once thought to be lost for
ever. It can be found lurking at the bottom of Keble Martin's
Plate 72, a small green weed among bigger weeds. He didn't
have an English name to give it. Back then, he had to make do

with its scientific one: *Halimione pedunculata*, which, Keble noted, occurs 'in salt marshes, E. England, very rare'. More than very rare, in fact, for no one had set eyes on it for half a century. Today, because all wild flowers – even the most obscure – must have an English name, it is called Pedunculate Sea-purslane, obviously a name invented by botanists. A peduncle is the stalk of a flower and, later, its seedpod. It is this character that distinguishes the species from the Common Sea-purslane, the small, bushy, green-grey plant that covers acres of the east-coast salt-marshes. It has also been called Annual Sea-purslane, to emphasise another difference from its perennial relative. Since Keble Martin's time, its genus has been removed from *Halimione* to *Atriplex*. This is in some respects a pity because Atriplexes, or oraches, are, if anything, even less exciting than sea-purslanes.

The lucky rediscoverer was a former colleague of mine, Simon Leach. He was inspecting a strip of salt-marsh behind the sea-wall, in 1987, when he suddenly spotted some strange stalked pods, held like tiny green butterflies on pins. They were attached to an odd, stiff little plant clothed in what looks like grey-green powder. Simon knew what it was, but he couldn't believe it. He told me he had to squat down on his haunches and take several deep breaths, his heart beating wildly. Nature had let him in on a secret: that, for some species, extinction isn't final.

That was thirty years ago. As we were to discover, Pedunculate Sea-purslane is still there, on almost the exact same patch of bank close to the tidal creek where Simon saw it, having neither increased nor decreased much in all that time. It is a very easy plant to miss. As an annual, dependent on temporary open conditions within the marsh, it has always tended to appear and then disappear. Moreover, it is late-flowering and most conspicuous in early autumn after many botanists have gone home. What had drawn Simon to this particular creek was not the possibility of finding extinct purslanes, but the presence of certain other uncommon species: a stand of Sea Barley, for instance, and a ditch filled with the trailing masses of Beaked Tasselweed. As Simon put it, 'you can't expect to find a plant like Pedunculate Sea-purslane. There's no point in deliberately looking for it. You have to *stumble across it.*'

A friend of Fred's, Tim Pyner, had offered to scout the place for us. We were delayed by the incessant Essex traffic, and by the time we arrived he was out on the marsh. You could tell from his body language that he had found something good. He was trying not to smile. 'Do you want the good news or the good news?' 'Oh, let's have the good news first.' 'Come and see.' The first bit of good news was that he had found the plant, and that it was in good nick. The second was that there was plenty of it. And the bonus was that we could lie down to appreciate its finer points, without getting covered in mud.

Rather to my surprise, I loved it. In the flesh, Pedunculate Sea-purslane looks as though it is constructed from something other than plant tissue; matchsticks, perhaps, painted pale grey-green, the colour of the underbelly of a Spitfire. The flowers are mere green blobs with tiny yellow stamens. It is the seedpods that catch the eye. As they ripen they turn into little claws, each one ending in a curious swollen tip that has left botanists grasping for a word. '*Obdeltoid,*' suggested Roy Clapham; '*obtriangular,*' offers Stace. Alternatively, imagine little wing-nuts, or a paper dart with a bobble in the middle. I was entranced. Moreover, our plant was the star in gorgeous company, full of flowers with 'sea' in their name: blue sea-aster, pink sea-spurrey against a rich purple backcloth of sea-lavender.

Does our lone patch of purslane – still the only colony known in Britain – represent the first stage of a new colonisation or the last stand of a species gradually pegging out? Either way, you get the sense of a plant that, like so many in my Last Fifty, isn't really at home here. It might have a tiny footprint in England, but we are not quite what it wants. Its real home lies across the wide sea on the marshy flats of Holland. Perhaps our plant was brought here on the legs, or in the guts, of Dutch geese. Or perhaps, as Fred thinks, it has been here all the time, and we just haven't been looking hard enough. Sooner or later, perhaps, it will turn up elsewhere too, probably somewhere on the East Anglian coast, now that people are aware of the plant and are looking out for it.

A man with a frisky spaniel came over to see who we were and what we were doing there. He was preparing to be cross. The dog jumped into the creek and splashed about, spraying water and mud at us. Fred showed him our written permission; we had been warned it might be necessary. The man nodded and stalked off without another word. He didn't seem at all curious why three men of mature age should be lying on their bellies in the middle of a marsh. What mattered to him was his privacy.

Discoveries like this generate action plans. The action in this case was to relocate the plant to other, seemingly safer, places where it could be looked after. One of these was a weapons-testing area owned by the Ministry of Defence where, it was reasoned, the Sea-purslane was less likely to be disturbed, except maybe by the odd explosion. Those plants were never seen again. It has also been grown in pots and planted out at Foulness

Island – only to be lost after a scrape for birds was dug there. Nature, I've often noticed, is better at finding 'suitable' places than we are.

It was now late afternoon and the sun was dipping towards streaks of cloud on the London horizon. The Quest was nearly over. A month ago I would have been relieved beyond expression. But, just now, I was sorry. Our day in Essex had been fun, thanks to Fred's eternal enthusiasm and botanical ebullience. I had enjoyed every encounter with a new plant; botany was not to blame for the tedious miles on busy roads, the race against the weather, the sleepless nights in strange beds. I was reluctant now to leave the secret creek, this commonplace mudbank rendered unique by a tiny, seemingly insignificant little plant. Left to myself, I would have stayed till dark, watching the shadows lengthen and clouds darken over the sea, feeling on the edge of things, right out here on the strand, where life begins and ends.

However, at this stage of The Quest, I was coming to realise, good things have to be paid for. It was some hours later, after I had said goodbye to Sue and Fred, that I realised I couldn't read the road signs. In fact I could barely make out the road at all without the help of overhead lights. It was as though I had lost my glasses and was motoring along without them. Driving ever so slowly on minor roads, with one pair of tyres in the gutter, I finally made it to the motorway and so blundered on blindly home.

Countdown

Four, three, two, one. The last four wild flowers. Where are they? What are they?

4

Thistle Broomrape
Orobanche reticulata

The Thistle Broomrape is a parasite of thistles with white flowers arranged in a spike on a brownish, leafless stem; searched for among thistles and tall grass at Ripon Loop by the River Ure in North Yorkshire.

3

Blue Heath

Phyllodoce coerulea

No. 3 is Blue Heath, an alpine relative of heather with single crimson, bell-shaped flowers held on curving stalks; searched for among rocks on the Sow of Atholl, Perthshire, with the help of Martin Robinson and Iain MacDonald.

2

Ribbon-leaved Water-plantain
Alisma gramineum

And No. 2 is Ribbon-leaved Water-plantain, which has clusters of pale lilac flowers and long, narrow leaves growing in
shallow (or sometimes deep) water; searched for in Westwood
Great Pool, Droitwich, Worcestershire, with the help of Nick
Button, Brett Westwood and Harry Green.

The Quest had failed first in the mist and rain on Skye and
then again on that fatal day on Coll when I decided not to risk
my shaking limbs and chattering teeth for the sake of the Slender
Naiad. Right from the start, I knew I was unlikely to succeed
in my mad attempt to see all the British plants, unless someone
in the meantime had found a Ghost Orchid and – even less
likely – had told me all about it, exactly where it was and in
good time, before a slug ate it.

But the Ghost Orchid is not the only impossible plant.
One of the year's low points was an afternoon by the River

Ure, near Ripon in North Yorkshire, inspecting thistles. There were plenty of thistles: the bank and adjacent meadow were choked with them, massed spiny stands pricked with purple cossack heads that would later fill the air with thistledown. But although it was clearly a good year for thistles, it had not favoured Plant 4, Thistle Broomrape, a white-flowered thistle-parasite about a foot high and shaped like a poker. Though widespread in Western Europe, both in the lowlands and in the mountains, in Britain the plant has always been confined to Yorkshire and in consequence is sometimes called the Yorkshire Broomrape – especially in Yorkshire, one imagines. Even here it is found only in half a dozen places, mainly in limestone grassland close to rivers. Like other broomrapes, it flowers well in some years, but not in others. In Britain, out at the limit of its range, it seems to be a very choosy plant.

I did my best. I did the research. I visited a place that in years gone by had produced scores of broomrapes. I searched. And searched some more, and found nothing. Shortly afterwards a team from the Yorkshire Wildlife Trust also had a day there broomrape-searching, and by the evening they had found just three plants, consisting of six stems. The previous year had been nearly as bad and, mark you, this was its very best site and was managed as a nature reserve. Was it something to do with the recent string of mild, rainy winters or, perhaps, two wet summers on the trot? We can only speculate, but in the meantime, what was to have been Plant 4 had been, to borrow a bird-twitching phrase, a total dip-out, another 'nemesis-plant'.

A few days later I was on the domed top of the Sow of Atholl overlooking Drummochter Pass, famous as a site – once the only site – for Blue Heath, an alpine plant better known by its scientific name, *Phyllodoce* (a name weirdly borrowed from a sea-nymph). The 'blue' is a translation of the Latin *caerulea*, but the bell-shaped flower is not blue, but crimson. Some say its leaves can take on a bluish sheen in certain lights, though more usually they have a coppery tint. Martin Robinson, the local botanical recorder, had warned me that we might be too early to see the flowers, but he hoped to show me the developing leaves at least (on which I earnestly hoped to find the odd bud). And Iain MacDonald from Scottish Natural Heritage had brought with him an aerial photograph of the hillside with the exact positions of *Phyllodoce* marked on it. 'It seems,' he said, 'to like late snow-patches, in mossy furrows among the high rocks that later turn into springs.'

We couldn't miss it, could we? However, we noticed, as we clambered up through short, deer-browsed heather, that a lot of rocks had fallen lately in the area where *Phyllodoce* grows. Apart from knocking over the plants, unstable masses of rock are not sensible places to roam, and especially not when they end in a cliff. All the same we gave that steep hillside a fairly thorough going-over, each of us adopting a different beat and combing the ground like police searching for clues. The trouble is, said Martin, that when Blue Heath is not in flower, the leaves look very similar to common crowberry, which grows all over the hill. Iain thought he remembered that the leaves of Blue Heath are *slightly* flatter and with slightly rough edges, but you would probably need to compare the two side by side to be sure. Well, we searched and searched and didn't find a single *Phyllodoce*, in flower or not. Martin looked worried, as well as frustrated. 'Don't worry,' I said. 'We've had a grand day on the hill, and it's only a plant.' Specifically it was Plant 3. And it was failure number four.

I spent another day with Brett Westwood, the Worcestershire naturalist Harry Green and Nick Button from Natural England hunting for Ribbon-leaved Water-plantain in a shallow lake near Droitwich. It is the only known site for this mysterious, seldom-seen plant, apart from a couple of deep dykes in the Fens, where it only flowers underwater. It is a private lake, but the kind owners not only gave us open access to it, they even lent us their boat. We were looking for a plant with a spray of fingernail-sized, pale-lilac flowers, each the shape of the ace of clubs, flowering in a welly's depth of water above floating, ribbon-like leaves. First, we decided to search the lake from the boat, jumping out to paddle in whatever shallow bay looked vaguely suitable. Failing to find any water-plantains, we then paced the shore, again jumping in wherever there were gaps in the dense fringe of sedge and reedmace. Nothing. Not so much as a bud or leaf. And what was more, not much suitable habitat, either. The dots on our map, which marked the places our plant had been seen in previous years, were mostly now dense sedgebeds. The plant may return from dormant seed persisting in the sediment, given a little help from mankind. But if there had been a single damn Ribbon-leaved Water-plantain flowering in that lake, I like to think we would have found it. It seemed as though Plant 2 had not deigned to appear this year. And so *Alisma gramineum* turned out to be something of a ghost too, another species sitting it out until its environment improves.

That left the Ghost Orchid, our most baffling and, it seems fair to say, rarest wild flower. I had searched for it before, in the deep, shaded woods near Henley. I had been to places where it had flowered. I once missed it by a matter of weeks, perhaps days. But so far the Ghost had eluded me, as it had eluded so many others — and, indeed, everybody since 1986. Could it still be out there, somewhere, in some darkly wooded corner where few botanists ever tread? It seemed to me more than likely but, as Simon Leach said of the Pedunculate Sea-purslane, and as I now understood, you can't search for plants like this and expect to find them. *You have to stumble across them by accident.*

1
Ghost Orchid
Epipogium aphyllum

The rarity of rarities may be still out there somewhere,
flowering fitfully or just sleeping, its bloated rootstock
ticking over

Searched for near Henley – ever hoping, never succeeding

The Return of the Ghost

In 2005 the Ghost Orchid was declared extinct in Britain. The
last official sighting had been on the bank of the wooded lane
where it had flowered more or less annually since Rex Graham
had rediscovered the thing, over the bowl of his pipe, back in
1953. But its wood had been badly damaged by the 1987 great
gale and subsequent clearing-up operations. No Ghost-hunter

has seen it there since, though plenty have looked. There were no certain sightings anywhere else, either, only rumours. In 2009 Plantlife, the conservation charity, decided to make this apparent extinction the subject of a 'declaration'. The loss of the Ghost is a warning to us all, they declared. It represents a challenge: we must do all we can to prevent the extinction of any other wild plant or, for that matter, any wild species. They called it the Ghost Orchid Declaration. The Ghost had become a kind of plant martyr. Goodbye, old Ghost. We won't forget you.

The ink was still drying on the Declaration when word on the street came that it might be still with us after all. Those in the know whispered that it had reappeared, not in its old haunts, but somewhere close to the Welsh border. It was true. By an extraordinary coincidence, a single tiny plant had been spotted just two weeks before Plantlife's press release. The finder's name was Mark Jannink. A man of rare dedication, his single-minded aim had been to search each and every one of the orchid's old haunts in the west until he refound it. The year – 2009 – Jannink had reasoned, was an unusually promising one for Ghosts. The coldest winter for many years had not been followed by a 'barbecue summer', as the weathermen had predicted. Instead it had been exceptionally cool and wet. The only sustained period of warm sunshine arrived late, in September. Ghosts, it is assumed, prefer cold winters followed by wet springs to encourage the growth of fungi in their roots, and then a warm spell in late summer to tempt the plant to put up a shoot. But even Jannink was ready to give up when at last, right at the end of the season, on 20th September, he stumbled across a tiny, barely visible flower. It was a Ghost. At that moment *Epipogium aphyllum* was no longer extinct. 'Hello, you,' he is supposed to have whispered. 'So *there* you are.'

It was growing under a line of oaks at the edge of a conifer plantation, enclosed in a hollow little larger than a footprint. The merest streak of a plant, almost the ghost of a Ghost, it was invisible except to the keenest eye. In a photo taken by a third party, Mark and a friend are pointing at the plant. I have the picture on my screen but, stare as I might, enlarge as I might, I still can't make out the Ghost. Mark likened the flower, not then fully expanded, to a snowflake. A friend shown it a few days later compared the apparition to a 'single leafless white violet'. This Ghost, the first that had been seen in Britain for twenty-two years, didn't look happy. It was growing at an oblique angle to the bank, so that its single open flower almost touched the ground. Some bug had gouged a hole into the spur where the flower stores its nectar. A few days later a hungry slug found the plant and selected the flower's main petal, known as the lip, for a snack. Having finished that, it went on to chew away part of the stem.

Only an inner core of active Ghost-hunters witnessed the resurrection. Two days after its discovery, five of them were standing there in a semicircle at seven-thirty in the morning. They stared. 'Some swore under their breath, others giggled with poorly suppressed excitement.' The now-open flower revealed pink spotting on its damaged, beard-like lip, the only dab of strong colour on its straw-coloured translucency. Over the next few days more witnesses watched it fade and turn brown. By the time of Mark's last visit the plant had become a corpse, bitten in two by that hungry slug. The remains were reverently collected and donated to the National Museum Wales. There, in the herbarium, the last British Ghost resides, a brown stem with a little mutilated flower: hardly more than an inch of former plant life, held down by strips of tape.

The Ghost's reappearance was announced to the world at the BSBI's annual exhibition in November 2009. Plantlife sportingly welcomed the 'wonderful news'. 'Applying the extinct label to a plant is always difficult,' explained its conservation officer, Trevor Dines. 'Plants can turn up from seed or following better surveys... But just as one swallow doesn't make a summer,' he warned, '[so] one Ghost Orchid doesn't constitute a viable, long-term population of a species.' The Ghost may not be extinct any more, but it is still 'critically endangered'. In retrospect, the surprise was not that the Ghost is still with us, but that anyone could have spotted this insubstantial wisp, this near shadow, in the shroud of earth and decaying leaves of its last resting place.

I met Mark on a fern-hunt in North Wales. Quiet, modest, hairless and fit, he was wearing a broad-brimmed hat. When not botanising, he builds performance-standard motorbikes. That day he was by far the most adventurous of us, scrambling up on to high ledges with confidence and an evident lack of fear. He had been given plenty of climbing practice by his next, post-Ghost botanical project: the Killarney Fern. Like the Ghost, this delicate, beautiful fern inhabits a world of secrets. It was collected to near extinction during the craze for ferns in the nineteenth century, and survives mainly in places the collectors had missed or were afraid to venture: holes and caverns in shaded gorges, rock underhangs, dark, splashy recesses tucked behind waterfalls. Mark showed me the dossier he kept of Killarney Fern localities. He had mapped each one in fine Wainwright-like detail, with notes on how to scale steep, slippery slopes, with or without a rope, and photographs of the various crevices and holes in which the fern seems to melt. Mark has probably seen more Killarney Ferns in Britain and Ireland than anyone alive – perhaps more than anyone who has ever lived. He kept a similar dossier for the Ghost Orchid, not of actual plants but of places where it had appeared, or might appear, but only in the one case where it actually did appear.

Of course I wanted to know more about the Ghost quest. What did it feel like to track it down? 'Well,' remembered Mark, 'for a start, I *didn't* say, "So, *there* you are." I was on my own and I don't talk to myself.' This misreporting had evidently irked him. What he might have thought, but certainly didn't say out loud, was: 'So now I can go home.' Like Rex Graham half a century earlier, he had felt more relieved than triumphant. And although the publicity was inevitable, he hadn't welcomed it. Mark was bothered that people would pester him for details, ask him to show them the plant, or at least tell them where it was. And word did get round in orchid circles, and more people came to see it than the place could support, without damage. Although the tiny plant was respected, the bare earth around it became trampled and punctured with camera tripods. And then brambles closed in, making further searches difficult and future ghostings unlikely. It had been a very ordinary spot, nothing special, just an earth bank under some trees. If the Ghost could appear there, it could appear anywhere. And probably will. Come late summer, the band of Ghost-hunters will be out in the woods again, searching hopefully. But Mark Jannink will not be among them; having found the Ghost, he had reached the end of that particular journey and moved on.

Was his Ghost really the only one? Such is the secrecy surrounding it that others could have been found, but not reported. The Ghost lurks on the frontier between rumour and fact. One Ghost-hunter, Sean Cole, referred to a number of unauthenticated sightings. The suggestive broken stem, for example, with a fat slug sitting where the flower might have been, which may or may not have been a Ghost. My own contribution to Ghost Orchid legend is a story told to me by an orchid-hunter from Connecticut. She had visited England about fifteen years back, she thought, and had been told of a Ghost in a wood somewhere, near a place beginning with 'C' (the Chilterns?), and not all that far from London. She went there and found a single plant with three flowers. It was inside a stockade... 'Whoa,' I interrupted, 'a *stockade*?' 'Yes, a stockade made of wood. There was a low door in which you had to kinda wriggle through. There was a man outside reading a book. He said it was okay to go in.' 'So he was *guarding* the orchid?' 'Kinda, I guess. He said, "Go right in." There were other orchids in there too – helleborines.'

I wasn't sure what to make of this. She did not strike me as a fantasist, and she was quite knowledgeable about orchids, especially from North America. She travelled distances to see rare ones. But I couldn't believe the *stockade*. A wooden rampart with a man outside, like the guard at Buckingham Palace, would not have remained unreported by our army of orchidophiles. Perhaps her memory was at fault and it had been thirty years ago rather than fifteen, in which case she might have been referring to the well-known Rex Graham site. Or perhaps she mistook the flower for something else – perhaps a Bird's-nest Orchid. But that is how these stories get around: misty, intangible, even unlikely, but surprisingly persistent.

I was hoping, rather than expecting, that the Ghost would reappear just in time for my quest. It would have made a good ending: the best kept till last – my last flower. I emailed my contact in the closed circle of Ghost-hunters. Anywhere, any time, I'd travel. I would swear never to tell a soul. They could blindfold me, if they liked. But it seems that the Ghost had never reappeared since that day in late September when Mark Jannink stumbled upon it. It may not be extinct, quite, but there does seem to be something wrong with British Ghosts. In Europe, in the Black Forest, say, or dark, mossy pinewoods in Sweden, the flowers appear fairly regularly, in some years more than others, but often in good numbers. Come warm, damp weather in late summer, up they nose through the decaying needles or leaves and put forth their spotty pink-and-yellow flowers into the open air. It may be that England is no longer Ghost-friendly; too winter-warm, perhaps, or without the right kind of pollinator. Something – who knows? Perhaps that steady parade of Ghosts in one Chiltern wood from the 1950s to the 1980s was not normality, but a freak; an unusually well-fed and active colony, eventually killed off by a very un-English hurricane. At the time of writing, no more Ghosts have turned up, and so the completion of my quest had been doomed from the start. Finding all the flowers is currently impossible: for me, for everyone, unless or until the Ghost decides to flower again. It haunts our inevitable failure. It sticks out its spotty tongue to empty space.

My health recovered slowly. With no alcohol and relatively little sugar to bother it, my liver healed itself, as livers do. There were no more internal screams for help, only a mild nudge, an alimentary hint now and then, usually after an occasional, illicit cocktail or sneaked bar of chocolate. Nurse Tracy pronounced herself pleased with my progress. As did the optician, who announced that my sight was back to normal after a couple of months of doubt. It would be wrong to claim I felt reborn. What I felt now was mortal. I realised there would probably be no more quests. Nature, in future, would be strictly for fun.

Of course I expected to suffer, and in a funny way I welcomed the midges, the trudges through wind and rain, the fretful, sometimes fruitless searches, and even, perversely, the outright failures. For they created a running narrative that took shape by the chance of events as if I were a fictional character in a book. I was prepared to take things as they came. Maybe it was bad luck to choose a year when the summer weather was, at best, changeable. And, of course, I could not have predicted the sudden, dramatic decline in my health, or the fatal illness of my mother. Maybe the pressures of near-continuous travel affected me more than I had bargained for. Maybe it wasn't sensible to have taken on so much botany in a single season. But challenges are, by their nature, not sensible or within one's comfort zone; they need to be difficult and uncomfortable or else they are not challenging. What I did not fully realise when I set out was the unexpected reward that comes from searching for wild flowers. Flower-finding is not just a treasure hunt. Walking with your head down, searching the ground, feeling close to nature, takes you away from a world of trouble and cares. For the time being, it is just you and the flower, locked in a kind of contest. It is strangely soothing, even restorative. It makes life that bit more intense; more than most days you fairly leap out of bed. In Keble Martin's words, botanising takes us to the peaceful, beautiful places of the earth. 'It is good fun and healthy'. It has only just occurred to me but offhand I can't think of a single field botanist who committed suicide.

And so I failed, but failure has its compensations too, in that the journey goes on. Maybe I will see all the wild flowers before I die, or there again maybe not. But in future I will go at my own pace. I will take my time. If I do ever see a Ghost, it will be a new experience, not a codicil to a failed quest. That bite no longer itches. Like the retired King Pellinore in the King Arthur stories, I am done questing.

Any prolonged encounter with wild flowers – or indeed wild anything – necessarily also becomes an investigation into the state of our natural environment. There are, as Jane Goodall would say, reasons for hope, but not all is rosy in this wild garden. Flowers and ferns are natural survivors. Our native species have been with us for the whole of human existence, and have adapted to the endless pressures and strains we place on them. But today they face unheard-of adversity. First there is the battle for physical space. Already pushed to the margins, many of our once familiar, once near-ubiquitous wild flowers are being squeezed into ever-tighter pockets of unused (or under-used) land. Nature reserves once seemed the answer – but even when plants are shut up behind a fence on protected land, it is impossible to isolate them from external influences, not least the slow, insidious build-up of nitrates and phosphates that promote aggressive brambles, nettles and hogweeds at the expense of more delicate wild flowers. Nor are they spared the consequences of climate change, with less frost and snow in winter and more rain in the summer, and perhaps more frequent floods and gales, too. I fear for the mountain flora in particular.

I wonder how much longer Norwegian Mugwort will last, up there on its exposed ridge; or Alpine Enchanter's Nightshade, in its eternal game of hide-and-seek with a larger relative eager to hybridise with it. We are living through the greatest fundamental change that wild plants will have experienced since the Ice Age. I hope their genes can cope with it. We all need hope in this business.

My trail of flowers was also a reminder that there are still wonderful places left in Britain, many of them defined by the presence of some elusive plant. I am happy to have stood on the frost-blasted ridge that is the sole domain of Diapensia, and to have walked the secret paths of the New Forest to glimpse lush, lipstick-red gladioli peeping from the bracken. I saw plants that I only knew from drawings and photographs, and usually found them lovely beyond expectation – for there are things even the best images cannot capture: the natural setting, the wind in your face, the sheer exhilaration of being there. I have travelled many of the wilder places of Europe, but still find something special about wild Britain, homely and rooted as it is, with its intimate scale, its detail, its mixture of ancient and modern, its sleepy corners and heart-tearing beauty. It is all the more special because it is ours, and who cares if this or that rarity is as common as chickweed on the other side of the Channel? We want them here because here is where they belong, and where they have been for thousands of years.

Above all, the days spent in the company of like-minded people were a reminder that, for the naturalist, there is no pleasure like a species shared. My quest would have been so much less successful, and far less fun, without the many kind, generous friends who were willing to act as guides and to share their knowledge and enthusiasm. When I think of those dedicated people, the backbone and heartbeat of British botany, I think of Mike Porter and his daily post of sedges, gazing into the latest ziplock bag with a look of rapture ('I think I'll need to count the stomata on *that* one'); of David Pearman getting up two, three hours early to do his botanical emails; of Tim Rich, high up on some cliff measuring whitebeam leaves; of Ian Strachan tramping the lonely hills of Westerness, Britain's last botanical *terra incognita*. Each of them has had their own quest, whether to write the definitive flora of their county, or to author-edit a national plant atlas, or to delve more deeply into the arcane world of micro-species, faithfully recording the small but significant particulars that define a species or a place. Sharing a passion is the ultimate joy. To others, the world of field botany might seem stuffy and preoccupied with unconsidered trifles; it may baffle and frustrate, with its funny names and technical jargon. It may at times seem irrelevant and even slightly bonkers. But to engage with wild flowers we need only look, watch and enjoy. If it interests us, and makes us feel good at the same time, I think the case for botany is already made. Flowers are precious not only in themselves, in their beauty and fascination, but because they are good for us too, and we need to look after them better, in our own interest as well as theirs. If you have enjoyed my botanical wanderings as a reader I hope that you too will find your own journey of flowers, perhaps a lifelong one. A journey that, in Keble Martin's words, allows plants to speak to us, and for us to find in them a new appreciation of life.

Notes

p.1 'The usual experience': Michael Foley, *Orchids of the British Isles*, Griffin Press, Cheltenham (2005), p.114. The most up-to-date history of the Ghost Orchid in Britain is Cole, 'History and status', as cited in the References

p.2 'parasitic piggyback': Fortey, 'Ghosts in a beechwood', p.172

p.5 'To be honest': I cannot trace the source for this quotation, though in my notes it comes under Cole, 'History and status'

p.6 'funny men in gaiters': Fortey, 'Ghosts in a beechwood', pp.170–71

p.7 'crept stealthily': Forty & Rich (eds), *The Botanist*, 2nd June 1926, pp.99–100

p.11 'The draughtsman's aim': Martin, *Concise British Flora*, Preface, p.7

p.13 'desire to know': Martin, *Over the Hills...*, p.44 (1968). He repeated the remark in *Concise British Flora*, Preface, p.8

p.15 'a mass of flower': Martin, *Over the Hills...*, p.54

p.15 'my fiancée': ibid, p.68

p.15 'This method': ibid., p.70

p.16 'walked miles': Martin, *Concise British Flora*, Preface, p.8

p.19 an autobiography... 'of quiet charm': Wilfrid Blunt, *Sketches for the Flora*, Michael Joseph, London (1972), Foreword (no page number) p.19 'rather noticeably': David Elliston Allen, *Books and Naturalists*, William Collins, London (2010), p.445

p.20 **I totted up**: Among the more surprising omissions were Scented Agrimony, Creeping Speedwell, Annual Mercury, Common Thyme and Common Reed.

p.25 'we commend botanising': Martin, *Concise British Flora*, Preface, p.8

p.26 **'gateposts with leaves'**: Oliver Rackham, concluding words in *Trees & Woodland in the British Landscape*, Dent & Sons, London (new edn 1990), p.208: 'Conservation is about letting trees be trees, not gateposts with leaves'

p.59 **'neither documented'**: Fred Rumsey, 'A review of conservation actions for *Bromus interruptus* with recommendations for future progress', unpublished report to Natural England (2014)

p.77 'slide imperceptibly': Miles Kington, *Nature Made Ridiculously Simple*, Penguin Books, London (1984), Preface

p.81 **'air anemone'**: Grigson, *Englishman's Flora*, p.338

p.93 **'bursts out along'**: Theophilus Jones, *A History of the County of Brecknock* (1805), quoted in *Craig y Cilau*, leaflet by Countryside Council for Wales (undated)

p.99 'Knowledge... makes extinction': Mabey, *Common Ground*, p.30

p.104 **'I feel like digging it up'**: Comment in *Mail* Online re 'Rubbish-filled ditch beside roadside burger van named as one of UK's 10 most important wildlife sites', www.dailymail.co.uk/sciencetech/article-1352489 (2011)

p.110 **'pastel shades'**: Mabey, *The Cabaret of Plants*, p.28

p.110 **'cream touched with'**: ibid, p.305

p.110 **'hopping with delight'**: ibid, p.306

p.149 **'The undisturbed nature'**: Halliday, *Flora of Cumbria*, p.442

p.160 'The crag is a place': Alfred Wainwright, *A Pictorial Guide to the Lakeland Fells, Book 6: The North Western Fells*, Westmorland Gazette (1964)

p.169 'all colonies are threatened': J. Wright, '*Polygonatum verticillatum*', in Wiggington (ed.), *British Red Data Books: 1. Vascular Plants*, p.294

p.173 'I never take a photograph': Obituary of Robert Moyes Adam by J. R. Matthews, cited by Carluke Parish Historical Society, www.carlukehistory.co.uk

p.175 'like old rock-roses': John Raven in Raven & Walters, *Mountain Flowers*, p.137

p.183 'would not dally': D. A. Webb, 'The hey-day of Irish botany 1866–1916', *The Scottish Naturalist* (1986), pp.123–34

p.184 'the most hostile environment': Jepson, 'Skye's the limit', pp.31–3

p.184 'an apparently endless scree': Raven & Walters, *Mountain Flowers*, p.134

p.206 'doubtfully native species': Pearman, 'Far from any house', pp.271–90

p.223 'warm sweetness': 'The Lake of Lilies', in Gerald Durrell, *My Family and Other Animals*, Rupert Hart-Davis, London (1956), p.218

p.226 'Twelve plants introduced': '*Schoenoplectus* on the Tamar Estuary', unpublished report by Panscape Environmental Consultancy (2014)

p.227 'Then a sentimental passion': Bunthorne's song in Gilbert & Sullivan's *Patience* (1881), Act 1

p.268 'Some swore': Garner, 'Haunted Herefordshire', p.7

p.269 'Applying the extinct label': Trevor Dines quoted in the *Independent*, '"So there you are!" Britain's rarest wild flower returns after 23 years', 19th March 2010

References

Allen, D. E., 'Botanical hotspots in Britain and Ireland: who revealed them and when?', Short Note, *New Journal of Botany* (2011), 1 (1), pp.58–61

Anon, *Robert Moyes Adam, Photographer 1885–1967*, Scottish Arts Council (1969)

Bentham, George & Hooker, Sir Joseph, *Handbook of the British Flora*, Reeve & Co., London (1858)

Boon, Christopher R. & Outen, Alan R., *Flora of Bedfordshire*, Bedfordshire Natural History Society (2011)

Brewis, Anne, Bowman, Paul & Rose, Francis, *The Flora of Hampshire*, Harley Books, Colchester (1996)

Chatters, Clive, *Flowers of the Forest. Plants and people in the New Forest National Park*, Wildguides, Old Basing, Hants (2009)

Clapham, A. R., Tutin, T. G. & Warburg, E. F., *Flora of the British Isles*, Cambridge University Press (2nd edn 1962)

Cole, S. R., 'History and status of the Ghost Orchid (*Epipogium aphyllum*, Orchidaceae) in England', *New Journal of Botany* (2014), 1 (4), pp.13–24

Cope, Tom & Gray, Alan, *Grasses of the British Isles*, BSBI Handbook No. 13, Botanical Society of the British Isles, London (2009)

Fortey, Richard, *The Wood for the Trees. The Long View of Nature from a Small Wood*, William Collins, London (2016)

—— 'Ghosts in a beechwood', *British Wildlife* (2017), 28 (3), pp.167–72

Forty, Michelle & Rich, Tim (eds), *The Botanist. The botanical diary of Eleanor Vachell (1879–1948)*, National Museum Wales (2005)

Garner, Peter, 'Haunted Herefordshire: the "Ghost" reappears in Britain after an absence of 23 years', *BSBI News*, Botanical Society of the British Isles (January 2010), 113, p.7

Gledhill, D., *The Names of Plants*, Cambridge University Press (2nd edn 1989)

Grigson, Geoffrey, *The Englishman's Flora*, Dent & Sons, London (1955)

Halliday, Geoffrey, *A Flora of Cumbria*, Centre for North-West Regional Studies, University of Lancaster (1997)

Harrap, Anne & Harrap, Simon, *Orchids of Britain and Ireland. A Field and Site Guide*. A & C Black, London (2005)

Jannink, Mark & Rich, Tim, 'Ghost Orchid rediscovered in Britain after 23 years', *J. Hardy Orchid Society* (2010), 7, pp.14–15

Jepson, Peter, 'Skye's the limit – an *Arabis* saga', *BSBI News*, Botanical Society of the British Isles (2004), 97, pp.31–3

Jermy, A. C., Simpson, D. A., Foley, M. J. Y. & Porter, M. S., *Sedges of the British Isles*, BSBI Handbook No. 1, Botanical Society of the British Isles, London (3rd edn 2007)

Jermyn, Stanley T., *Flora of Essex*, Essex Naturalists' Trust, Colchester (1974)

Lusby, Philip & Wright, Jenny, *Scottish Wild Plants. Their history, ecology and conservation*, Stationery Office, Edinburgh (1996)

Mabey, Richard, *Flora Britannica*, Sinclair-Stevenson, London (1996)

—— *The Common Ground. A place for nature in Britain's future?*, Hutchinson, London (1980)

—— *The Cabaret of Plants. Botany and the Imagination*, Profile Books, London (2015)

—— & Evans, Tony, *The Flowering of Britain*, Arrow Books, London (1980)

McClintock, David, *Companion to Flowers*, Bell & Sons, London (1966)

—— & Fitter, R. S. R., *Collins Pocket Guide to Wild Flowers*, William Collins, London (1956)

Marren, Peter, *Britain's Rare Flowers*, T. & A. D. Poyser Natural History, London (1999)

—— 'Lost and found: the resurrection of an "extinct" British plant', *British Wildlife* (2017), 28 (4), pp.248–52

Martin, W. Keble, *The Concise British Flora in Colour*, Ebury Press & Michael Joseph, London (1965)

—— *Over the Hills...*, Michael Joseph, London (1968)

—— *The New Concise British Flora*, Ebury Press & Michael Joseph, London (1982)

—— & Caldwell, John, *Sketches for the Flora*, Michael Joseph, London (1972)

Murphy, R. J., *Fumitories of Britain and Ireland*, BSBI Handbook No. 12, Botanical Society of the British Isles, London (2009)

Noltie, H. J., *Wild Flowers: A sketchbook by Charles and John Raven*, Royal Botanic Gardens, Edinburgh (2012)

Page, C. N., *The Ferns of Britain and Ireland*, Cambridge University Press (2nd edn 1997)

Pearman, D. A., 'Far from any house' – assessing the status of doubtfully native species in the flora of the British Isles', *Watsonia* (2007), 26 (3), pp.271–90

—— & Preston, C. D., *A Flora of Tiree, Gunna & Coll*, privately published, Dorchester (2000)

Plantlife, *The Ghost Orchid Declaration: Saving the UK's wild flowers today*, Plantlife, Salisbury (2009)

Poland, John & Clement, Eric, *The Vegetative Key to the British Flora*, privately published (2009)

Preston, C. D., *Pondweeds of Great Britain and Ireland*, BSBI Handbook No. 8, Botanical Society of the British Isles, London (1995)

—— & Croft, J. M., *Aquatic Plants in Britain and Ireland*, Harley Books, Colchester (1997)

——, Pearman, D. A. & Dines, T. D., *New Atlas of the British & Irish Flora*, Oxford University Press (2002)

Raven, John & Walters, Max, *Mountain Flowers*, Collins New Naturalist 33, William Collins, London (1956)

Rich, T. C. G., *Crucifers of Great Britain and Ireland*, BSBI Handbook No. 6, Botanical Society of the British Isles, London (1991)

—— & Lockton, A. J., '*Bromus interruptus* (Hack.) Druce (Poaceae) – an extinct English endemic', *Watsonia* (2002), 24, pp.69–80

Rich, Tim, Houston, Libby, Robertson, Ashley & Proctor, Michael, *Whitebeams, Rowans and Service Trees of Britain and Ireland*, BSBI Handbook No. 14, Botanical Society of the British Isles, London (2010)

Rose, Francis, *Colour Identification Guide to the Grasses, Sedges, Rushes and Ferns of the British Isles and north-west Europe*, Viking, Harmondsworth (1989)

Scott, Michael, *Mountain Flowers*, British Wildlife Collection 4, Bloomsbury, London (2016)

Shaw, Andrew, 'Stanner Rocks NNR. Reserve Focus', *British Wildlife* (2014), 26 (2), pp.99–105

Stace, Clive, *New Flora of the British Isles*, Cambridge University Press (2nd edn 1997)

—— & Crawley, Michael J., *Alien Plants*, *New Naturalist Library*, William Collins, London (2015)

——, Preston, Chris D. & Pearman, David A., *Hybrid Flora of the British Isles*, Botanical Society of Britain and Ireland, Bristol (2015)

Stewart, A., Pearman, D. A. & Preston, C. D. (eds), *Scarce Plants in Britain*, Joint Nature Conservation Committee, Peterborough (1994)

Stroh, Peter et al. (eds), *A Vascular Plant Red List for England*, Botanical Society of Britain and Ireland, Bristol (2014)

Tennant, David & Rich, Tim, *British Alpine Hawkweeds. A monograph of British Hieracium section Alpina*, Botanical Society of the British Isles, London (2008)

Webb, D. A., 'What are the criteria for presuming native status?', *Watsonia* (1985), 15, pp.231–6

Westwood, Brett et al. (eds), *The Nature of Wyre. A wildlife-rich forest in the heart of Britain*, Pisces Publications, Newbury (2015)

Wigginton, M. J. (ed.), *British Red Data Books: 1. Vascular Plants*, Joint Nature Conservation Committee, Peterborough (3rd edn 1999)

Woods, R. G., *Flora of Radnorshire*, National Museum Wales, Cardiff (1993)

Acknowledgements

A journey like mine relies heavily on the generosity of fellow naturalists, and the warm spirit in which so many old and new friends responded to it will remain with me for the rest of my days. To all who took part in The Quest, my warmest thanks. My principal helpers and guides were, in alphabetical order, Ashley Arbon, Steve Berry and Pat Millard, Ian Bonner, Chris Boon, Alan Bowley, Andrew Branson, Nick Button and Kate Stephen of Natural England, Andy Byfield, Clive Chatters, Bob Gibbons, Ben Jones, Richard Mabey, Iain MacDonald, Cat Owen-Pam, Tim Payner, David and Anita Pearman, George Peterken, Mike and Julie Porter, Alex Prendergast, Martin Rand, Ivor and Jane Rees, Tim Rich, Martin Rickard, Jeremy Roberts, James and Joanna Robertson, Martin Robinson, Fred Rumsey, Michael and Sue Scott, Andy Shaw, Jonathan Stokes, Ian Strachan, Peter Stroh, Graham Tomlinson, Ray Woods, Will West and Brett Westwood. I owe a particular debt of thanks to Bob Gibbons for saving my bacon on the return from our ill-fated journey to Coll.

Others helped with information or in other ways, notably Patrick Barkham, Ian Bennallick, Karen Birkby of RSPB, Brian

Davis, Trevor Dines, Lynne Farrell, Lady Rosemary FitzGerald, Isobel Griffiths of CCW, Dick Hornby, Mark Jannink, Andy Jones, Simon Leach, Graeme Lyon, Mike McCarthy, Liz McDonnell, Chris Miles, Jeremy Mynott, Sharon Pilkington, Chris Preston, Dominic Price of the Species Recovery Trust, Phil Pullen, Martin Sanford, Rebecca Tibbets of Natural England, Fiona Walker, Laura Watson of Yorkshire Wildlife Trust, Belinda Wheeler and Barry Yates. My thanks to them all.

I owe a debt of gratitude to the late Penny Hoare for reading the draft with such care and suggesting so many improvements. I will miss her wisdom, insight and sympathetic understanding. As others have said, there are not many left like her. I thank Rosemary Davidson for her encouragement and support, and also her successor at Square Peg, Rowan Yapp. I am also grateful to Harriet Dobson for piloting the book from manuscript to neatly designed pages, to Stephen Parker and Dan Mogford on design, to Mandy Greenfield for her careful and thoughtful copy-editing, Anthony Hippisley, for his eagle-eyed proof-reading and Alex Bell, for his very thorough index.

This book is dedicated to David and Anita Pearman for their kindness and hospitality over the years, chasing the wild flowers of Dorset, Cornwall and the Outer Hebrides, and having such fun in the processs.

A Note on the Illustrations

The drawings of plants at the head of each chapter and section are from two main sources. The older are line drawings by Walter Hood Fitch (1817–1892) made for George Bentham's *Handbook of the British Flora* in 1863–5. These served the Handbook and field botany in general until well into the twentieth century. Most of the remainder are by Stella Ross-Craig of Kew, published as *Drawings of British Plants* between 1948 and 1973.

The drawing of Downy Rose in Chapter Two is a sketch by Keble Martin, which, as a full watercolour, occupied a prominent position on the dust jacket of *The Concise British Flora*. It is taken from *Sketches for the Flora* (1972) by W. Keble Martin, p.72. The drawing of Radnor Lily on p.33 appeared in *Flora of Radnorshire* by Ray Woods, reproduced by the author's kind permission. That of Suffolk Lungwort on p.44 was specially commissioned for this book by Fred Rumsey. That of Interrupted Brome was drawn by C. E. Hubbard for his book *Grasses* (1954) and reproduced by permission of Penguin Books. The leaves and berries of Ley's Whitebeam on p.98 were drawn by Tim Rich and reproduced by his kind permission. Proliferous Pink, on p.113, was drawn by James Sowerby for *Smith's English Botany* in 1801 and is in the public domain. Leafless Hawk's-beard on p.147 is from a coloured drawing by Jacob Sturm in *Deutschlands Flora in Abbildungen* (1776), also in the public domain. Estuarine Sedge on p.199 is from The BSBI Handbook, *Sedges of the British Isles*, with the permission of BSBI.

Index

penguin.co.uk/vintage